THE GRIT

THE STORY OF LOWESTOFT'S BEACH VILLAGE

by Dean Parkin & Jack Rose

with illustrations by Paula White

To Anne & Michael

Paula White

CORNER STREET

Dean Parkin

21/9/2019

It was a community on its own, but
though they call it the 'Beach' now,
what we called it was 'The Grit'.
We used to say we were born on The Grit.
LENNY 'WINKY' NORMAN

Published in 2019 by Corner Street
Unit 4, 8 New Cut, Halesworth IP19 8BY
cornerstreet.co.uk

First edition 1997, reprinted 1998
Revised and updated 2019

Paperback edition 978-1-9162055-0-5
Hardback edition 978-1-9162055-1-2

Designed and typset by Silk Pearce.
Printed and bound by Leiston Press, Unit 1,
Master Lord Industrial Estate, Leiston IP16 4JD.

This book is dedicated
to all those who lived on
THE GRIT

ACKNOWLEDGEMENTS

On behalf of Jack Rose I would like to thank everybody who has helped with the two editions of this publication: those who spoke or wrote to us, those who lent photographs and those who have put us in contact with others or pointed us in the right direction.

Those who assisted the first edition in 1997 are still very much appreciated – Ernie Childs of Great Yarmouth Pottery, Anna Hogan, David Johnson, Robin Summers and especially Christine Johnson and Panda Books.

Thanks go those who have contributed time, knowledge or skill to the 2019 edition – Nathan Berry, Bob Collis, Christ Church (Rev Matthew Payne and Monica Brewster), Christine Johnson, Michael Laskey, Jo Leverett, the Lowestoft Heritage Centre (Lesley Bunn), the Lowestoft Maritime Museum (Jim Aguss & Colin Dixon), Lowestoft Record Office, Becky Marshall-Potter, Maggie Menzies, Nicola Parkin, Chloe Pearson, Peter Spedding and Mischi Vernetti. Thanks also to Phil Aves (Lowestoft Rising CEP), Jayne Austin (Suffolk Museums Development Manager) and Jayne Knight (Suffolk County Council Arts Development Manager) for their help with The Grit project which paved the way for this publication.

I am also grateful to Ivan Bunn for for the reproduction of his maps and his ever helpful assistance; David Butcher for his contribution on The Denes; Russell Walker for discoveries of photos and documents; Lucy Martin on the Beach Village Lowestoft Facebook page for ongoing online detective work. I am indebted to Colin Dixon for his encouragement and support at the beginning of the revision process and for putting me onto the Capps-Jenner manuscript, and to Bert Collyer for generously sharing new reproductions of the cleaned-up old negatives.

Special acknowledgements go to Jack Pearce at Silk Pearce and the rest of his team – Rob Steer for his wonderful re-imagining and new designs supported by Anthony Blease and Ian Coote; Paula White for all her work on the fabulous illustrations; Naomi Jaffa (at Poetry People and Corner Street) for her diligent management of the whole Grit project and this publication. A final big thank you to Jack Rose's daughter, Jackie Emery and her husband Bob for their generosity and enthusiastic support.

IMAGE CREDITS

Most of the photographs in the 1997 edition were from the Jack Rose Collection. We were grateful to the following who kindly permitted the use of photographs: Glennis Barnard, Matthew Boardley, Olive Burwood, Vina Capps-Jenner, Harry Collins, Lydia Cullen, Claude Dalley, Alan Doy, Ray Durrant, Iris Gibbs, Roger Gouldby, Oliver Guymer, Jessie Hitter, Ron James, David Johnson, Ada Jones, Billy Keith, Benny Knights, Peter Larter, Bob Maltster, Ivan Meadows, Edna Mortensen, Charles Oldman, George Osborne, Joy Pearce, Bert Prettyman, Ian G Robb, Clifford Temple and Alan Weller.

The 2019 edition includes 120 new photographs. Thanks are due to: Pam Burwood, Beryl Capps, Bert Collyer, Martin Ellis, Caroline Hall, Mel Hall, Brian Horne, David Waterman and Robert Whybrow. Additional gratitude for the use of specially commissioned photographs from the Heritage Centre and Nigel Purdy (Beach Village Model), Rob Howarth (The Excelsior Trust at The Ness) and Peter Everard Smith (GritFest and *Pearls from The Grit*).

CONTENTS

Dean Parkin and Jack Rose, August 1997.

1997 INTRODUCTION

Compiling this book has been like working on an enormous jigsaw. The idea for it arose from the first Beach Village exhibition, which took place at Christ Church in 1995, where people began to ask about the possibility of a long overdue book devoted to the subject.

Once we decided to go ahead with the project, the framework was provided by notes gathered from many years of research, in addition to newspaper articles, essays and booklets from authors long since dead, such as Hugh Lees, whose research proved invaluable. The appeals for information, photographs and recollections, which were made at Beach reunions and in the *Lowestoft Journal*, were also fruitful and soon letters began to arrive and contacts were made. Dozens of interviews followed, hours of tape recordings and tens of thousands of words. Many of these stories overlapped and therefore needed editing, but piece by piece they fell into place and a true picture of The Beach began to emerge. With the book still growing and more people getting in touch, projected publication dates came and went, and for a time it seemed as though we would never finish!

The people we spoke to are the last generation of 'Gritsters'. Jack grew up amongst these people. As children they all lived on The Beach and although they were aware that life was hard for their parents, they at least enjoyed the benefits and security of growing up in a close-knit community. We realise that had this book been attempted whilst their parents were alive, the story may have been rather different. Nonetheless, the importance of a record of this unique community was sadly illustrated by the death of several contributors during the preparation of the book.

Though there are still pieces of the jigsaw missing, possibly lost forever, we trust that this book gives a faithful account of what life was really like on The Beach. Our thanks to all the Gritsters who contacted us and were so willing to help. Their friendly nature is still very much in evidence and their stories and history are at last captured in this book.

JACK ROSE & DEAN PARKIN, SEPTEMBER 1997

The cast of Pearls from The Grit: Tim FitzHigham (Billy), David Redgrave (Ned), Dean Parkin (Narrator), Sally-Ann Burnett (Ruby), Maurice Horhut (Tickler Sam).

2019 INTRODUCTION

It's been a long journey back – 25 years since Jack Rose and I started writing *The Grit*, and two decades since he died. Revising the book, out of print since 2003, has been a poignant experience without Jack. Our first edition contained 50,000 words and 150 photos, with a popular painting by Ernie Childs on the cover. This new edition has 65,000 words and 250 photos, nearly half of which I'd never previously seen before. And I'm thrilled that Lowestoft artist Paula White has come on board to provide the evocative cover and chapter illustrations that capture so perfectly the unique spirit of the place.

These days I earn my living as a writer, poet and workshop leader. Over the last ten years my work has had an East Anglian focus and two particular ventures inspired The Grit revival. In 2016 I was commissioned to write a book about the residents of Stowmarket's post-war prefabs which were due for demolition. The similarity to the Beach Village was striking. In 2017 I was part of the Arthur Ransome heritage project, welcomed by the Shotley Peninsula community. Perhaps something similar could be done in my home town? Because one thing that doesn't change is Lowestoft people's passion for their history.

And so – supported by the National Lottery Heritage Fund – The Grit project to celebrate the fishing village became a reality and a runaway success. It has proved a rich source of new stories and photos fuelling the appetite for a revised, freshly-designed edition. As part of the project, we toured my theatre show *Pearls from The Grit* with a cast of professional actors. They had genuine Suffolk accents so could 'talk proper' to bring stories from the book to life on stage. The show included recordings of Jack Rose's own inimitable voice – needless to say, his jokes still got the biggest laughs from the audience.

Today people are living on The Grit again, building houses, converting old net stores into flats. Modern industries too – renewable energy firms, a landmark wind turbine. Where once you were ashamed to say you were from The Beach, in the era of *ancestry.com* people are excited to discover relatives who had been skippers or fisher girls. As I get older I think of my own links with the place ever more fondly – in the 1970s my Dad ran his plastics factory at 261 Whapload Road, and on both sides of my family I have relations who lived on The Grit.

It's half a century since the fishing village was demolished, but out of sight has never meant out of mind. I've loved this opportunity to revitalise the story, collecting together the photographs and memories of the people who lived there from 1900 to the 1960s to create this authentic oral history record. The Grit is definitely back on the map.

DEAN PARKIN, SEPTEMBER 2019

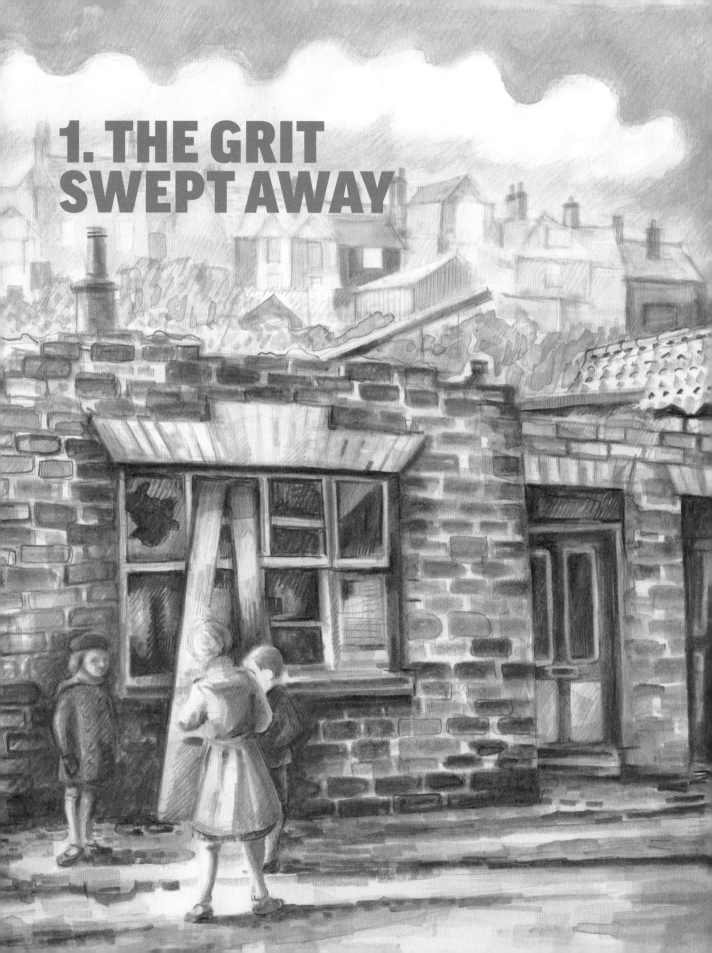

1. THE GRIT SWEPT AWAY

I was like most of the Beach boys, we all drifted
away as soon as we could ... when I came back
to Lowestoft I took my wife down to show her
where I was brought up and couldn't believe it
... Birds Eye and all the neat business premises
now, and I couldn't even find where I lived in
Anguish Street, it was all gone ... E J DAY

'It could have been a wonderfully pretty little place down here still,' Bob 'Umshi' Norman told the *Eastern Evening News* in September 1966. 'I shall be glad to get away now... Everywhere is smashed up and no-one does a thing about it.'

The Beach Village had become a ghost town, with only a few people living amongst the tumbledown streets and derelict houses. 'Slum clearance' had gone on for some time, but in the 1960s this process was accelerated in an optimistic new era which sought to sweep away much of the old. At this time the Beach Village represented a grim, dark, depressing age of hardship and in 1964 was described as 'a relic of less prosperous days' by the *Eastern Daily Press*. The end was best symbolised by the demolition of the last two long-serving public houses – the *Gas House Tavern*, demolished in October 1967 and the *Rising Sun* soon after, with its last memorable night on 4th November 1968 when the place was drunk dry.

By the beginning of the 1970s there was little to remind anyone of the huddle of cottages and houses and narrow streets which had been home to 2,500 people in 1900, and significantly more every autumn when the Scots arrived for the herring season. At that time the strong feeling of independence among the Gritsters was understandable – there was no need to venture up into the town – as every shop and service was available within this community, not to mention 13 pubs! The Beach was even an ecclesiastical parish, with its own church in addition to a chapel. The residents worked there too, the men mostly as fishermen while many of the women worked in the fishyards and net stores or mended the fishing nets at home. There were smoke houses, rope and twine-spinning sheds, all related to a booming fishing industry, but although the crews and labourers were never well paid, their hardships shared and a strong community emerged.

The demise of the Beach Village had set in by the 1930s. The slump of the fishing industry and the general economic depression of this period caused further deprivation to the Beach between the Wars and in some cases the living conditions of these people were terrible. An example of the worst of these dwellings is given in a 1933 inquiry into a clearance order on four houses in Anguish Street. One of these properties, said to be typical of the rest, was stated as being poorly built and laid out and now had 'crumbling walls and a leaking roof…'.

(Top) Christ Church and Whapload Road during the last days of the fishing village in the late 1960s. All the buildings to the right in the photograph were soon to be swept away.

(Bottom) Derelict properties in Nelson Road, next to the Church. Alan Youngman lived in Ethel Cottage (left) in the 1960s and remembers, "We had a little courtyard at the back and there'd be a dustbin in there, no back gate. So the dustman had to come through the house, through the hall, out the back door to pick our dustbin up and then back again!"

(Overleaf) Christ Church and the south-end of Whapload Road during the heyday of The Grit, circa 1910.

(Right) The Almshouses in Whapload Road were built in 1838 for £600 for aged and infirm fishermen. Their demolition on 14th February 1968 is widely regretted.

(Below left) Cumberland Square contained some good examples of the cobbled houses built using stones from the beach. These five cottages were pulled down in October 1967.

(Below right) Cumberland Square was near to the *Gas House Tavern* off Wilde's Street. At the entrance to the Square was Sadie Villa (the house on the right), named after its resident, fisherman Sadie Springer.

The rear of the rooms was overshadowed by a factory and '…the living room and one of the bedrooms was in a state of perpetual semi-darkness with no window ventilation and two of the bedrooms had ceilings that sloped down to just over four feet. The scullery floor was over six inches below street level and there was one tap with no sink, the water dripping on the brick floor.'

In defence, the owner of this property pointed out that the tenant of the house had lived in it for 33 years and had raised a family of eleven and suggested that improvements could be made with the demolition of the rear of the house and the erection of a lean-to kitchen. However, the Borough Surveyor Sidney Mobbs fiercely disagreed, saying that the house was unfit for habitation and he would not keep a dog in the living room! The clearance order went ahead and the tenants were rehoused.

Unfortunately, the fashion for modernisation came about 50 years too late for The Grit. In the 1930s the Town Council began a scheme of slum clearance on the site, with the idea of building a council estate in its place. In September 1937 the Lowestoft Corporation Redevelopment Scheme started and ended in Lighthouse Score, with new council houses being built to replace the picturesque old cottages which were still occupied. However, the Second World War thwarted any further redevelopment.

The Grit found itself on the front line and some families were evacuated and part of the village became uninhabited. Born in 1929, Jack Moore lived in East Street and spent his childhood in the Beach Village. "People had moved out of a lot of the houses because of the bombing; the army took over and used them for street training. Blown-up and shot-up and everything else. They used a lot of those old houses for house-to-house combat. One of the reasons many buildings were pulled down after the Second World War was because the army wrecked them. They had the old beachmens' shods (sheds). They had those. That's why they had to be pulled down after the War. That was the beginning of the end down there."

The north beach was sealed off and became an immense minefield, as a result of which the sea wall was off-limits. Not everyone appreciated these dangers and on one occasion, having heard that a cargo boat had been sunk off Lowestoft with a load of butter washed up on the beach, Ronny 'Titch' Wilson, Jack Rose and John Wooley decided to look for it. Finding a gap in the barbed wire, they walked onto the Denes and made their way to the sea wall. About half way across they heard someone shouting and looking back, saw a man in a peaked cap, together with three or four sailors, all waving their arms. Ignoring them, Ronny, Jack and John carried on to the beach but found nothing there. On the way back they met the man and the sailors who collared the three boys, telling them they'd just walked through a minefield!

"We left the Beach when I was seven in 1940," says Danny Burwood who lived at 65 East Street, "as my mother was frightened of the gasworks being hit. We were within a hundred yards of it and there would have been an almighty explosion." The Germans certainly did target the gasworks and there were many air raids in this area. Joy Pearce lived in Rant Score East,

(Above) Bomb-damaged houses at the rear of Strand Street, looking south from Fishery Street – probably the result of the 250kg bomb which fell at the rear of East's Garage, Whapload Road on 4th June 1941.

(Right) Looking down Rant Score East, towards the gasworks. The gap at the end of the row of houses on the left is where a bomb fell during the Second World War, showing how close the gasworks came to being hit.

close to this target. "It was handy living right near to the gasworks because we used to be able to hear their crash warning, which was a three minute warning before the enemy planes came over, a little bit before the normal sirens, so we could get in the shelter first." Thankfully, the gasworks were never directly hit, but the near misses did turn many surrounding properties into ruins. "We suffered structural damage," Mrs Pearce continues. "I was up with some friends in Reeve Street in the town. My grandfather was in the merchant navy but my grandmother was at home and the ceilings came down. We had to move out and took most of the stuff up to Camden Street in a tin bath, while the heavy stuff was moved by Hailey's."

'Bimbo' Osborne lived at 18 Rant Score East next to Binks' Bakery. His house was bombed on 3rd July 1940 and the two people next door were killed. "My brother worked at the gasworks and saw the bomb drop just off the gas holder and ran to his house to get his wife out."

This was Lowestoft's first daylight raid and the first fatal casualties of the Second World War. There was no warning and Mrs Baster, her daughter (aged 14) and her nephew George Youngman (aged 18 months) were killed. 'Falling masonry' was given as the official cause of death, but Sonny Smith remembers it differently: "I was near Binks the bakers when they tried to hit the gasworks, and the blast blew this baby right out of the pram, and it landed on the railings, it was hanging there, so I picked it off and all the brains fell out."

The same plane then circled and dropped another 12 bombs on the town centre, resulting in the Co-op burning down and another death. This was the second of 105 raids on Lowestoft during the War and the Beach Village suffered its share of damage.

On 3rd May 1941 the blast of a parachute mine which fell on the sea wall caused structural damage to 450 houses. Wilde's School building which was being used as the headquarters of the Lowestoft Air Training Corps was also struck. More tragically, on 13th June 1941 two bombs hit the Central School where soldiers had been sleeping, killing 15 and injuring six. "I was digging the bodies out of Central School after that got hit," recalls Ronny Wilson. "My father and I went round. We were digging them out about three o'clock in the morning. They were all soldiers down there but they left the lights on. I think they got a direct hit and one of them was found right up in the High Street."

"Our Anderson shelter was opposite the Little Bethel," recalls Jean Mitchell (née Keable). "During the heavy air-raids we used to run from our house in Wilde's Street to the shelter in East Street. When it got really bad we practically lived in the shelter. My Mum used to cook potatoes and boil kettles on a round oil heater. This caused condensation where the water ran down the metal frame of the shelter making the bed we slept in very, very damp..."

Jack Moore also remembers the shelter in East Street, although his family never used it. "The Eagle Brewery was where we used to go. The brewery used to let all the Lowestoft people and Beach people in their cellars. You'd take a blanket and stay all night. And there was a bloke with a violin who'd play tunes all night. Those cellars were well down in the ground. Hundreds went down there. They did that every night 'cos the siren went every night. It was a good shelter, that was."

(Above) Work progresses on the new sea wall in April 1947. The previous wall had fallen into severe disrepair during the Second World War, finally collapsing as a result of a strong north-east wind in March 1946.

(Right) On Friday 20th August 1941, eight high-explosives fell on East Street, Nelson Road and Fishery Street, destroying a blockhouse with a machine gun post. The two houses on the right were 65 East Street, where the Burwoods lived next door to the Crittens at 67.

(Right) On 13th June 1941 two bombs hit Central School, where 14 soldiers and one civilian were killed, and another six people injured.

(Below) Bomb damage to the interior of the hall at Central School. This is a stereoscopic photograph mounted on card which when seen through a viewing device gave a primitive 3D effect.

52. Central School, Interior of Hall. 13/6/41.

Many families never returned to The Grit after the Second World War and there was no attempt to renovate or repair any of the houses. After 1946 new industries started to be encouraged onto the site but redevelopment was slow and in the meantime, the housing shortage prompted new people to move into the Beach Village, attracted by its cheap 'temporary' accommodation. Some would live there for up to 20 years but they rarely had any connection with the fishing industry.

The arrival of Birds Eye Foods in 1949 would prove significant. Originally just a small depot opened for the preparation and packaging of fruit for the Great Yarmouth factory, the Lowestoft operation subsequently went from strength to strength, expanding over much of the site of the old Beach Village.

The War had caused untold damage to The Grit, both structurally and to the community itself, although perhaps the most immediate problem was the sea wall. Prior to the War it had been supported on the landward side by sand hills covered in marram grass, but these disappeared during the occupation by the naval and military authorities and it was feared that the sea wall might collapse.

Gradually the sea did undermine the wall and on 23rd March 1946 under the headline, 'Lowestoft Wall Breached', the *Eastern Evening News* reported, 'A change in direction of the wind on Sunday brought relief to those who had previously been anxiously watching at the north sea wall since Saturday. Flooding has been averted but extensive undermining was revealed.'

The Borough Engineer, Geoffrey Gentry, along with Sidney Mobbs, the Engineer to the East Norfolk Rivers Catchment Board, who was the original surveyor when the wall was built, visited the scene and both were concerned by the state of the six foot flood wall. Mobbs pointed out, 'The continual pounding of any defences will find weak spots. That is what has happened to this wall; for six years the sea had free play, because the maintenance work could not be carried out. Thousands of tons of sand have been scooped from beneath the wall as if it had been tunnelled, hence the collapse of 300 feet of the decking some 40 feet wide. The subsidence is anything up to six feet...'

Although the sea wall was patched up to prevent any immediate breaching, the faults in the structure were irreparable and it became obvious that a new one needed to be built and Geoffrey Gentry was given the task of designing it. At 11 feet 3 inches high and 6 feet wide, with 18 groynes extending into the sea at intervals, this is the wall that still protects the area today.

Many of the villagers had experienced flooding by the time the notorious 1953 surge occurred. "Normally flood water came through the drains," remembers Matthew Boardley who lived at 1 Jubilee Terrace on Whapload Road. "The tide would come up and it would all go through the drains and we'd get flooded. My mother would send me out to see if the water was coming up through the drain, and as soon as it did I had to run in and tell her so that she could put the flood-boards up. The 1953 flood was different though – a wall of water swept down Whapload Road."

It was the most disastrous flood the east coast had ever seen. A new record high tide of 26 feet split Lowestoft and Oulton Broad in two. The Beach Village was the worst affected area, the low-lying streets soon waist-deep and the water level on the pickling plots and the net drying ground soon rose to four or five feet. With other men from the village, Mr Gus Jensen, the then licensee of the *Rising Sun*, made a round of all the houses to warn occupants and kept an all-night patrol with Willie Boothroyd and Dan Dyer, waist-deep in a current of water that kept knocking them off their feet. Indeed, it was for this brave night's work that Gus received the British Empire Medal.

The Tucks lived in Wilde's Street where the water came up as high as 3 feet 3 inches in the house. "I remember them coming and measuring it afterwards by the water marks on the walls," says Beryl Clover (née Tuck). That night her mother was in the *Gas House Tavern*, while sister Norma was in the house with her other sister and her boyfriend. "As mother got home the water was gurgling in the drains," recalls Norma. "To me, as a child, that was exciting. I remember looking out of the window and seeing things floating past, but I wasn't at an age when it worried me. We were getting the furniture up, putting the settee on the table and the chairs upside down on the settee, and as we were trying to do this, the water started coming in the door. So we went upstairs. We stayed up all night. Father had chickens outside in the shed and he went out and opened it up so they could get on the roof or something high but I think we still lost four."

Beryl continues, "We had a little fireplace upstairs which we were trying to keep alight all next day to dry off things that were wet downstairs. There was nothing you could do, the whole area was mud outside, you couldn't put anything on the line, it was just mud, so everything had to be dried inside."

John Day lived at 2 Canary Cottages, Whapload Road and was ten years old when the 1953 flood occurred. "The night was very angry with screaming winds, and in the early morning lots of dead horses and pigs were found not far from our house. My father knew one of the coastguards, and we went to see him at the little look-out near Hamilton Dock. Everywhere was covered in thick, gooey, sticky, clinging, stinking mud and we saw more dead animals."

Colin Dixon recalls, "During the 1953 flood my grandfather was at sea and whenever he was at sea, my grandmother came and stayed with us, and by that time we had moved up to St. Peter's Street to Sparham's Buildings. When grandmother went to go home this particular Sunday, she met her milkman who asked where she was going. She said, 'I'm going home,' and he replied. 'You'll never get down there, Kate, it's been flooded!' So she came back home and we all went down to the Beach Village."

"I was eleven at the time, and when we reached the road down there, there was still water. Grandma was worried about the contents of the sideboard, where she kept some money, so a neighbour waded with me on his back from Maltsters Score through Salter Street and we went into Wilde's Street, into the house, got into the sideboard, got the things we wanted and then back. Everything was topsy-turvy, all the furniture had been thrown about by the water.

(Left) 1st February 1953 – the Sunday morning after the worst flood the east coast had ever seen. Water was still lapping at the door of Christ Church.

(Below) Further down Whapload Road, the back gardens and the net racks were still under water.

After the flood, she did go back to live there though. The family all got together, in those days they did, and everybody rallied round, and they went into Grandma's house, stripped everything out, washed and scraped off all the mud, and she went back to live there for a number of years."

Joan Reynolds moved to Whapload Road a year before the flood on 6th February 1952, which was the day King George VI died. She recalls, "I lived there with my husband Jack and our two little lads, Christopher and Paul. As I remember it, the actual day of the flood was very, very windy, there was a strange atmosphere, it was really a peculiar sort of day." Jack was at work that night and Joan thankfully managed to scramble to safety with her children up the cliff. "Next morning Jack put on some high waders and managed to get through to the house," Joan continues. "He wanted to retrieve money and personal items before any looting started, which did happen. I didn't go back for quite a while though."

"When I did go back, there was still water in the kitchen. When you think of it, I had had the sea in my house! There had been about five foot of water and the damage was horrendous. It was like a wet bombing raid. The front door had gone, the garden wall had gone, the front windows had been smashed. I had other people's furniture in my house, my own furniture had been swept away and disappeared. The sideboard had been turned on its side and smashed on the floor. We had mostly lino then, but where the sea had swirled round that had all been churned up into little fragments. The joint of beef we'd been going to have on the Sunday was still in the kitchen, bobbing about in the water, and my knitting was still on the table with one ball of wool hanging in the water, turned all black. They had to knock a hole in the wall to drain the water out of there. We lost so much that couldn't be replaced, like our wedding photographs."

"We lived with my mother for three weeks until we came back and lived upstairs. The RAF came along and helped us to dry out. We had food parcels and a carpet from Canada, there was a Lord Mayor's fund which gave us a little bit of money, but we had no insurance. We got it all together again though and lived there for another ten years."

The 1953 flood proved to be a huge blow to the Beach Village, causing many people and businesses to leave the area for good. "Within six months of the flood we were out of the Kumfy Kafe," remembers Ron James. "We had just opened a fish and chip shop the night before, next to our Kumfy Kafe, and it was only open one night!" His wife Doris recalls, "We'd paid for all the pans in the fish and chip shop and of course, when we got up next morning, all the pans were full of water but no fish in them! They were ruined. We were very lucky though really. We were the only business down there that was insured for sea flood and the only reason we were was because the Prudential agent pointed it out to us. 'Do you want to be insured for sea flood?' he said. 'If you don't specifically state it, you won't get it,' and it cost another half a crown a year. So he put it down and so luckily we were covered. We were flooded out on the Saturday night and the Prudential were knocking at the door on Monday morning with an open cheque. They were very good to us."

(Above) "We had seven foot of water in that pub," remembers Alice Coleman, landlady of the *Gas House Tavern* (pictured, centre). "After the flood, whenever it was windy I used to get nervous. So when the *Blue Anchor* in the High Street came on the market I went for that."

(Right) The sea rushed through the low-lying streets of the Beach Village at 10pm on that Saturday night and still hadn't receded from the Denes by the next day.

(Right) The debris in East Street, post-flood. The logs had been stacked near the pickling plots and were swept around the Beach Village, ramming against many of the properties.

(Below) The 1953 flood affected the businesses in the area too. The ladies at the Steam Laundry were quick to retreive the laundry boxes which they gathered outside the premises and left to dry out.

"The only thing that wasn't covered was the car, a little Austin 7. I could just get this Austin 7 into an Anderson shelter, which I used as a garage, and of course, when the water came it lifted the bloody thing up and we couldn't get the car out. Of course, we did get it out eventually, and the seats were floating inside and were jammed into the roof. We got compensation from the flood fund for that though."

Those that did stay tried to get on with their lives in the ailing village. Jean Mitchell lived at 19 Wilde's Street. "When the water subsided it left behind filthy sludge, very smelly. All my Mum's furniture was ruined, it took many weeks to get some order back and many months to get everywhere clean. We didn't have trauma clinics then. You all had to get stuck in, pull yourselves together and get on with life."

Property was damaged, belongings lost, and people, fearful of another North Sea surge with fatal consequences, were rehoused in the town. The flood certainly hastened the demise of the Beach, and in 1955 the local press announced details of the 'First Stage of Slum Clearance Programme' which included the whole area east of Whapload Road from Marsh Cottage in the north to the Bath House at the corner of Hamilton Road in the south. Familiar buildings and roads were now disappearing and existing streets, like East Street, Spurgeon Street, and Fishery Street, became overshadowed by the growing Birds Eye Food factory.

In the early 1960s the remaining residents began to drift away, houses were boarded up, and some derelict properties became 'the haunts of winos and unsavoury characters'. The area was run-down and in a sorry state, with the Chief Public Health Inspector, Mr Cormack, commenting at the time that '... the Beach Village does not even possess a veneer of olde worlde charm.'

The Beach was doomed, and in these final days many old Gritsters took one last sentimental walk around the derelict streets. 'See that little house over there,' 'Umshi' Norman gestured to a reporter in 1966. 'A family of seven boys and a girl were brought up there. Only two bedrooms, they were a lovely family … It was a real community down here when I was a boy.'

(Top right) With smashed windows and doors off their hinges, Anguish Street had been allowed to fall into a dilipidated condition.

(Middle left) Like so many of the little cottages, 65 East Street, on the corner of Rant Score East, was in a state of disrepair.

(Middle right) Looking south from Gasworks Road, derelict property at the east end of Wilde's Street.

(Bottom left) *The Princess Royal*, once the pride and joy of landlord Wilfred Jones was left boarded up for many years.

(Bottom right) The ruins of the Bath House in Hamilton Road. Built in 1824, it provided hot and cold showers and sea water baths to local who did not have bathing facilities at home. Long out of use, the building remained much the same until its demolition in the late 1960s.

(Right) The 1970s brought the new era of the Beach Village Industrial Estate – the houses on the east side of Whapload Road had been cleared and the streets relaid.

(Below) Looking south towards the last remaining houses in Salter Street with East Street in the foreground, in the late 1960s.

2. THE TOWN BELOW THE CLIFF

The Beach area had an old world charm all its own... many of the cottages were flint-faced and had pantile roofs of that warm red shade of the days gone by... HUGH LEES

It was in 1791 that the first primitive houses were built on the Denes, to the east of the town. Edmund Gillingwater records that 76 tenements were erected here over the next 15 years, which was the birth of what we now know as The Grit, the Beach Village, or simply the Beach, a town below the cliff. At first these dwellings were outnumbered by the many fish-houses which were located there. A guide book from 1812 records that at the bottom of the cliff these buildings were so numerous that 'had they been built more compactly, they would have been sufficient to form a small town of themselves.' A small town was exactly what would evolve over the course of that century.

All of the Denes were privately owned and permission to build on the Beach had to be obtained from the Lord of the Manor, as the whole of this site was considered to be his wasteland. The Corporation bought the manorial rights to the Denes in 1889, but originally strict conditions were applied to these buildings which could not exceed a certain height, and rent was due from those occupying the land. An example of this comes to light in various deeds from the early 1800s concerning Matthew Colman, who had to obtain a licence from the Lord of the Manor to build Ethel Cottage which stood at 1 Nelson Road, known at the time as Nelson Score East.

Ethel Cottage was still standing and in use after the Second World War. "My father was Charles Hall and he was born down there. He lived near Christ Church in Ethel Cottage," recalls Joan Hall. "I think there were five brothers and six sisters, all in this two-bedroom house." Later the Youngman family would live there.

The fishing industry was responsible for the growth of the Beach Village. This had always been an obvious area for such activities, and fish-houses could be found along the base of the cliff in the 16th century. In the mid-17th century cod livers were boiled on the Denes in large iron coppers to extract the oil, and when Lowestoft became involved with whaling that same century, it was here they boiled the blubber for its oil. The decline of the Dutch fleet and the end of the Napoleonic wars in 1815 freed the North Sea for fishing operations. 'Before the harbour was made, the beach was busier than now,' comments Arthur Stebbings in his *Guidebook to Lowestoft* in 1886. 'The fish were all brought ashore and sold on the beach, and great indeed was the stir.' The harbour, built in 1831, wasn't a success until it was acquired by Samuel Morton Peto who developed it alongside a railway in the 1840s. Now the fishing industry began to expand, causing more houses to be built with a pattern of streets forming. In early documents the area is referred to as the 'Beach Village', but by the late 19th century it was known to the locals as 'the Beach' or 'The Grit.'

(Top) Mid-19th century engraving of Beachmen in their shods on the north beach, overlooked by the low light.

(Middle) In 1829 John Kirby noted in his *Topographical and Historical Description of the County of Suffolk*, 'At the bottom of the (hanging) gardens there is a long range of buildings erected for the purpose of curing fish... [from which] escapes the disagreeable effluvia arising from the herrings whilst under cure.'

(Bottom) An early photograph taken around 1870 showing Lighthouse Score and the previous lighthouse which was replaced by the current one in 1874.

Leading down from the High Street to the Beach Village were the 12 'Scores' where many of the Beach families would live. Unique to Lowestoft, the Scores are believed to have ancient origins and were no doubt formed over a period of many years. Footsteps wore paths into the soft sloping cliffs down to the Beach and tracks were eventually formed, with proper wooden steps added to a few.

Although the exact origin of 'Score' is unknown, it is thought the word could be a corruption of 'scour', or possibly from the Old English 'scora', related to the Norse 'skor' which means to make or cut a line. Road surface conditions in the Scores were notoriously poor and in winter months would be dangerous and sometimes impassable. The steps were irregular too – in those Scores that had them – and were usually beside flowing open drains.

Many of the Scores took their names from the people or the public houses located close by, although the general title of Mariners Score would seem to be an exception. Names were frequently changed over the centuries and sometimes Scores were known by more than one name. Street names on The Grit were no doubt derived in much the same way, but it wasn't until the 1860s that they were officially titled. In a meeting of the Lowestoft Improvement Commissioners in 1863, names for streets on the east side of Whapload Road were suggested by the Paving Committee. These were Rant Score East, Anguish Street, Wilde's Score East (later known as Wilde's Street), Cumberland Square, Nelson Road, Coleman Square and Neave Court (which may have been an earlier name for Barcham Square). Anguish Street was named after the Rev George Anguish (1763-1843) who was Lord of the Manor, living at Somerleyton Hall before Sir Samuel Morton Peto. On some maps the name was corrupted to Anquish – probably because no-one could believe a street would be called Anguish, but it was named after a person rather than any 'misery, pain or suffering'. Even in the 1920s there was some confusion regarding street names, as illustrated by Hazel Boardley (née Disney). "I lived opposite the *Rising Sun*. Our house had two numbers, 56 Whapload Road and 1 Spurgeon Street, as we had doors on both roads, so that was all a bit confusing!"

As the Beach Village grew so the fishing industry continued to expand, but the fleet consisted entirely of drifters until the arrival of Kentish men in 1860, who brought trawling to Lowestoft. A little over a decade later, there were 111 trawlers accounting for 30 percent of the town's fleet. However, few of these fishermen from Ramsgate and Kent settled on The Grit; the majority of them were either skippers or masters and could afford to live in better parts of the town, such as Denmark Road and Clapham Road. In the 1880s, as many of the local skippers who lived on The Grit became prosperous, they also moved into the town to new houses which were being built in Worthing Road and Sussex Road which became known as the 'Skipper Rows'. The 1860s also saw the arrival of the first Scottish vessels. Originally these were just from the Firth of Forth, but by the 1890s the fleet had grown to an invasion from Scotland's east coast. The Scots brought their 'womenfolk' down too, arriving on special trains, and their job was to gut and pack the fish, which they did with stunning dexterity. More Scots settled locally than the Kentish trawlermen, and many of the Beach people spoken to in the course of writing this book had Scottish connections. It was

(Right) Malsters Score in the early 1900s, showing the cottages and traditional crinkle-crankle walls. In 1999 the Score was refurbished and the walls extended.

becoming increasingly inconvenient for larger craft which were still landing their catches on the north beach. To cope with the influx of the Scottish fleet each autumn, a fish market was opened in 1872 as there simply hadn't been enough room at existing quays for both trading vessels and fishing boats.

The Denes were purchased by the Corporation in September 1889 for around £2,500 from the trustees of the last Lord of the Manor, Mr Richard Henry Reeve, after his death in 1888. Many plans were subsequently put forward concerning the use of this land. In 1897 a possible route was proposed for a railway line between Yarmouth and Lowestoft which cut straight through the Denes, and although the Council were in favour of the idea, there were too many protests from the public.

There were also proposals for a pier to be built opposite Lighthouse Score, and in 1897 the Duke of Cambridge visited the town for the purpose of cutting the first turf for this structure. This was to be part of a larger scheme which would involve a winding road from

the High Street to Whapload Road, and a fine approach road to the pier wide enough for trams, to be flanked by shops and restaurants. There would be three ornate gateways, the third leading to the pier itself and situated at the end of which would be a grand entertainment hall holding 2,000 people. This was to cost £60,000, but after the initial turf-cutting ceremony nothing happened, and although the North Pier was referred to at a few subsequent Council meetings, the project sank without trace. How different the north end of Lowestoft would have been if this vision had been realised! Although whether a North Pier would have survived two World Wars and the post-war planners is another matter.

The long tradition of fairs held on The Denes dates back to the 15th century. In the early 1900s, Old Spillings Fair took place around Easter on the site which would become the pickling plots in the mid-1920s. Originally known as Pilling's Fair, it was named after the police sergeant responsible for choosing the site after an application was made to hold a fair in the town.

In April 1887 another fair was held on the Denes which attracted a considerable number of visitors, especially youngsters to the roundabout rides. It is said that one of the showmen lost a valuable horse when it fell and drowned in the Warren Pond, situated near to Warren House.

As early as 1844, there are reports of Lowestoft Cricket Club playing matches on the Denes. A permanent enclosed ground was established in 1853 and built at the seaward end of a ropewalk, with a pavilion that stood opposite Lighthouse Score. A deep perimeter ditch was dug to prevent vehicular traffic and stray horses and cattle wandering onto the pitch. However, in 1894 the Cricket Club also moved to the new Crown Meadow following an agreement with Lowestoft Town FC.

(Far Left) Frost's Alley Score was the oldest of the Lowestoft Scores, built over for the new police station in the late 1970s.

(Middle) Wilde's Score was once the home of a school and a crinkle-crankle wall, but is now incomplete: the lower section was built over by Birds Eye in the 1970s and its path diverted into Cumberland Place.

(Right) Mariner's Score in the early 1900s, still has its distinctive archway at the top and for nearly 90 years was also the location of a school, until it closed in 1934.

At the north end of Whapload Road was the summer home and park of the Sparrow family. Robert Sparrow co-founded the Lowestoft lifeboat with Rev Francis Bowness at the beginning of the 19th century and his estate, which also included two fish-houses and the fishermen's cottages in Lighthouse Score, was known as Sparrows Nest. Auctioned in 1897, it was bought by the Corporation for over £11,000 and the following year let to Frank Stebbings, the High Street printer, who erected a stage in the grounds where he presented a circus and variety show.

The entertainment took place under a large tented awning in the lower garden which lasted until it was destroyed by a gale in 1912, when a new pavilion was hastily built under the supervision of Sidney Mobbs (the council engineer who was later responsible for the sea wall built in 1923). The Sparrows Nest Theatre opened in 1913 by which time the gardens had become a public park.

In August 1919 large marquees were set up on the North Denes for a 'welcome home' feast for 3,500 soldiers and sailors returning from the First World War. Liquid refreshments included 30 barrels of beer and 115 gallons of mineral water and after the feast, the men were joined by their 'wives and sweethearts' for an entertainment at Sparrows Nest.

In 1920 Lowestoft Corporation decided a new recreational area would be built on the North Denes, partly on land that had been allotments for 60 years. A model yacht pond had already been installed nearby in 1889, which in winter was also used for skating and fancy dress carnivals illuminated by coloured lanterns. Now, over 30 years later, enclosed grounds for cricket, tennis and hockey would be added, plus the construction of an outdoor swimming pool. The main instigator of this plan was none other than Borough Surveyor Sidney Mobbs – designer of both the Sparrows Nest theatre and the sea wall. He also happened to be Vice Captain of the Cricket Club and was the driving force behind this costly plan to provide the town with a first class venue for cricket.

As part of Mobbs' plan, the swimming pool was the first to be built, and it opened on 7th July 1921. Containing water pumped direct from the sea, the open-air pool was 150 feet long by 100 feet wide, with depths varying from three to six feet, and it had a diving board and a water chute. Although the pool suffered bomb damage during the Second World War and was subsequently filled in, it was hugely popular amongst the children who lived in the Beach Village in the 1920s and 30s.

The cricket and hockey pitches took longer to be constructed. In 1922 the Denes Oval ground was levelled and in 1924 the Norfolk Cricket Association employed cricketer Mr G A Stevens (of Norwich Wanderers Cricket Club) to give expert advice on the laying of the new cricket square and outfield. It wasn't until the following year that first match was played at Denes Oval – on 6th June 1925 against Norwich Wanderers Cricket Club, with Mr Stevens in the team. It is not recorded if Sidney Mobbs played that day. Another sport was added the following year to the area's list of outdoor pursuits; a golf course was laid out partly on the Denes and partly on the cliff-top and Corton Golf Club was established. If you wanted leisure activities in Lowestoft, the Denes was the place to go.

(Right) The early 19th century thatched summer residence of Robert Sparrow. In the 1890s, the Council bought Sparrows Nest Gardens which became a popular venue for concerts, with a 1300-seat theatre built in 1913.

(Below) The Ravine in the early 1900s. Dividing Lowestoft and Gunton, it led to the more prosperous houses on North Parade with access to Belle Vue Park.

(Above) The Lowestoft Corporation created a new recreational area on The Denes in the 1920s starting with an open-air swimming pool in 1921 right next to the North Sea. Damaged during the War, the caravan park now stands on the site.

(Top right) In the early 20th century, the north beach was as popular as the south beach for bathing.

(Middle right) A new Bath House was built in 1824 on the southern boundary of The Grit on a site where baths had been available for many years. *White's Suffolk* (1844) describes it as 'an oblong building with rusticated angles and has a spacious reading room, and hot and cold baths.'

(Bottom right) In September 1927 the new sea wall was used for motor cycle and car speed trials. The 60-foot wide decking, a mile and a half long, was declared ideal but trials were never held again, although the following year motor cycles did race round the gravel perimeter of Normanston Park.

Until the Second World War, the north beach was as popular as the south beach for bathing, and there was evidence of the increasing popularity of the seaside holiday in the 19th century, even when shared with a fishing area such as the Beach Village. From the early 1800s there was a Bath House on the Beach where bathers were provided with heated sea-water. By 1824 it was deemed necessary to build a new Bath House, which was larger and offered more facilities, such as 'sulphureous medicated baths', and was run by 'four gentlemen' who sold it to a Mr Walter Jones in 1830. The advertisements of the day made it plain that the baths would operate only during the summer season and it seems likely that they were built for the summer visitors rather than the locals. By 1884 the Bath House had passed into the hands of the Cook family, who had had a long association with this area, hiring bathing machines from the north beach since 1768. In 1901 there was an attempt to convert the Bath House into a hotel, joining it with two other nearby properties, Kent House and Beach House. The scheme would have cost £9,000 and was put forward by Frank Stanley Dorling who applied for an order to move the full licence of the Albion Stores in the High Street to the new hotel. The local magistrates refused and the plans were scrapped.

The early 1900s saw the building of the first of the three sea walls for the north beach. Although all of these structures succumbed to the North Sea on various occasions, they all provided an invaluable breakwater for the force of the water which, had there not been a sea wall in place, would have proved devastating. On 26th November 1925 Mobbs' wall faced a record high tide of 24 feet and the whole of the Beach Village was flooded to a depth of about two feet, with thousands of herring barrels washed through the streets. In all, 250 houses were flooded to a depth of three feet. It seems likely that this is the occurrence that Ruby Timberley (née Dalley) remembers, "I was about six years old, attending Mariners Score School. I think it was in the early afternoon when a man came round ringing a bell and telling mothers to collect their children from Mariners Score School and get them upstairs, and our mother came along with other mothers to collect us. The sight will remain with me always of when I looked out of the bedroom window to see fish barrels floating in Anguish Street with driftwood and seaweed. The sea was very deep and was splashing against the walls of the houses and coming indoors to about three feet high. We children were terrified. I think the adults were too. Of course, everywhere was soaked in sea water. Gradually the tide turned and the sea went back. The council of the day allowed each householder one hundredweight of coal free to help dry out."

Historically, the 'town below the cliff' had frequently suffered from flooding. Edmund Gillingwater recorded that in the early 1700s if a spring tide coincided with a north-west gale, the sea would force its way over the beach and sweep across the Denes into fish-houses and approach the hanging gardens which were the back gardens of properties in the High Street running down to the bottom of the cliff.

Over the centuries, the sandbanks which once acted as breakwaters diminished and the sea gradually encroached. The evidence of this erosion is recorded by Gillingwater in 1790, who states at the time he was writing his history of Lowestoft, there were at least three fathoms of water over an area which had been dry land in the reign of Henry VIII. At the beginning of the 19th century there were still visible sandbanks. After the Battle of Waterloo in 1815 an effigy of Napoleon was placed there, and by 1861 Beachmen even used to run trips to Holm Sands where on one occasion a cricket match was played. There had been a lengthy beach beyond Ness Point where you could find the Marram Hills, named after the grass which grew there, holding together the sand which was gradually being washed away.

A flood in November 1897 must have served as a warning to the Council who subsequently began to consider the erection of a substantial wooden wall along the sea front, running a distance of 1,800 yards, from Ness Point to the boundary of Mr Colman's estate at Corton. The lowest tender for this work was £6,900 but the Council decided to consult an expert in these matters. Mr William Tregarthen Douglass was the engineer they turned to. He had been resident engineer at the new Eddystone Lighthouse and had recently constructed, a sea wall in Cromer. Douglass charged 30 guineas for his consultation which consisted of two visits to the site before he drew up a plan and quoted £34,356 to carry out the work. The main part of his scheme was the construction of a concrete retaining wall, costing £10,500, which would run the whole length of the front to the Ness. Douglass maintained that the wall would keep the sea from flooding the Denes, and that the groynes would prevent the encroachment which had been so marked during the previous ten years. The committee was not satisfied with this at first, as a concrete wall of the length he proposed seemed a rather substantial affair and they deferred their decision for further discussion, but eventually the plan was accepted and the Douglass Wall, built in 1902-3 withstood the pounding of the North Sea until the early 1920s.

In 1922 a new sea wall was constructed. Designed by Sidney Mobbs, this included a roadway which became a popular promenade. A bus service ran along it in the summer, giving the seasonal visitors a closer look at the Beach Village. In 1927 this roadway was also used for both car and motor cycle racing, with a mile-long course laid out, with tuning pits situated on a site which later became the Corporation depot. On one occasion, a magnificent cup was donated by the town council and a crowd estimated at 6,000 saw the cars and motor cycles hurtling along the sea wall. It is said that one racing car reached a speed of 100 mph in the days when lorry drivers were being fined for exceeding the 12 mph speed limit in the town!

The sea wall was also where many people gathered on 7th June 1931, when Lowestoft suffered an earthquake. It was felt that the vibrations had come from the sea and there were fears that the fishing trawlers could be damaged. An anxious wait followed before they all returned safely to harbour. Although there was no serious damage, George Wilson, who lived on Whapload Road recalls, "During the earthquake in the 1930s our chimney fell off and dropped on our shed!"

(Above) The houses in Newcombe Road were some of many that suffered flooding on Sunday 28th November 1897 when the town 'was visited by a tide that had never been known before'. This prompted the building of the Douglass sea wall in 1902.

(Right) Despite the new sea wall The Grit was still flooded although the wall certainly reduced the force of the waves. High tide in 1905 brought with it water across Whapload Road, northwards of the Steam Laundry (right).

3. THE BEACHMEN

**Everyone took an interest in the Beach Companies
in those days, and the almost deserted Beach
was soon all alive when the cry
of 'Running Down' was heard.
LETTER TO THE *LOWESTOFT JOURNAL*, 6TH FEBRUARY 1897**

When one strolls on the Beach,' writes Arthur Stebbings in his *Guidebook to Lowestoft* in 1886, 'the Beachmen may be remarked by their absence, for look where you will not one is to be seen, do not imagine they are not all at hand. They are like the warriors of Roderick Dhu, numerous though not seen; let a ship strike the sands or come ashore, and out of the cavernous depths of the 'shods' they pour in goodly numbers, equal to any emergency and ready for any deed of rescue. The visitors do not often witness these scenes for they come in fair sunny weather…'

The Beachmen were fishermen, supplementing their income with salvage work, assisting the sailing ships which ran into trouble off the coast. They also picked up work carrying fish to markets in London, in addition to taking the pilots from the shore to ships which required guidance coming into the harbour.

Edward Capps-Jenner (1887-1974), son of the coxswain of the lifeboat, remembered the late 19th century Beachmen of his childhood in a 1960s typewritten account of his life as 'someone who came off The Grit'. 'The Beachmen, of whom there were in my boyhood a large number, were organised in three 'Beach Companies', each had a shed (pronounced 'shod') on the beach, and each had a yawl (pronounced 'yoll')… These boats were kept pulled up on the beach near the appropriate shed, and were owned and worked by members of the appropriate Company, and used for salvage work in helping stranded vessels (mostly sail), which got into difficulties very frequently on the beach or outlying sandbanks.'

In his Guidebook, Arthur Stebbings described the shods as, 'well furnished with sails, spars, ropes, excellent though odd-looking telescopes, through which the Beachmen do not look into the middle of next week exactly, but by which they know that a ship is on the sands before the ship's crew know it and they launch their gigs and are halfway to the rescue before the crew know in what jeopardy they are. These sheds are painted with the gayest of colours, and the figureheads of vessels whose crews have been saved are displayed thereon.'

The tradition of the shods continued well into 20th century. Jack Rose, born in 1926, remembers his grandfather taking him as a child to the Young Company shod near the gasworks. "This old building seemed to be held together with tar, and was adorned with old ships' figureheads and name plates from wrecks. To a young boy though, it seemed dark and spooky with a strong smell of salt, tar and sweat."

In the 19th century whenever a ship was spotted in distress the yawls would be launched from the shore and there was a frantic race amongst the three Beach Companies, with the first yawl to make contact with the endangered vessel being rewarded with the job according to the laws of salvage. There was money to be made from salvage and as a result, there was no shortage of assistance for troubled vessels. In the early days the Beachmen were also linked with smuggling and had a notorious reputation, seen as little more than scavengers and branded 'longshore sharks and pirates'. However, the Beachmen were needed and saved many lives from stricken vessels, especially in the days before lifeboat stations and harbour tugs which would, in time, take over their role. Lowestoft's first lifeboat was established in 1801, built by Henry Greathead at Shields for £105. The Beachmen were obvious choices for the lifeboat crew but they refused to use her, claiming she was unsuited to this particular part of the coast. After much discussion a replacement boat, *Frances Ann*, was built in 1807 for £200 by Mr Barcham who had his yard in the Beach Village. This vessel, built locally, was obviously preferred and served until 1859, saving 300 lives during that period.

Edward Capps-Jenner records how the Beachmen's role changed during his childhood in the early 1890s. 'At the time of my early recollection, salvage work was falling off, owing to many of the sailing coasters and larger sailing ships having been replaced by steamers, which latter, according to my father, could find their way up and down the coast on their own and it seems were almost expected to do so! They were, you see, never 'wind-bound', as the old sailing ships so frequently were and all trying to get away as soon as a favourable wind occurred, pushing one another onto the sands as the saying was. There were not always, by any means, lives to be saved, but there were anchors to be run off and laid, and other assistance to be rendered, which could well be done by a beach yawl or gig.'

'We beach boys all had, of course, an allegiance to one or other of the Companies, the 'Young Company', the 'Old Company' and the 'North Road Company', which owned yawls named respectively *Georgina*, *Happy New Year* and *Lady Sophia*. The Old Company also had a small yawl, then going into decline, called *Success*. Members of these Companies formed the lifeboat crew, and only such members were allowed in the lifeboat, which in those days 'went off' only in 'lifeboat weather'. In fine weather the rescue or salvage work was done by the Companies' own boats.'

'If the lifeboat did a salvage job, the RNLI did not make any charge for the use of the boat, but only for the cost of repairing any damage which she might sustain or replacement of any damage which she might sustain, or replacement of any gear which might be lost. Neither, of course, did the RNLI make any payment to the men, they taking such salvage as they could get as payment for their work.'

The Beachmen continued to combine manning the lifeboat in addition to their salvage work and, in many cases, fishing-related work. However, by the time Jack Rose was a child in the 1930s, the Company shods had evolved into little more than clubrooms for the lifeboatmen. During the Second World War the two remaining historic shods were used by the military; both suffered bomb damage and all the old pictures, name-plates and

(Top left) John Coleman, Matthew Coleman and 'Sheppey' Hook playing cards in the Old Company shod.

(Top right) The Old Company shod, shown in the early 1900s, was adorned with salvaged figureheads from ships and name boards all recovered from the North Sea. The Company members lining up outside are (far left) Peter Smith, 'Brock' Ellis (with telescope), 'Sheppey' Hook, Dixon Peek (seated), Harris Allerton and John 'Painter' Swan.

(Bottom right) The Young Company shod, pictured in the 1920s, was situated near to the gasworks and proudly displayed a small salvaged cannon outside.

figureheads were taken away. After the war, compensation was received for the damage to the Beach Company property and a Nissen hut was erected near the sea wall, to the north of the coastguard look-out. This was called the 'Lowestoft Lifeboat and Life Saving Apparatus Social Club' and subsequently moved to the former Ayers' net store in East Street and then to premises at the end of Hamilton Road in 1962 before the lifeboat crew broke away and formed the 'Lowestoft Lifeboatmen's Crewman's Association'. These clubs were the last link with the Beachmen and their Companies.

The earliest mention of any Lowestoft Beach Companies is in 1762, with references to Companies run by two brothers, Thomas and Nicholas Martin, and another owned by John Masterson. This was followed by the arrival of three new Beach Companies in the 1780s to cope with the increase in salvage and pilotage work. Denny's, Reed's and Lincoln's were owned by private individuals, pilots who were also publicans in the cases of Joseph Denny and William Lincoln. Originally Beachmen merely crewed the boats but in 1835 the pilots left and the Companies were all reorganised, the Beachmen buying shares in the boats. The oldest, Denny's Company, which was by then known as 'Denny's Old', was now re-named the Old Company, while Reed's and Lincoln's amalgamated and became known as the New or Young Company. A third, the North Roads Company, named after the area where it principally worked, is believed to have been established in 1837 although some sources claim that the date was 1845. Each had around 60 to 80 members and any man who wanted to become a member had to purchase a share of the yawls, have his name entered in the books and he was then entitled to work the boats and form one of the lifeboat crew. Widows were allowed to put a man into the boats to work the shares owned by their late husbands or be looked after in some other way. The younger men would only take half a dole until they reached a certain age. A veteran Beachman was appointed to look after the sails, gear and shed and another member looked after the financial side of the Company, keeping the books and paying all the bills for repair. With money at stake, the rivalry between each Company was intense, and although the Old and Young Companies joined up in the 1850s to form the United Beach Company, the partnership was short-lived and they soon returned to their separate identities.

The Beachmen would receive their wages or 'doles' in one of the public houses. The Lowestoft Beach Companies had their own pubs dating back to the days when Joseph Denny owned the *Herring Fishery* and William Lincoln owned the *Jolly Maltsters* next to Maltsters Score. The North Roads Company had the *George and Dragon* which from 1850 to 1875 became known as the *Norwich Arms* in the High Street.

Each Company had two or three yawls and a smaller vessel called a gig was used in calmer weather. The yawls were tarred originally, but over the years were painted instead. At first, their top sides were black, with red or blue bottoms, then white bottoms with a deep black top was the fashion until all white with a black top streak became popular. Yawls could be launched quickly and because they were light, could achieve a speed of 15mph with a good wind. Stones were used for ballast which could be quite useful for ammunition if you were racing a rival Company!

(Right) William Benjamin Burwood (1836–1907), known as 'Happy Will', was a member of the Old Company. It seems likely that he is the William Burwood who in his youth lived close to the Bath House and who married Matilda Critten in 1857.

(Far right) Two old beachmen in the 1890s. In 1892 the Lowestoft Journal reported, 'There are now eight members of the Beach Companies 80 years of age and upwards, and five others over 86 years' This was at a time when the average life expectancy for men was 44 years!

The Companies took a pride in their yawls, and the names of these vessels became well known around the Beach Village. Between 1837 and 1894 the Old Company had four yawls by the name of *Happy New Year*, others being *Princess Royal*, *Southern Friends*, *Beeswing*, *Mosquito*, *Bittern* and *Success*. The Young Company had the *Lord Nelson* and in later days, the *Georgiana*, while the North Roads Company had *Victory* and *Lady Collyer*.

In the early 1880s nearly 300 longshoremen belonged to the three Lowestoft Beach Companies, the biggest being the Old Company which had 119 members, while the Young Company had 90 members and the North Roads Company 70. By this time, some family names had been on the Company books for three generations. The most frequent names in the Old Company were Burwood and Mewse, with Ayers, Cook, Yallop, Coleman and Smith following closely behind. There were three men called James Ellis and three William Burwoods! In the Young Company, Tyrrell, Capps and Hall were the most common names, while in the North Roads Company Rose and Knights were the most repeated. The Old Company was living up to its name too, and among its members had veterans such as James Yallop, who was recorded as being 88 years of age, Ben Butcher was 85, Stephen Butcher 84, H. Spurgeon 82, John Clark 80, Ben Taylor 79 and Tom Ellis 76.

Famous Lowestoft photographer Harry Jenkins did much to capture this generation of Beachmen, with stunning portraits which he sold as postcards and which are much sought after today. Harry arrived in the town in 1896 and soon set up shop at 2 Pier Terrace and

(Above) Three portraits of Ned 'Nitty' Ellis by Lowestoft photographer Harry Jenkins.

(Overleaf) A montage showing portraits of the Beachmen from the Old Company created by Harry Jenkins in 1914.

was succeeded in the business first by his son, Ford, and then by his grandson, Peter, who was still trading in the 1990s.

Harry's most instantly recognisable Beachmen portrait adorned the window of the shop in the 1970s and 80s. It featured Edward 'Ned' Ellis, pictured with two young children (who are the young Ford Jenkins and his sister), but few know the story of this fiery character's life. Ned was born on 22nd June 1843 and was also known as 'Nitty' to his family and friends. He married Anna Moore in 1866 and they had 10 children, living on The Grit at Newcombe View, to the south of the village in the area of the Bath House and the Coastguard Station.

Ned seems frequently to have got into arguments and disputes, but the Harry Jenkins photo brought with it national acclaim in 1905 when it was used to advertise Lifebuoy soap. In 2019 his great great great great grandson, Martin Ellis, shared the story. "My family has it that he was asked to pose again for the adverts a year or so later for the next campaign but he refused, telling them he had never been paid for the first shoot, which Lifebuoy refuted. He therefore didn't pose for them. For subsequent adverts they used a facsimile of Ned and then a cartoon type depiction of him." Ned seems to have got into more trouble in his later days. Martin explains, "There is an issue of him disappearing off the radar late in his life. He was no longer on the census for 1911. It was suspected that this was because he was in prison before he died in 1920."

In Memory of a Few Members

J BUTCHER 1879-1912.

SAM MEWSE

1815 TOM ELLIS, "BROCK" 1899

1828. ROBE

E ELLIS 1796-1861

H ALLERTON.

1837. JOE FLETCHER "POSH"

PETER SMITH

THE OLD

1837 J.S.COOK.

1914

W. ALLERTON.

T BUTCHER.

1832. NODDER YALLOP.

1823.T COLEMAN.

TH

he Old Comp. of Beachmen, Lowestoft.

1846 EDWARD ELLIS.

S. AYERS.

1827 JOHN FLETCHER 1888.

1799 THOMAS COLEMAN 1874.

1835 W BURWOOD 1909.

1837 J MEWSE.

1837 J.AYERS.

FLETCHER AYRES. T COLEMAN

W HARRIS

1846 JOE SWAN 1911.

1828 JAMES BURWOOD 1912.

1830. W HOOK. 1912.

H. JENKINS.
PHOTOGRAPHER
LOWESTOFT.
COPYRIGHT

Ned's wife Anna remained on The Grit though. She seems to have been quite a character too. In David Butcher's *Living from the Sea*, Annie Short recalls, 'If anybody was ill, everyone mucked in. There used t' be an old lady down there, ow Ned Ellis' wife. She wuz just like a doctor, that woman was. She used t'do all sorts o' things. She had an ow parrot an' if anyone went t' the back door you'd hear that ow thing sing out "Anna, you're wanted!"'

With the demise of sail the Beachmen's role was diminishing by the latter half of the 19th century. Many trading vessels now had their own pilots aboard and with steam tugs operating from the harbour the yawls had strong competition. The Beachmen had to find other work, and the increasing popularity of the seaside holiday in Victorian times provided an opportunity for taking visitors on pleasure trips along the coast. By the end of the 19th century, the large yawls were being kept purely for the prestigious Lowestoft Regatta races. This event was dominated by the Young Company yawls – *Eclipse* and later the *Georgiana* – which were presented to them in 1892 by the 'Committee of Gentlemen Admirers of the Beachmen'. In response the Old Company got their own new yawl, which took the name *Happy New Year*, but had to wait 15 years and 15 *Georgiana* victories until it won the very last yawl race in 1907.

'This yawl race was for Beach people the event of the day,' writes Edward Capps-Jenner remembering his childhood in the 1890s. 'There was much argument and strong language from beginning to end of this event and it was sometimes a thankless task to be chosen to 'take', that is to steer the boat, unless of course she was the winner, when the beer was plentiful and free. The Regatta days were half-holidays and so the highlight of the year with us beach boys.'

The Beach Companies dwindled from the start of the 20th century. In 1901 the North Roads Company amalgamated with the Young Company and there would be another attempt at combining the Old and New Companies in 1922, but this lasted just a year. The Young Company eventually closed its books in 1939, the same year that the Old Company launched its last yawl, before closing in 1940. In 1935 one of the last shod concerts was held in the Young Company shod. These annual concerts were known as 'smokers' and were peculiar to Lowestoft, but by this time had become more of a nostalgic affair, recalling the past glories of the Beachmen. The *Lowestoft Journal* reported on this particular smoker, stating that there was 'an excellent concert programme' that night. The Company still had 60 members, amongst them the Coxswain Albert Spurgeon, and it is recorded that the highlight was a duet sung by the brothers Welham, 'Happy' and 'Brassey', which caused much amusement, while 'refreshments, liquid and otherwise, were provided in abundance, together with plentiful supplies of tobacco, cigarettes and fruit dessert.' The concert evenings were always a success and there would be many songs sung into the early hours. The Old Company also held smokers, where 'Posh' Fletcher is said to have often sung a rousing chorus with the rest of the Company joining in the refrain:

Don't forget your shipmates,
Don't forget your shipmates,
I 'on't forget my shipmates,
With a whack-fol-the-riddle-lol-the-ri-do!

(Right) The yawl race at the 1853 Lowestoft Regatta was watched by large crowds on the beach and the North and South Piers. The Eastern Counties Railway ran excursion trains to bring visitors to the town for the regatta, which was an event not only for yachtsmen but also for the Beachmen, whose yawls competed for prize money totalling £30.

(Below) Beachmen in the Old Company shod in the 1930s. Harris Allerton (far left) lived in East House, the most easterly house in the country.

(Right) Robert Hook, coxswain of the Lowestoft lifeboat for 30 years and a member of the Old Company, with his brother William 'Sheppey' Hook (far right).

(Below) As part of his election campaign in 1910, Conservative MP Harry Foster was pictured with the Old Company. He found a supporter in local hero, coxswain and Old Company stalwart, Robert Hook who appeared on promotional postcards with the message –'Vote for Foster – the true friend of all Lowestoft Fishermen'.

Despite the demise of the Beach Companies, the presence of Beachmen in the lifeboat crews continued. Throughout the early history of the lifeboat in Lowestoft, the coxswains lived in the Beach Village. Robert Hook is a fine example, having been coxswain of the lifeboat from 1853 to 1883 and a member of the Old Company too. By the age of 16 Bob was six foot three inches tall with a 'Herculean frame' and he was already helping to save lives at sea. By the time of his retirement he had twice won the Institution's Silver Medal. Hook retired in 1883, owing to a dispute with the Lifeboat Institution over paying his crew in his pub called the *Fishermen's Arms*, opposite the the *Rising Sun* (premises that would later be Hammond's fish and chip shop). Hook came from a Beach Village family and had a brother who was known as 'Sheppey', supposedly because he wore his tan 'slop' (a fisherman's smock) so long that he looked like a shepherd. In the *Lowestoft Journal* on 11th September 1886 Robert Hook explained a little of his famous history; 'I was born on 4th June 1828 and am therefore just over 58 years old. My father was Robert Hook, a fisherman and Beachman who died a few years ago aged 86 years. My grandfather was 87 years old when he died in 1844 and both had been long connected with lifeboat service in one way or another.' Robert Hook died on 28th June 1911 aged 83, and was survived by his wife Sarah Ann Hook, who died seven years later on 18th January 1918.

Hook's successor as coxswain was William Capps-Jenner, who was appointed in 1883 and held the position until his death on 10th February 1901. His son Edward wrote, 'Over our front door when I was born was a blue board with black letters, bearing the inscription, 'Royal National Lifeboat. William Capps, First Coxswain.' His appointment was the result of a discreditable affair in 1882, which came to be known as 'Black Saturday' when lives were lost in shipwrecks owing to some sordid dispute about payment to the lifeboat crew, and the boat was not launched as she should have been. As a result of the row which followed, a change of coxswain was made, and my father undertook the job, which nearly drove him mad, but being the man he was he determined to stick it out and get the station onto a good footing again, and this he did although he never received public credit for this very fine work, which only a man of exceptional strength of character, determination and goodwill could have done.'

'To get back to the lifeboat (*boat* pronounced to rhyme with *put*), in those days the coxswain called out the crew by maroons (a type of rocket which made a loud noise) fired from a post set up on the beach and operated by the signalman, one Billy Stone. But if the weather was bad my father and other Beachmen would hang about the pier 'in case anything happened'. One night he and my three brothers were all doing this, but Bob got fed up and came home early, remarking to my mother that nothing would happen that night. He had just turned in when the maroons went off, and he missed the boat to his intense annoyance.'

'It was not unusual in the early days for my father and three brothers all to be in the boat together. The crew were 19 in number and each had to secure a belt, (cork lifejacket) to qualify for 'going off'. There was great competition for these belts among the best and keenest members of the Beach Companies.'

'My father had in common with other Lowestoft lifeboatmen two silver medals – one presented by the Austrian Government for the rescue on 13th January 1877 of the seven-man crew of the Austrian brig *Osip* by the lifeboat *Laetitia*; the other a local award for the rescue of the *Berthon* on 14th November 1882.'

One thing that Billy Capps-Jenner did change during his tenure was how the men were paid. His son explains, 'There was a system whereby the RNLI paid each member of the crew a fixed sum, according to the time of day or night and time of year. Also a fixed sum for 'launching-money'. As the Lowestoft boat was always afloat in the harbour, this latter money was intended to remunerate those shoremen who not having secured a belt, assisted in un-mooring the boat, putting in the sails etc. and getting her away, and then re-mooring upon return. The maroons of course gave notice to everybody that the boat was going on service, and at times the number of shoremen was very high, reaching about two hundred on at least one occasion.'

'A purely local custom was to pool all the money received from the RNLI and to share it – two shares to a man in the boat, one share to a shoreman. I have heard my brother Jack say that he has received as little as one and sixpence for going off the boat.'

'My father decided to reform this method, and not to allow the possibility of a slacker turning up after the boat had gone, standing under a lee somewhere and drawing half as much for doing nothing as the man who risked his life. He therefore got the men to adopt a tally system. Any man who put in an appearance before the boat was cast off from her moorings got a round brass 'tally', none of these being issued after casting off. The names of the holders of these discs were then recorded on a slate in the shed on the pier, and when the money was 'doled' they were paid accordingly.'

'This 'doling' of all salvage awards, launch money and other RNLI payments for lifeboat work was done by the coxswain in the lifeboat shed on the Beach. 'The signal that a 'doling' was to take place on a certain day was to lash a certain burgee flag mounted on a boat-hook to one certain post in the middle of the Beach. It was an extremely efficient 'bush-telegraph'.'

'At that time a new coxswain was chosen by the members of the Beach Companies. This however could get confusing because family names were so common on the Beach Village and many men had the same name – one of the reasons why nicknames were so important. 'On one occasion, when a ballot was organised to chose a coxswain, the voters' list had to give all the nicknames of the members of the Companies to ensure that the right Jack, Billy, William, John, Robert etc. was identified. The coxswain so elected was John S. Swan.'

That would have been in 1911 when John 'Jack' Swan, born 1857 and a member of the Old Company, was chosen to replace the late William Capps-Jenner. Swan came from a large Beach family which it is said at one time had three generations in the Company. From an early age Jack was involved with yawls and he was a member of the lifeboat crew for 52 years and in 1911, at the age of 54, he was appointed coxswain of the Lowestoft lifeboat.

One of the most spectacular rescues with which he was involved was when the lifeboat *Agnes Cross* put to sea in a fierce gale in response to a distress call from the *Hopelyn*.

(Below) In addition to the Company shods, some Beachmen had their own personal hut where they kept their own fishing gear. Harris Allerton's shod (top) was next to one which belonged to Jack Rose's father. These were close to Harris's house in East Street (which can be seen overlooking the two wooden properties).

(Right) Born at 2 Cumberland Square, William Capps-Jenner (1840-1901) was lifeboat coxswain from 1883 till his death.

(Bottom right) 'Watcher' Turrell was a well-known Beachman and lifeboatman and the great-grandfather of Joy Pearce.

The vessel had run aground on Scroby Sands and had been battered by huge seas. Despite jagged parts of the wreck sticking up all round, Swan managed to steer his lifeboat right up close and save 24 lives and the ship's cat! Swan was awarded the RNLI Gold Medal for this service and the house where he lived, which was next to the Almshouses on Whapload Road, became known as Hopelyn Cottage as a result of this rescue.

In June 1942 Swan retired after helping to save 258 lives in Institution boats with over 70 launches as coxswain. He had been awarded two Silver Medals in addition to the Gold, and he was further honoured by King George V with an OBE on 30th June 1924 at Buckingham Palace. During his retirement Jack became an elder statesman for the RNLI and spent his time supporting the service by presenting prizes, or speaking at theatres and cinemas in London, and was even heard on the radio. He died on 2nd February 1935 at the age of 78, and three of his sons followed him into the lifeboat service.

Jack Swan was fondly remembered in the Beach Village and was still well thought of in the 1990s. Ron James remembers him as an old man, "He was a fine old fellow with a white beard. I was in Lowestoft Hospital with him. I lay in the next bed to him and as he'd won several awards he had a lot of influential friends who used to bring him fruit which was a luxury in those days. When they'd gone he'd say, 'Come on boy, you have these!' He was a nice old chap, he was. He used to say, 'Take 'em all round the ward!'"

Swan's successor as coxswain was Albert Spurgeon. As a crew member of the *Agnes Cross* he received the Bronze Medal in November 1922 for his part in the *Hopelyn* rescue, and in 1924 he took over the command. In November 1927 he was awarded the Silver Medal for his rescue of the crew of the ketch *Lily of Devon*. He became coxswain of the *Michael Stephens* in 1939, and in November 1943 he was awarded the Bronze 2nd Service Clasp for his rescue of the crew of *HM Minesweeper No. 106*. He retired in 1947 after 23 years as coxswain. Charles Ellis recalls that Albert Spurgeon was the proud possessor of a pair of binoculars, given to him by a German captain during the First World War. "He reckoned that the L52 Zeppelin came down off Lowestoft and the lifeboat picked up the survivors. Spurgeon pulled the captain into the lifeboat and he had a set of night-glasses round his neck. He said, 'Thank you very much,' and taking the glasses from his neck he hung them round old Spurgeon's neck and said in first-class English, 'You might as well have these, I shan't need them any more in this war.' And Spurgeon always had those glasses."

The bond between the Beach Village and the lifeboat continued into the 1960s and beyond. Harry Burgess lived on The Grit, and was a lifeboat crew member from 1931 to 1936 and bowman from 1937 to 1946. In 1947 he was made second coxswain and in the same year was appointed coxswain, the youngest on the east coast at that time. More recent coxswains have been Peter Gibbons and John Catchpole, both of whom had connections with The Grit.

Vernil Tuck was typical of this breed of Beachmen and lifeboatmen. Said to have been the last surviving member of the Old Company, Vernil lived with his wife and three daughters at

27 Wilde's Street but later, in the early 1960s when this property was demolished, he moved with his wife to Lighthouse Score until his death on 3rd August 1987. One of his daughters, Beryl Clover, recalls her father talking about his early days in the lifeboat. "Because his name was Tuck, they used to call him 'Friar' Tuck. He was in the lifeboat from a very early age. He used to go there to sweep up at first, because he wanted to get in the lifeboat." Her sister Norma takes up the story, "He went there when he was 15 and we don't think he was credited with all the years he was there. Because he was known as 'Friar' some of his early years were credited to Friar instead. Later on he was known as just 'Tucky'." His first name, Vernil, was unique to the Beach Village. Beryl explains, "When he was born in 1907, he should have been Vernon, but they spelt it wrong at the christening, or at least, that's what he always said!"

"I can remember when my father used to go out on the lifeboat," adds Norma. "When the rockets went up we all had our own little jobs, one had to get his boots out ready for him, while the other was getting his bike out of the shed. My Mum used to get his coat, Sheila used to get his tobacco and that, we all knew our jobs, then he used to get on his bike, and we all used to race down beside him. There was a slipway by the lifeboat shed and we raced with my Dad and all the children in the road used to go as well, and we'd all stand on the sea wall, and the lifeboatmen would wave on their way out. We used to wait for them to come in and sometimes our hands were all frost-bitten."

Yvonne Scriggins' father John Scriggins, who was also known as Jack or 'Pimp', died in January 1996. At one time he was a lifeboatman on the *Agnes Cross*. "When on lifeboat duty Dad was knocked up to go to a rescue, more often than not he would have to put on wet trousers which had been drying in front of the fire. They were his only pair."

Ron James' father was also a lifeboatman. "I've known a time when my father would go to the pub and have a couple of pints, come home and be just going to bed and the lifeboat guns would go, and he'd run like hell down there and that was supposed to be his day off, and he'd be out in the lifeboat! They used to run right along to the North Pier, we used to call it the Old Extension, they used to have to run all the way and I don't know how many, but people have died just running there, collapsed with a heart attack I suppose. We didn't know much about that then, they were dead and we just buried them!"

(Right) John Swan was coxswain from 1911 to 1924 when he retired aged 72. He won the Institution's gold medal, the silver medal twice and was also awarded an OBE. His successor was Albert Spurgeon (far right) who was coxswain from 1924 until his retirement in 1947. Albert won the Institution's silver medal and twice won the bronze.

(Right) Most of the lifeboat crew had connections with the Beach Village. Here the crew are pictured on the boarding boat with the lifeboat Frederick Edward Crick in the background. (From the top, clockwise) Billy Capps Jenner, Billy Thorpe, Harold Robinson, Jack Rose, Harry Kirby, Harry Burgess (coxswain), Peter Gibbons, Jock Stoddart, Vernil Tuck.

(Opposite left) After the Second World War the Beach Companies regrouped and renamed themselves 'The Lifeboat and Life-Saving Apparatus Club' with new headquarters near to the coastguard station. (Back row) Mr Gooch, Gus Jensen senior, Jack Saunders, Vernil Tuck (partially hidden), Billy Capps-Jenner, unknown, Arthur Swan, Jack Capps-Jenner, unknown, Harry Burgess, George Burgess. (Middle row) Arthur Swan, 'Twee' Swan, Mr Campbell, unknown, George 'Pongo' Wilson, unknown, Bobby Capps-Jenner, Reg Stigles, Benny Ayers. (Front row) Lenny Swan, Frank Searby, 'Lordy' Howe, Fred Menhennet, unknown, Johnny Swan.

Thomas 'Brock' Ellis weighed 24 stone and was described as the biggest man in the port. It seems likely this is the Brock Ellis who in October 1835 was one of the crew of a beach yawl which capsized off Yarmouth whilst putting men on board a stricken Spanish brig, the *Paquette de Bilboa*, to help pump her out and pilot her into the harbour. However, the ship went down and after swimming for seven and a half hours and covering 15 miles, he was picked up by the brig *Betsy* of Sunderland. Brock was in bad shape, his throat was inflamed and swollen, his neck, chest, hands and feet completely flayed. He was the only survivor.

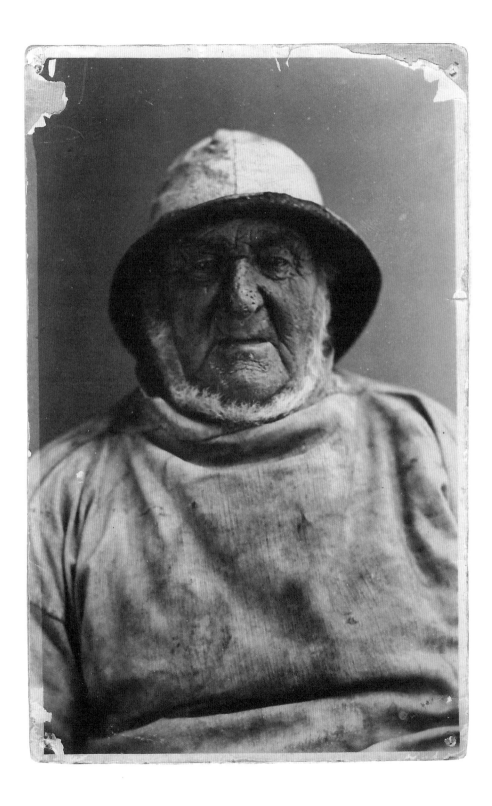

4. OLD FITZ & POSH

BILLY: Old Fitz and Posh. A funny old pair.
NED: Yew know what they were? A pair of rummins.
But they dint do yew no harm.
from PEARLS FROM THE GRIT (2018)

Perhaps one of the most unlikely stories to come out of the Beach Village was that of the poet and the Beachman, or 'Old Fitz' and 'Posh' as they became known among the fishing fraternity. When the two met, Edward Fitzgerald was a 55-year-old poet and writer living on Market Hill, Woodbridge with a failed marriage and a reputation for eccentricity. He would later become world-renowned for his translation of the *Rubaiyat of Omar Khayyam*. Joseph 'Posh' Fletcher was his complete opposite, a 25 year old Lowestoft Beachman, who lived at 8 Strand Street, earning his living trawling and long-lining supplemented by salvage work with the Old Company.

It was Fitzgerald's fascination with the Beachmen and their stories that formed the basis of this remarkable friendship which began with a chance meeting in 1864 as a result of Joe's father's shrimp boat being stolen. The boat was spotted by coastguards further down the coast, moored on the Deben near the Felixstowe Ferry, where Joe and his father were to collect her. When they arrived the next day Fitzgerald's yacht happened to lay alongside the shrimper and, having heard the news about the boat, Old Fitz invited them aboard.

Fitzgerald struck up an immediate rapport with young Joe, who was full of the sea-lore that Fitzgerald found so interesting and would enthusiastically send to his famous friends such as Tennyson and Carlyle. In his schooner, the *Scandal*, named after, as he put it, 'the staple product of Woodbridge', Old Fitz made regular visits to Lowestoft and always stayed at 12 Marine Terrace in London Road North in the days when the front of the house was what is now the back, close to the harbour and his new-found friend. However, Fitzgerald knew the town before he met Fletcher, once writing that he used to wander the town's shore hoping to come across a Beachman, whom he could befriend to learn more of their hard life. Later it was found that Joe had noticed his strollings but didn't like to approach the poet at first as he didn't think it becoming.

When in town, Old Fitz and Posh, as he became known, might roam around the North Denes or the harbour or more likely pay a visit to the *Suffolk Hotel*, the old poet's favourite haunt, where he would sit and smoke and listen to tales of Posh and his friends, their tongues loosened no doubt at Old Fitz's expense. However, they would never go over the bridge to Kirkley as neither fancied mingling with the 'aristocratic gentility,' although the pair did once go to church together in Great Yarmouth. Fitzgerald also had Fletcher's portrait painted by Samuel Lawrence and even persuaded Posh to pay a visit to a theatre in Lowestoft for a performance of *The Merchant of Venice*, during which it is said that the fisherman slumbered peacefully!

Fitz described Posh as 'a man of the finest Saxon type... blue eyes, a nose less than

(Top) Edward Fitzgerald (1809–1883), pictured in 1873, was an English poet and writer, best known for his translation of *The Rubaiyat of Omar Khayyam*.

(Bottom) Joseph 'Posh' Fletcher (1839-1915). To commemorate their friendship, Fitzgerald commissioned artist Samuel Laurence to paint this portrait of Posh around 1870. The painting's whereabouts has been unknown for many years and only a photograph remains.

(Right) The herring lugger *Meum and Tuum* (LT244) in Penzance harbour. Fitzgerald bought the boat for Fletcher for £360 and the two men began an ill-fated business partnership.

Roman, more than Greek, and strictly auburn hair that any woman might sigh to possess…
a man of simplicity of soul, justice of thought, tenderness of nature, a gentleman of nature's
grandest type.' Born in Lowestoft on 20th June 1839, Joseph Delly Fletcher was however
very much a Beachman, and like many of his kind was always fond of his drink.

One man who knew Posh Fletcher well was Harris Allerton, a fellow member of the Old
Company, who in 1959 at the age of 85 was interviewed by Charles Goodey for an article
concerning the friendship which appeared in the *East Anglian Daily Times*, on 31st March
that year. At the time he could even recall having seen Fitz, remembering, 'He was a big old
man who used to go about with a great shawl around his shoulders.' Harris recalled Posh
well; "He was a very nice man was Joe, what anybody else may say about him. He was a
nice old cock – one of the best. He wouldn't harm a cat. He was a man anybody would like
provided they were sociable. He was not a bully and was very fond of a joke. He was a fine
upright man right to his last days. He was one of our best seamen – a very good fisherman."

In 1867 the friendship of Posh and Old Fitz led to a business partnership when Fitz
bought a herring lugger for £360 and Posh contributed the fishing gear as his part of the
enterprise. Fitzgerald, ever the poet, named the vessel *Meum and Tuum* (Mine and Thine),
which is perhaps derived from the old Beach saying, 'What's thine is mine and what's
mine's my own.' Although the name painted on the stern was *Meum and Tuum*, locally
she was known as the *Mum Tum*! Registered on 3rd August 1867, this vessel was 47 feet 4
inches long with a 15 foot beam and a 6 foot 7 inch depth of hold. She had a black

hull with yellow beadings and her name on the transom was picked out in gold letters on a scarlet background.

Despite the catches showing a profit of £450 at the end of the first year, Fletcher was never a businessman and all the money was spent clearing debts which he had allowed to mount up. Things didn't improve and eventually the partnership broke up and the 'Mum Tum' was sold and continued to fish the North Sea until she became unseaworthy. She was broken up in 1888 and her nameboard purchased and donated to the Omar Khayyam Club. Posh took over another boat, the *Henrietta*, with Fitzgerald as mortgagee, but soon after New Year's Day 1869, Fitz was back in Lowestoft writing, 'I came here two days ago to wind up the lugger's account.' This too was sold with Fitzgerald receiving the proceeds.

One of the main problems of this partnership was revealed by Albert Spurgeon, a coxswain of the Lowestoft lifeboat, who was also interviewed by Goodey for his research. Spurgeon was a longshoreman who spent his whole life on the Beach and as a lad knew Posh. 'I used to be his lapdog as a boy. He used to lay his boat alongside ours and I used to see after it for him, especially when he used to get his 'dowry' as he called it from Old Fitz. He used to go on the booze when it arrived and I wouldn't see anything much of him until the money had gone.'

Harris Allerton could also remember seeing the 'Mum Tum' in and around the port, but did not agree that alcohol was the only problem. 'I wouldn't say drink was his downfall. Of course he liked his pint, but I think his worst trouble was his wife. She was one of those hell-cat women and was forever scrubbing her linen props [washing line] and those sort of things and that was what made him get an extra pint aboard at times.'

Mason Ayers was Fletcher's last surviving relative, a veteran fish market merchant and also a trustee of the Fishermen's Bethel. Ayers was living on The Grit when he gave Charles Goodey on alternative verdict on his uncle. 'He was a fine-looking chap in his early days, that's probably why he got the nickname Posh. When he first became skipper he was a very good fisherman but all that changed after Old Fitz bought him the 'Mum Tum'. He was properly spoiled by the old man who used to take him to some of his posh dinners and made rather a fool of him. They used to go a lot to the old *Suffolk Hotel* where Fitz used to treat him to drinks and he got so he did not go to sea when he ought to have done. Drink was his worst enemy and Old Fitz properly ruined him, there's no doubt about that… You wouldn't call him [Posh] a likeable man. My father didn't think much of him, not when he gave way to drink and he left my aunt in a bad way. They had five or six children but most of them died of consumption. His downfall was drink and, in many ways, that was due to Fitzgerald.'

After the failure of the business, Fitzgerald and Fletcher drifted apart, although Fitz did keep in touch for a while with letters and the old poet, about to go to Lowestoft in 1877, could still write kindly of his friend. 'The Great Man is yet there; commanding a Crew of his own… His Glory is somewhat marred; but he looks every inch a King in his lugger now. At home (when he is there and not at the Tavern) he sits among his Dogs, Cats, Birds, etc. always with a great Dog following all around and abroad. This is the Greatest Man I have known.' In 1893 Fitzgerald died and was buried in Boulge churchyard in Suffolk.

(Left) Strand Cottages in Strand Street, pictured here circa 1900. The cottages were just off Anguish Street and in the 1870s Posh Fletcher lived with his wife Sarah at No 8 – the doorway where the woman stands with a baby.

After the break-up of the partnership Posh fished on other luggers but in the end was reduced to scraping a living from shrimping and whatever else he could pick up. After his wife died in 1892, Posh lodged for the next fourteen years with Mrs Capps at 2 Chapel Street and was often to be found in one of two beer houses in the north of the town.

Life was not kind to him in his last years, as Albert Spurgeon described, 'He lived at one time in Duke's Head Street, but later lived in an old bathing machine on a bit of land near my home in Newcombe Road. He took off the wheels and laid it on four stones off the beach and when the Corporation tried to shift him, he claimed squatter's rights and they couldn't move him.' Indeed, the last time Mason Ayers saw his Uncle Joe was when he was 'cooking herring over Beamish the blacksmith's fire down on the Beach.'

By this time the letters from Fitzgerald that Posh had amassed were worth a small fortune, or they would have been had he kept them intact and handled them wisely given how much the poet's reputation had grown since his death. Seemingly unaware of their potential value, Posh had frittered them away over the years, telling author James Blyth, who was writing a book about Fitzgerald and Fletcher, that he had 'torn up sackfuls of 'em and strewn them to the winds.' Others had been given away for a pittance with Fletcher complaining to Blyth about one man who called to see him. "He axed [asked] me about the guv'nor," explained Posh, "and for me to show him any letters I had. He took a score or so away w'im and I told him a sight of things, thinking he was a gentleman... he gave me one drink of whisky and that's all I see of him. He was off with the letters and all and never gave me a farden [farthing]. I heerd arterwards as the letters was sold by auction for thutty pounds."'

Harris Allerton had also come across some of these precious letters and told the story to Charles Goodey in 1959. 'He finished up in a shed big enough for one man to sit in, not far from my house,' said Harris, 'and I used to go and have a talk with him. He had sold his bigger shed to Burrows the boat-owner when he was hard up and I saw Burrows clearing it out. There wasn't much in it and I asked Joe if he still had any letters from Old Fitz. He said he couldn't remember but as I sat outside mending my nets one day I saw Burrows come out of the shed with a kipper box and a shovel. He dug a hole and emptied the box in and, being curious, I went back later and unburied the stuff. I found 40 or 50 letters Old Fitz had written to Joe and I knew they must be worth plenty of good money. I read some of them – I remember Old Fitz asked in one about a new stove he had fitted in Joe's cottage. I could have kept the letters myself – it wouldn't have been stealing, would it? But I thought, 'Poor old Joe, he's hard up. They won't do me any good.' He used to bring me bits of stuff out of his shed and sell them to me and when he came next morning I gave him the letters.'

'I told him: 'You know they are worth money, don't make a fool of them.' I knew where he would take them. He thanked me and went to Fred Ecclestone's pub up in Crown Street and sold them to someone for £20. Three days after that, I went back to the hole to see if I could find any more and dug up another four or five that had been spoiled through being left in the ground. Still, they were readable and I kept them until a few years ago when I happened

to catch my sister just about to burn them on the kitchen fire. I rescued them and sold them for £1 to Mr Mallett who used to write in the papers about us old Beachmen.'

Life continued to be a struggle for Posh and at one time when he was ill, he was taken to Oulton Workhouse but came back to his little hut again. In 1909 he obtained an old age pension but on 17th September 1915, at the age of 76, Posh died a pauper in Oulton Workhouse from 'heart failure due to senile decay and chronic bronchitis'.

Reading the story of Fitzgerald and Fletcher in 2019, it's hard not to see the relationship as a love affair between two men. In the Victorian era such behaviour was against the law and could result in a prison sentence. Although Fitzgerald married, he and his wife quickly separated and lived apart. It's his letters to Posh and his correspondence with friends where he writes with a passion about the man who is 'fit to be King of a Kingdom', that are still widely quoted in books and articles with titles such as, *The Gay Love Letters of Edward Fitzgerald*.

Joseph 'Posh' Fletcher was the most well-known of Lowestoft fishermen in his day – almost celebrity status – but was unable to handle his brush with fame or deal with his relationship with Fitzgerald. Despite the rumours of homosexuality and his alcoholism, the Beach Village community did not turn their back on him and many spoke up for him. No matter what anybody said about Posh, he was off The Grit. 'He was even defended by the coxswain of the lifeboat. "He was a real old Beachman,' said Albert Spurgeon, 'Not a scrounger like some of them but a real good old sort.'

There were differences of opinion about Joseph 'Posh' Fletcher, pictured here towards the end of his life. Harris Allerton described him as 'a fine upright man' whereas his nephew Mason Ayers said, 'You couldn't call him likeable'. But there is no doubt he was a colourful character and respected as a Beachman.

5. GRITSTERS

**It is fairly true to say that every person
on the Beach was a character in their own right.
LEONARD ADAM**

The Lowestoft Beach population are in every sense of the term a peculiar people,' said an article in the *Lowestoft Journal*, in the early 1900s, 'from the earliest childhood inured to hardship and contention with the cruel sea, which they regard as the natural enemy, the merciless devourer of their kindred, and many widows and orphans. They acquire a sturdy independence of character unknown to the citizens of inland towns. They have inter-married for generations amongst their own particular class, and there are few Beach families, we believe, which are not like the Highland clans. They are generally speaking a quiet unobtrusive class of persons, but when the latent 'Viking' spirit is aroused in their breasts, they are like the ocean in a storm.'

This independence on the Beach was sometimes taken to such a degree that people from the town would not mix with those who lived below the cliff. There was a feeling that the town folk looked down on people from the Beach – and not just literally – which served only to isolate this small fishing community and fire up its spirit. Alan Doy recalls a story which illustrates this isolation from the rest of the town. "My grandparents' name was Cullum, and they lived at 3 Rant Score East and had several children, one of whom was my mother, Agnes. Boys from the town wouldn't take out Beach girls and if they did there would be a bit of a fuss. When my mother started dating my father she didn't want him to know where she lived so when he used to take her home, she would say goodbye to him at her friend's house in the High Street. Then she used to go through to the back of the house and slide on her bottom down the cliff and go home that way!"

"My father's father was quite wealthy and when he found out that his son was going out with a Beach girl he didn't like it. He threatened to cut him off from the family so my father told him to stick his money. When my parents married they lived in Kimberley Road in the town and my mother's sister went to live in Tonning Street, but as soon as their husbands had gone to work the girls went back to the Beach; that's where they belonged."

Beach people were known by a variety of names, such as 'Pea Bellies', 'Sand Chompers' or 'Gritsters' and they certainly proved themselves to be a unique breed, showing great strength of character in times of adversity. Generations of families lived on the Beach, and some surnames had long association with the place, such as Mewse, Capps, Rose, Ayers, Liffen, Cook, Burwood, Swan, Hook, Norman and Dalley.

Beach families frequently used the same first names across the generations, which could lead to confusion at times. This was why nicknames were so important. Edward Capps-Jenner wrote, 'On one occasion, when a ballot was organised to chose a coxswain, the voters' list had to give all the nicknames of the the members of the Companies to ensure that the

John Rose, who lived in Vigilant Cottages and later in the Almshouses, was a Beachmen and lifeboatman. Here he is talking to a young Harry Burgess who would later become lifeboat coxswain.

right Jack, Billy, William, John, Robert etc. was identified. The coxswain so elected was John S Swan'.

'In my own family the names William, John, Robert and Edward were used in various combinations so that we had Billy's boy Jack, Jack's boy Johnny, Bob's boy Billy, Bob's boy Bob, Billy's boy Billy, the boy Bob's Bob etc. and my own three Christian names were given to Bob's boy Ted. Order was got out of this tangle by giving the relationship – Brother Billy, Uncle Ted, Brother Ted, etc. My wife was first to introduce something new, in the shape of Harold, which did not meet with family approval as 'none of thy family is called by this name'.'

Edward also went on to recall some of the many nicknames he could remember during the early 1900s. He wrote, 'The nicknames, very prevalent in this district, of some of the old men may be amusing although I know very little of their origin: 'Wire' Rose, 'Dobin' Cooper,

'Twee' Swan, 'Grandfather' Saunders, 'Luff' Turrell, 'Curly' Dann, 'Dearly' Gurney, 'Prince' Allerton, Tom 'Canny' Swan, 'Chi' Harper, 'Slum' Turrell, 'Tom Duncan' Coleman, 'Little Ditty' Butcher, 'Blowgy' Burwood, 'Bussey' Ayers, 'Crawney' Mewse, 'Joe Painter' Swan, 'Bob Bridley' Ayers, 'Matthie' Butcher, 'Tommy' Jones, 'Paddy' Mewse, 'Mun' Capps, 'Chawfey' Turrell, 'Pipman' Ayers, 'Tute' Cooper and many others.'

One of the oddest nicknames was Tom 'Tar-the-Clock' Liffen. It seems that Tom was painting the front room and painted over the clock too! Michael Duncan didn't discover the origins of his father's nickname 'Tishy' until after he died. "My Uncle Dick and my father, both fishermen, joined Harry Tate's Navy as my father told me, for the duration of the Second World War, and both returned to a life-time of fishing afterwards. My father's friends were all from the fishing fraternity and his name was Charlie but most of these people called him 'Tishy'. It never occurred to me to ask why and I didn't find out until after his death at the gathering of family and friends on the day of my father's cremation. I asked my Uncle Dick why they called my father 'Tishy'. He said that when they were young boys, they used to play along the Denes with their mates and on one occasion they were playing along the top of the area above the Denes Oval and had a race from top to bottom. My father came last and apparently a few days before a horse named 'Tishy' came last in a big race, I think he said the Grand National, so they nick-named him after that."

One of the most popular and memorable characters in living memory seems to be Arthur 'Happy' Welham. Happy was born around 1858 and by 1891 lived in the Fishermen's Cottages at 16 Lighthouse Score until he died in 1937. Lenny 'Winky' Norman remembers, "Now Happy never did wash, only if it rained! He used to have a chimney sweep business but in the fishing time my Dad used to say that he'd go along and cart all their gear for them at a tanner a time or whatever they could afford. He'd cart the oilies and boots and that back to the houses, his dog with him… when the cart was full, his little old dog would run along underneath. I've seen old Happy that drunk that the little dog would have the reins of the donkey in his mouth and drive all the way along Whapload Road till they got home. The dog would take old Happy home!"

In addition to carrying the fishermen's clothes to the docks in his cart for a few pennies, during the First World War Happy performed similar services for the Navy. It was around this time that he retired his faithful old donkey and bought a little black and white pony, but his donkey obviously meant a lot to him as it is said that during one of the many floods on the Beach Village he took her upstairs into a bedroom for safety! Happy also had a little terrier dog, called Spot, who always used to travel around with him, sitting alongside him in the pony trap.

One particular story occurred in 1916 when the German Navy bombarded the town. An unexploded shell fell into Lighthouse Score and Happy, never one to miss an opportunity, is supposed to have grabbed a broom and rolled the shell into his garden, charging passers-by tuppence to see the new exhibit! However, not everyone agrees with this version of events.

Benny Knights explains, "This yarn about Happy Welham rolling it into his garden and charging tuppence, well, he couldn't move that in his garden! I'll tell you what happened to that. I was seven years old at the time and I was running along Whapload Road on that day and as the guns went off I jumped in the air. When the shell hit the wall and fell onto the road, it faced Happy's garden wall, so he came out with a broom and swivelled it round so that it faced the Denes in case it went off! The Navy came about three days later with a lorry and took it away!"

During the summer months Happy would put a notice above his front door saying, 'If you are dry, Come in and try Happy's Home Made Drink.' This was a wine that he and his wife, who the local children used to call Aunt Phoebe, made in their kitchen along with lemonade for which they charged halfpenny a bottle.

Happy died in 1937 aged 79 shortly before his cottage was due to be demolished. Ronny Woolner recalls, "It was one Christmas. We realised that nobody had seen Happy or his wife for two or three days. I lived in The Shoals, just at the bottom of Lighthouse Score, and nobody had seen them. So my father and another man fetched a ladder and got through their window. They were both lying there ill. They took Happy away and he died but his wife was okay and she moved away and lived until after the Second World War."

Bill Cooper lived at 38 Whapload Road and remembers, "There were two chimney sweeps on the Beach. There was Happy Welham of course, and Jakie Smith. There was another character called Rackham who used to walk about with a basket of smoked fish on his head, selling them. Then there was the Old Pot Buyer. This was a bloke who used to push this handcart full of old chamber pots. Plain ones tuppence each, the ones with flowers on three pence."

Another notorious Gritster went by the name of 'Daisy Dinks', who seems to have been quite a girl in her day. Daisy lived on the Beach for many years, right up until its demise. Jean Mitchell remembers, "The last year we lived on the Beach, 1965, I worked in Squire's shop on the corner of Whapload Road and Wilde's Street. Mr Squire was just winding down the business and his best customer in that last year was 'Old Daisy' as she was known. She was particularly known by our American Allies during the war and often gave Mum a tin of spam or corned beef for our dinner. Although my Mum didn't approve of her way of life, she never refused these tins, as they were a luxury during the war."

Godfrey Girling was a barber in the Beach Village in the 1930s and came across all sorts in his line of work. He recalls 'Dickie-Bird' Rose, a distant relation of Jack Rose, who lived next door to one of Jack's uncles in the Almshouses in Whapload Road. "He used to come in mine. I used to say, 'Hello, Dickie' I thought that was his name, but it wasn't. Some bloke said to me, you shouldn't call him that! He got had up once for saying to the kids, do you want to come and see my little dickie-bird?"

Godfrey also remembers Joe Catchpole. "He came in mine one morning, poor old fella, he was a little bit slow, but a good old boy really. I said to him, 'How are you getting on, Joe?' and he said to me, 'I want you to do me a kindness, I want you to cut my throat!' So I said, 'If that's

(Left) Happy Welham pictured with his donkey and Spot, his terrier. "I've seen old Happy that drunk," says Lenny Norman, "that the little dog would have the reins of the donkey in his mouth all the way along Whapload Road till they got home."

Lowestoft. The High Light.

(Above) On the side of Happy's house in Lighthouse Score was a sign which read, 'Fire! Fire! Fire! Arthur Welham chimney sweep'. Ever the entrepreneur, the bottom line advertises his 'sweetest wine'.

(Right) Happy lived at 16 Lighthouse Score, the end cottage nearest to Whapload Road, for over 70 years. He also owned the fine allotment seen in the foreground, complete with makeshift sheds and a rabbit hutch.

On 25th April 1916 the German Navy bombarded the town and an unexploded shell fell near to Happy Welham's house in Lighthouse Score. The story goes that Happy moved the shell with his broom – either to charge passers-by to look at it or to point it away from his house. These recently unearthed pictures confirm the shell was definitely moved from the bottom of the Score (right), to outside his garden wall (stereoscope photo below) where it drew a crowd. However, Happy seems to be keeping a low profile from the cameras!

Unexploded 11.7 shell fired by German cruisers into Lowestoft.

what you want, I'll oblige you!' and he kept running on about having his throat cut. So I got him in the chair and lathered him up, and I got this old cut throat razor, dipped it in boiling water, shut the razor up, and said, 'Are you sure you want me to do it, Joe?' He said, "Yeah, go on,' so I said, 'Right,' and drew the closed razor across his throat, and that was hot. He grabbed his throat and jumped out of the chair, yelling like hell. I was just as mad as they were!"

"Another great character down there," recalls Lenny Norman, "was Nathan 'Slasher' Pickess. He was as big and broad as anyone could be, strong as an ox and he liked his beer. He was that strong he could pick a barrel up and sling it in the air. His son Freddie was another notable character; if he didn't like you he'd hit you!" The Norman family themselves were Beach folk, Lenny's parents running the *Suffolk Fishery Tavern* in the 1920s. Lenny's father Robert and brother Bob both took the same nickname 'Umshi' and although the family left the Beach Village, they always had links with the place and Bob returned in the 1950s and took a house alongside the *Gas House Tavern* where he lived until it was demolished in the 1960s.

Ron James can remember another man who had connections with a public house in Nelson Road on the Beach. "Billy Jones' mother used to keep the *Princess Royal* but Billy was a lorry driver for Arthur and Sam Boardley and I believe he was the first man ever to drive a lorry from here to Aberdeen with a load of fish nets. You see, when they were fishing, they used to do so many weeks up there but during that time the nets had to be repaired or tanned, as they called it, to preserve the nets. So Billy had to take a whole fleet of nets up and bring them back and he was the first bloke ever to do it. And you think of those little roads in them days, from here to Aberdeen was a heck of a long way."

"Then there was old Billy Day," Ron continues. "There was a firm down there called Gooderham, he was a coal merchant. Now there was a little fella who worked for them, he was very little. I suppose he was well under five foot and poor old boy he was a lovely lad,

Aerial view of The Grit in the early 1920s.

but the coal merchant used to have his horse and he never got off the cart to deliver it but he used to say, 'Billy, hundredweight up here, hundredweight there, run, you bugger, run!' And he used to have a sack of coal on his back and he used to run everywhere. The merchant couldn't get his horse and cart up Spurgeon Score so he used to stay at the bottom and poor old Billy used to run all the way up and back with a hundredweight of coal and he'd be running like this all day. He was a real hard grafter… They used to slit one corner of a sack and wear it like a hood and then sling a sack of coal over their shoulder, but that empty sack was heavy, without the coal as well!"

George Wilson lived in the same street as Jack Moore, who recalls, "The Wilsons lived three doors down from us. I can remember the sons, Tom and George, and their mother Maud. Her husband worked on the fish market. They were the first black family in Lowestoft, but we never made a fuss about it. They lived in East Street, down the bottom, the road going down towards the Gasworks, nearly opposite the *Gas House Tavern*."

Ron James also remembers George Wilson, who worked as a binman. "He used to get as drunk as a lord at the *Rising Sun* or somewhere like that every other Saturday and they used to go and get his missus and put him in a wheelbarrow and push him home. There were no drinking and driving problems in those days!"

According to Jack Moore, one of the best-known men on the Beach Village in the 1930s was Albert Chapman, also known as 'The Watchman'. Albert worked at the Corporation's storage yard near to the sea wall for 42 years, looking after the equipment used for repairing the wall and the groynes. Jack explains, "Albert was severely disabled, with only one leg, but he got about very well on crutches or in a three-wheeled invalid chair, it was the type with a long rod handle on each side which he pushed back and forward to propel it all along. His son said he lost his leg when sweeping the mines in the First World War – one destroyed the boat he was on."

"While he was watching this place he had an old hut to shelter in from the bad weather, he had a fire and was able to make a pot of tea. Although Albert only had one leg he would soon chase after us in his wheelchair if we got out of hand and gave him any cheek. He never caught us, but I don't think he ever tried very hard, it was all in good fun. Whenever you saw Albert he had his little dog with him, if he was on crutches the dog would walk just behind, or if he was in his wheelchair it would always run beside him on a lead."

Ronnie Wilson recalls more Gritsters. "Like Deafy, he used to come along the Beach with a golf ball, and knock the golf ball right from where the fish market is, right the way up to the golf course, he was deaf and dumb. Then there was an old tramp, called 'Puggy' Utting. At one time he lived in the opening where Boardley's carts used to be."

Mr E J Day remembers, "There was the rat catcher, old Bob Stigles. He lived by the church, and another well known man was the one-armed barrel organ man who used to play outside pubs and he used to let us play the organ while he went round with his hat."

Charles Ellis, who lived in Scarle's Buildings, recalls another typical Beach character. "Mrs Palmer had been our next-door neighbour for years and she had many run-ins with old Scarle, our landlord. I think he was a solicitor by trade, lived in Norwich, and you've seen those Victorian cartoons of the old rent men? Well, he was just like that. He had a big, bulbous, red nose, and he always had a Gladstone bag which he put the money in. Times were hard and Mrs Palmer had a family to keep and her old man, Billy Palmer, had one eye. He used to wear a bowler hat and a patch over his eye. He was just a hanger-on down the fish-market, he'd pick up a bob here and a bob there. I mean he never had a real job so they were bloody hard up. Scarle came after the rent one day, when they owed several weeks rent and said, 'I've come for the rent Mrs Palmer,' and she say, 'You'll get your rent when I get some money, my family comes first.' He said, 'Mrs Scarle and I were never blessed with children.' 'Your old woman,' she say, 'she ought to have married a fisherman, she'd have plenty of kids then!'"

"I know for a fact that she owed £46 for bread, and in those days that was a lot of money. Her boy Percy went into one of the top boats, the ones that always earned the money, and he did well once and she paid off every penny. She wouldn't avoid paying. Old Scarle went round there once near Christmas. And he say to her, 'What are you going to have for Christmas dinner?' She say, 'Well, it's like this Mr Scarle. If the boats do well we're going to have a turkey and a Christmas pudding. If they don't do very well we'll have red herring and close the curtains.'"

Charles remembers that when Mrs Palmer died, a rumour began to spread around the Beach that her house was haunted. He continues, "Mrs Palmer had been a big woman who always used to wear a white apron, spotlessly white, and some people said that they saw her standing in the doorway with this white apron on. In the house doors would open, they'd hear footsteps, that sort of thing. I used to think it was a guilty conscience, you know, they felt guilty they hadn't done enough for her when she was alive. After school, the kids used to go round to Scarle's Buildings to see if they could see her ghost. One night my father wanted some tobacco, so he say to me, 'Here you are boy, go and get me some cigarette papers,' but it was dark so I stood in the doorway and I wasn't very keen on going. So he say, 'What the hell is up with you?' So I say, 'I might see Mrs Palmer.' He say, 'Come you here. You knew Mrs Palmer when she was alive. She used to give you sweets, didn't she? Did she ever do you any harm?' I shook my head. 'Well then,' he said, 'if she didn't do you any bloody harm when she was alive she isn't going to do any when she's dead. Go and get me my tobacco!' I always remember that, because after that I was never scared."

"The keys for the front doors in Scarle's Buildings would fit the other houses in the row, and our key fitted Mrs Palmer's door. One night about ten o'clock, just before my old man was getting ready to go to bed, there was a knock on the door, and there three or four of these clients that reckon they can see ghosts. They had packs on their backs with all that paraphernalia. My Dad said, 'What do you want Mister, this time of night?' So one of them say, 'Well, we hear that there is a ghost two doors away, where Mrs Palmer used to live, and we want to see for ourselves.' You see, with the house being empty, they wanted to sleep there the night, and one of them said to my old man, 'We understand that your key will fit the door.' But he wasn't having none of it. He say, 'You get off my doorstep, you'll not get my key, and if you get in that bloody house, I'll come and kick you out. If Mrs Palmer's ghost is there, you leave her alone. She lived there all them years and if she want to stop there that's her business, not yours.' This bloke and his mates, they scuttled out of the yard, they were gone out of sight right quick. My old man soon put a stop to them."

During the depression of the 1930s, Charles worked in Ayers' fish-house as a way of getting some money. It was here that he encountered more fiery characters who lived on the Grit and remembers one in particular. "They were hard down there all right, but they had to live that way because that was how it was. Old Maud Wilson worked with me at Ayers; she was a West Indian and weighed about 16 stone. She was a nice woman really, but she didn't stand any nonsense. She was one of the women cutting the herring for kippers, and these women were each allotted a girl who was paid about half as much to pack the fish. Well, the women used to be there sometimes before six in the morning, so they could get their day's work done. Betty, she was a cheeky little beggar, was allocated to Maud, and she was never on time. She couldn't get up I suppose, and it was a hell of a time to get up in the morning. So Betty was always late and it put Maud late and she got fed up with it. So eventually she say, 'Betty, if you're late tomorrow morning, I'll show you what we used to do to the girls at Sayer and Holloway's.' Well, the next morning Betty was late again. When she turned up Maud say, 'You're late again, girl!' and she say, 'Yes, Maud,' and before Betty could say anything else, Maud grabbed hold of her, and lifted her with one hand, straight across the bench face down. She was up with this girl's skirt, pulled her knickers down, so there was her bare behind. There were these plates that were used with a stiff brush and black lead to stamp the fish boxes. Maud slapped one on her behind and put 'Best Bloaters' across her, and then she pulled up her knickers and said, 'Now be late tomorrow'…"

The 'sturdy independence' and the 'latent Viking spirit' described in that *Lowestoft Journal* article is perhaps best illustrated in the life of Samuel Capps, a Gritster born in 1844 who ended up in America, fighting in the Civil War and embracing the life of a rancher. The story was discovered by Beryl Capps, a member of the Suffolk Family History Society and Secretary of the Lowestoft Group. Beryl explains her family connection: "My husband was an estate agent (Wiseman-Capps) and the Capps were a big family on the Beach Village and had a big net store on Whapload Road." In the early 1970s Beryl was contacted by Evelyn Capps-Walker, who lived on a ranch in Colorado, who was keen to know more of her father's family history. Evelyn was born in 1897 and her father came from Lowestoft, starting life as fisherman living on the Beach Village and so the story unfolds.

Samuel John Capps was born on 2nd March 1844 at 5 Rant Score East. The Capps were a Beach Village family – his mother Susannah was a Burwood (another strong Beach family). His father owned several drifters and when Samuel was 11 years old he went to sea as his father's cabin boy. In 1862, at the age of 18, Samuel Capps left Lowestoft never to return. Beryl Capps takes up the story, "It looks as if he joined the Merchant Navy fleet. He once said he had a very cruel master and that must be why he jumped ship at New York and joined the Union in the American Civil War. He changed his name to John Burwood, his mother's maiden name, to prevent him from being traced, because he was told that the British Navy would find you anywhere in the world if you went absent."

Samuel Capps (seated, with beard) was perhaps the only 'cowboy' to be born on The Grit. Pictured in the early 1900s with his wife Amelia (to his left) and their family at the Capps family ranch in Colorado. Evelyn is sat in front of her father.

Samuel's daughter Evelyn often visited Beryl and Lowestoft in the 1970s to discover more about her father's origins. On one visit in June 1985, when Evelyn was 88 years old, she told Samuel's story to the *Lowestoft Journal* and how her father, having fought in the American Civil War, joined the Pacific Union railroad. While guarding some horses, he had arm-to-arm combat with a Native American Ute Indian. Evelyn said, 'My father saw feathers on the brow of a hill. They were unusual because they were not moving. He crept up and jumped the Indian who was waiting with his knife to kill him and take the herd.'

After battling across the untamed plains of the New World, Samuel Capps met the girl he would marry – only to discover that she was from Norwich, less than 30 miles from his home town and had relations born on The Grit. Amelia had come to America with the Mormons and he married this 'local girl' on Christmas Day 1876 and began a 50,000 acre cattle ranch in Colorado. Samuel and Amelia would go on to raise a family of two boys and six girls, the youngest being Evelyn.

In 1882 the Capps family moved to their own ranch and Samuel became a big public figure in the town of Santa Clara, serving as as Justice of the Peace and elected Mayor twice in 1907 and 1913. He died in January 1923 at the age of 79. His wife Amelia died at the grand old age of 94 in 1948. Beryl says, "Samuel started off as a poor fisher boy from the Beach Village and he ended up in America and his own huge ranch. I always thought I'd write this story one of these days. I got the title – *From Fishing Boats to Cowboy Boots*! The Capps' ranch of Colorado is still there but not in the family now. All this from a Beach Village boy."

6. CHILDHOOD

LT 293

In the Beach Village there was plenty for children to do, but you made it yourself. There was no rowdiness like today.
BILLY KEITH

Growing up on the Beach in the early part of the 20th century was very different from children's lives today. With the whole of the Denes to play on, the north beach nearby and freedom to roam the streets, many of the people speak of their childhood happiness in spite of the hardship of the time. Although they may not have had the computers and toys of today's younger generation, the Beach boys and girls made their own fun. However, even in the 1920s and 1930s, children's games were subject to fashion. Ruby Timberley remembers, "There always seemed to be seasons when certain toys were the 'in' thing. When the shops started selling wooden tops and whips every child wanted a top and a lot of fun was had in seeing who could whip their top and make it spin the longest. Then the time came for wooden hoops with a stick to bowl them along Whapload Road. No problem with traffic in those days, we could see and hear the odd horse and cart coming, and we just let it pass and carried on bowling or whipping. Sometimes if the weather was hot, the tar melted on the road and stuck to your shoes, or feet if you had no shoes on. Then marbles were 'in' and no end of fun was had. We children had bags to keep them in and there were different kinds of marbles, the glass ones were called alleys."

"As the weather got colder, skipping for girls was the thing. Single skipping ropes with wooden handles costing one penny were a girl's pride and joy, and mothers' clothes lines were very handy when a number of girls wanted to skip on the pickling plots (before the Scots girls came). Two girls would each hold one end of the rope and turn it, calling their comrades to run and jump in and skip, usually to a rhyme or number, then change over so every one had a turn."

Mrs Jessie Hitter (née Harper) was from an earlier generation, born in 1903, but she also used to play marbles, "Me and Esther Garrod used to play on Christ Church Square, we used to make a hole to play marbles, but she always used to win. We also used to play with skipping ropes and wooden tops." During the summer, children would spend hours on the beach. "The boys used to run down the beach with no bathing costumes on, while the girls used to go in the sea with flannelette drawers on, we never had bathing costumes... we used to run down the beach with no shoes on. In the summertime the boys never had shoes or socks on, we couldn't afford them."

Ethel Baker (née Thompson) remembers, "I used to play around the boat sheds or on the pickling plots. We were given a bottle of water and bread and lard sandwiches and told to stay out all day."

"We spent hours on the beach," recalls Ruby Timberley, "running or walking barefoot from home to the beach, we made sandcastles, designs made of pebbles in sand – we leap-frogged,

(Left) Two schoolboys lurking in Lighthouse Score. Edward Capps-Jenner wrote about his 1890s childhood, 'We beach boys went about in gangs, which often clashed but nobody got hurt. When my mother discovered I was likely to borrow her plunger as a weapon that was the end of my gangster career with the 'Church Boys'!'

(Right) A little girl plays in a boat on the once vast north beach, circa 1890. In the distance are heaps of stones which were gathered for making roads and building houses. The stones would be broken up and then youngsters would cart the cobbles to local builders for a farthing a barrow-load.

jumped off the sea wall, and ran in and out of the sea, and lots more. In the afternoons the mothers came with the babies, and to gossip with each other. This all sounds very nice and I think we were very fortunate to live so near the sea, although when the sea was rough in the winter we could hear the roaring and splashing of the waves indoors. Sometimes we saw a horse being brought down to the sea in hot weather to walk through the sea to cool its feet with the man still sitting on the horse."

Edward Capps-Jenner also wrote about this happening earlier, in his childhood of the late 1890s. "Boardley's horses were taken down to the sea to wade in the waves and favoured boys were allowed to mount them whilst they were so doing."

Born in 1928, Mr Eric Horne also has fond memories of those far-off days of sunshine. "In the summer holidays, whole days would be spent playing on the beach with a packed lunch taken along, consisting of sandwiches and a bottle of home-made lemonade. My eldest brother sometimes had a Sunday swim in the sea off what we called the Second Denes. I would sit on the beach beside his towel and clothes, and afterwards he would give me a piggy-back all the way to the shop near the bottom of Wilde's Score and treat me to a halfpenny ice-cream cornet, served from a two-compartment wooden affair on wheels, which stood outside the shop. There was a difficult choice to be made between vanilla and strawberry."

Ronny Wilson was born on The Grit, and lived at 4 East Street, opposite the *Rising Sun,* his mother running a sweet shop. "My mother took up a business at the bottom of Spurgeon Score, a sweet business in a shop that used to be Cook's the butchers. My father was a fisherman, a chief engineer, so we were a little bit richer than the others, so I was the one who paid tuppence to go in *The Regent,* and go down the back to the toilet and open the window to let all the others in. About 20 of us in for tuppence!"

Ronny fondly remembers the Denes swimming-pool, "And outside of that you had a children's playground with swings and roundabouts and the boating lake. We used to go swimming from the beach though, and, in fact, when I was a boy we used to sleep on the beach. We slept down there right through the summer period, we spent four weeks down there and never went home, except to wash our clothes out. My mother used to give us a few spuds and a bit of lard, and we slept down there in an old sack tent behind the gasworks. We used to go down on the market, knock off a couple of herring, light a fire, split them, put them on the fire and roast them for our dinner. There was me, I was called 'Titch' Wilson, 'Hockey' Pickess, Troy Harper, there was Harry Harper, Claude Dalley and the Prettymans."

This gang included Bert Prettyman. "That's where we used to be all the summer," remembers Bert, "in our tent on the beach, the whole lot of us. Our mothers knew where to find us."

Benny Knights, although older, also spent the summers of his youth camping out in this area, "The foreman at Gourock Ropeworks used to give us boys a bell tent which we used to pitch on the Denes and in the summertime we used to live down there, every night. We used to get potatoes and stew up; we had a hell of a time."

The Shingle Mill stood on the North Extension from the late 1930s and extracted shingle for road building until diminishing supplies was causing erosion by the late 1950s. The Mill had also provided an impromptu children's 'pool'. Billy Keith lived in Cook's buildings and recalls, "The cranes dug out a huge area, 10 to 15 feet or deeper, and the tide would come in and fill it up. We used to stand on the quay and dive in; we had our own swimming pool!"

Ronny Wilson also took part. "While we were there 'Penny' the copper used to wait at the other end for us, so we had to climb on the sand wagon, bury ourselves in sand and breathe through a straw till we jumped off and go home. 'Course he used to wait for us. Penny was all right, he was a good policeman. He'd give you a boot up the backside, but if you told your father, you'd get another one, so you used to keep quiet about it." Children kept playing at the abandoned Shingle Mill until a boy was tragically killed there. Demolition followed in 1960 and the lads turned their attention elsewhere.

"There were some rafts down there too," Ronny continues, "that were used for painting the boats. They used to leave them in the harbour, tied up, and we used to get them and go out on them. One day we were on one of them, there were three lots of rafts, and we were stuck in the middle. So old Penny, he come along and say, 'Right! I want you lot!' So I say to the others, 'You go that way and we'll go the other and get ashore, and when he comes chasing after us, you can get ashore,' but he never even bothered! He just wheeled our bicycles up the police station and waited there till we came to get them back!"

(Far left) Picnic by the drying nets – Mrs Ethel Horne with one of her three boys.

(Left) Eldest brother Frederick (left) pictured with Eric Horne (right), with the old Eagle Brewery wall as the backdrop. The Hornes lived at 4 Rant Score and Frederick died aged 23 in the Second World War serving with Royal Army Medical Corps during the fall of Tobruk.

(Above) The Shingle Mill on the North Extension.
1. Billy Stone's pier
2. Hamilton Dock
3. Royal Pier
4. Lifeboat shed (washed away in the 1953 flood)
5. Coastguard Station
6. Shingle Mill
7. Crane
8. North Pier
9. Jackaman's Corner
10. South Pier.

(Right) Boys on the harbour beach, 'borrowing' one of the rafts which were used to paint the boats.

The boys were certainly mischievous but strong discipline was always forthcoming as a result. Billy Keith remembers one incident when he climbed up on the roof of Sayer and Holloway's fish-house, the place where his father worked as foreman. "I climbed up and fell through the roof," recalls Billy, "and went straight into the red herrings. But I had killed the dye, the pickle was broken, and they had to dump all those fish, the whole lot. My father, being in charge, really scalped me!"

Ronny Wilson admits that he was always in trouble as a boy. "I was always getting wrong for something," he reveals, "like the time I had a stick, I made it myself, and when the man used to come along to light the lamps along the street, I put them all out, and he used to go round to my father's house and say, 'Your bloody boy has put all the lamps out!' and I used to have to go round with my father and relight them and he'd give me a right clip over the head. Another time, I threw a stink bomb across the road to my mate, but as it went across the road Bingham's van went past and it went right in the window! My father had to pay for all the cakes and he gave me a clip round the ear, but it was accidental, I just threw it and it went straight in the window, bang! And then there was a big lorry there one day, with 50 pigs in it, and I just couldn't resist it. I just let the back down, and all the pigs went all round the roads, everywhere. Everyone was asking, 'Who let those pigs out?' but I never owned up. It took about six hours before they got them all back again!"

Charles Ellis recalls that there was briefly a salt factory near Ness Point. "When they cleared the site, they left the wall that went round the outside and that area was used for making Klondike boxes, big boxes to put the herring in. There was huge stacks of boxes on that site when it was cleared, thousands and thousands of boxes. The kids used to get in there and make hides and tunnels through the boxes. After that Scots girls had it for barrels, but that factory stood empty for a while and as kids we were always getting in there. Near the chimney there was a huge wooden structure, which had a set of steps to the top where there were steel wires attached on each corner, running from the top down to the ground. We kids weren't really supposed to play on this thing and the police were always after us. One day we were on top of the structure and three or four policemen came after us. They thought they'd got us; all they had to do was block these stairs. So a couple of them went upstairs after us, and do you know what we did? We all had cloth caps, so we put them round the wire and slid down it and ran away! We used to do that, slide down these wire guys [guy ropes]. We were lucky really because the wire was years old and rusty, with pieces sticking out of it. If it went through your hat you would get it in your hand! And that was high too!"

Money was scarce and pocket money for children was mostly unheard of. If you wanted money, even as a child you had to work for it. Billy Keith says, "We used to sit down near the Coastguard and see the boats come round and say, so and so is on that boat, someone else is on that one, you go to that house, you go to that one, and we used to run to their house and tell them that their husbands were coming home and then we'd get treated. And then you'd go and tell the men as they were getting off the boats that we'd let their wives know and they'd treat us as well."

Ronny Wilson remembers, "I did some kitbagging before I was old enough to go out to work, outside the Sparrows Nest. With a barrow on the back of a bike, we used to carry 12 kit bags strapped up, roped up. I got a farthing once for taking some to St. Lukes, a farthing! But usually you'd get a penny or tuppence or sixpence. I once got a quid for carrying one for a Scottish skipper from the bottom of The Ravine to the top."

Bert Prettyman recalls some of the sporting activities. "We had a cricket pitch outside our house," he explains. "There was a telegraph pole there that we used to chalk the stumps on and our football pitch was Sharman's Opening. One side was the path, the other side was the wall. I wanted a pair of football boots badly and my mother said, 'I can't afford to buy you any; you'll have to write to your brother Charlie.' So I did, and I got them and so I was captain for the day in my brand new boots."

Ruby Timberley also remembers the boys playing football and cricket, "with make-shift footballs and cricket balls and of course make-shift wickets and goal posts, but they still enjoyed their games. Some sat on pavements flicking playing cards or five flat stones. All harmless fun, keeping children out of mischief and costing nothing."

Ron James recollects that the Beach had its own Christmas traditions too. "For years I had my Christmas breakfast in the Beachmen's shed, but we were only allowed in there then, all the kids used to go down there. We never had Christmas trees, we had hoops. They used to have one hoop going one way and one going the other, tied in the middle, and then you put your crepe paper round that and decorated it with baubles and little bars of chocolate and hung it up in the window. We had our hoop made by my uncle because he was a cooper. That was our Christmas tree."

"Christmas morning, all the old boys used to walk round each other's and have a drink and then go into the next one. Well, that only went on till the pubs opened at 12 noon on Christmas Day, and then they'd start again and most likely finish up round one of them playing cards all of Christmas afternoon."

Eric Horne has his own festive memories, "At Christmas, I remember puddings made and boiled in cloths for many hours in the brick copper or in large cast iron saucepans. I can't remember us having chicken for Christmas dinner, but a piece of roast pork was certainly a luxury. I recall Hannant's toy shop a little way down the High Street, where I would spend ages gazing through the window at the masses of toys mostly priced beyond the reach of Village people. However, with her hard work throughout the year, my mother made sure that we always had a good Christmas. One present I particularly remember was a metal van big enough to sit on, which I used to ride down from the top of the Score. I was sharply rebuked one day by a dear old lady in a Victorian bonnet. Rant Score was the only score wide enough for traffic and we did get the occasional vehicle or horse and cart passing through... In the summer, events took place on the old Battery Green, which was then a rough patch of grass in front of the Coastguard Cottages. One event featured men on horses, galloping around to the tune of 'All the king's horses and all the king's men'. The annual carnival route also went past here."

(Right) Barrow boys outside the main gate of the Sparrows Nest park. During the War years, boys used to cart the sailors' kit bags, charging threepence for trips north of the bridge and sometimes getting sixpence for south of it.

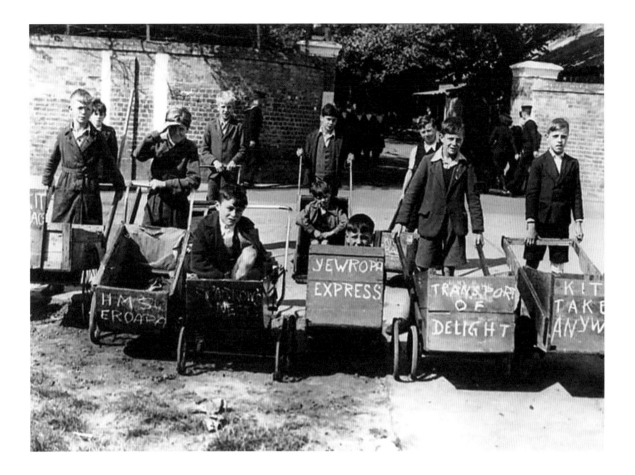

Mrs Hitter fondly remembers the Easters of her childhood, "Good Friday, Mother used to make saffron buns, we used to call them saffron dingers... Mother used to give us a piece of bread and margarine and a hard boiled egg, marvellous to have an egg then, and we used to go on the Denes all day long, swing on them net posts, play on them, it was lovely. There was also a big fair down on the Beach when I was young, down Hamilton Road where the Scots girls used to have their barrels. Then there was May Day and the maypole. I used to love dressing up as the May Queen. My mother used to do my hair up in ringlets, a bit of curtain for a veil. We used to dress up in paper frocks, spend days making these paper frocks, and we all used to sing, 'Climbin' up the walls, Knockin' down the spiders.' We used to go to people's doors and sing and get pennies. We used to have a little tea party if we had enough."

Eric Horne continues, "On May Day, children would roam around together banging tins or saucepans, and chanting a ditty which went, 'Climbing up the walls, Knocking down the spiders, Cabbages and turnips too, Put them in your aluminium saucepan, And we'll have a rare old stew!' Children dressed up in old clothes, blackened their faces with burnt cork and walked round the streets after tea singing this song, which was sung to the tune of a Salvation Army hymn which started off with the words 'Turn to the Lord and seek salvation.' They knocked on doors, tin can in hand, for any small donations."

"The boys used to dress up in any old thing, and go about the Beach knocking on doors," says Matthew Boardley, "but one old girl in Old Nelson Street used to make us sing, 'Now is the month of May...' and we got money for that!"

Ethel Baker recalls singing that song too. "I remember May Day. We had a May Queen and about six others all dressed in paper dresses which we kids made and we sung 'Now is the month of Maying, when merry lambs are playing...' Then we had a tea party when the week was out."

The Beach Village gave children freedom and the community gave them great security. "They were happy days," remembers Benny Knights, "because we had the whole of the Denes to play in." Ronny Wilson adds, "We had such great fun, so wonderful, it was the best part of my life, living down there."

(Below) The Coronation Day party at the *Gas House Tavern*, 2nd June 1953. The photograph was taken at the rear of the pub, with many of the younger attenders in fancy dress. Coming just five months after the devastating flood, the Coronation Day was a chance for the Beach community to join in a celebration.

(Opposite right) Beach boys on the pier. Cecil Wilson (second left) lived in Maltsters Score and said, "Like the kids take car numbers, we took boat numbers."

(Bottom left) Beach boys on the harbour beach in the 1920s, with the drifter *Boy George* in the background. Edward Capps-Jenner wrote, 'The boys were a great nuisance in taking away small boats. It was said even if you chained and locked the boat at both ends these boys would take away the middle!'

(Bottom right) The 'Gasworks Gang' as they were known, pictured here in 1956. Left to right, (top row) Valerie Harper, Jacqueline Jensen, Jean Hill, Denise Peters. (in front) Sadie Springer, Marlene Jensen, Sandra Coleman, Glennis Baldry, David and Doris Davis, Leslie Harper.

Reggie Howe   Cecil Wilson   Freddie Wilson   George Wilson   Berry McNeil   Lenny and Bobby Howe

A BEACH BOY'S LAMENT

When we were a lot younger
we knew starvation and hunger.
We were all poor, yes, down an out,
if we were naughty, we got a good clout.
Mum was boss whilst Dad was at sea,
condensed milk sandwiches with sugar for tea.
We went to the bakers, and asked for stale buns
and off to the butchers for bones we did run.
A Sunday dinner we seldom had,
times I'm afraid were hard and very bad.
Second hand clothes were what we wore,
these had to last, as we got no more.
Holes in our shoes and down to the uppers,
we never worried about any suppers.
Down to the Market for an old cod's head,
this would be mixed with a swede and some bread.
Everything was asked for in hope of a meal
we were told always ask, never steal.

JACK ROSE

7. SCHOOLS

Train up a child in the way he should go
and when he is old he will not depart from it.
PROVERBS 22, VERSE 6

Most of the children went to school with no boots or shoes," recalls Mr E J Day who was born in 1903, "but each year before the bad weather the parish used to send boxes of clogs to the school and if our mothers could afford it, we all got a pair for threepence."

The children of The Grit were poor, and their life at school was a struggle. They were never far away from hardship at home and many can remember how every Friday afternoon the sons of the fishermen would be excused from lessons to go and get their fathers' wages from the company office to save the postage money.

There were a number of schools connected with the Beach Village, but after the First World War just three remained – Wilde's School, Mariners Score School and Central School. Prior to this were also Annott's School and Christ Church Infants, but the histories of all the schools in the area seem to overlap and some were amalgamated to add to the confusion.

Wilde's School was established as the result of a bequest from John Wilde who stated in his will made on 22nd July 1753 that, after the death of his niece and housekeeper, Miss Smithson, part of his estate should be put in trust for the building of a school. This estate included dwelling houses, fish-houses, yards and gardens in Lowestoft, and also land and property at Worlingham, all bequeathed by Wilde with the intention of opening a school for 40 boys, with preference to be given to the children of fishermen. The will also instructed that an annual sermon should be preached at the parish church of St. Margaret's on 23rd December, and this was fulfilled for 150 years, the text being, 'Train up a child in the way he should go and when he is old he will not depart from it.'

John Wilde died in 1738 and upon the death of Miss Smithson (by then Mrs Perryson) on 7th December 1781, the trustees erected a building for a school in the score named after him according to his wishes. The original construction went up in 1788 and the first master was Alexander Payne, appointed in 1790 to teach 40 boys at this new free school which opened a year later. Another school room was built later at the bottom of Wilde's Score, which could be entered from Wilde's School playground. It seems likely that this was constructed in 1831, as this date was marked out with the bottoms of dark bottles in the wall and this building became known as the 'Bottle Shed'.

Among the headmasters at Wilde's School was William Douglas who held the position for 24 years until October 1892 when he was succeeded by George Arthur Amoss. Edward Capps-Jenner started attending Wilde's School in 1894 and had memories of both men. He wrote, 'The head of Wilde's when I arrived, and at the time I left, was Mr Arthur G Amoss, who had the reputation of being 'stingy' with the cane. He did not, however, compare in that

(Left) The 'Bottle Shed' school room was at the bottom of Wilde's Score and thought to have been built in 1831, the date that was marked out using the bottoms of dark bottles in its gable end wall.

(Below) The interior of the 'Bottle Shed'. Condemned by the School Medical officer in 1924, the room was taken over by Walter Larke in the 1930s who renamed it the Hiker's Rest when he turned it into a billiard room.

WILDE'S SCHOOL, LOWESTOFT.

respect with the previous Head, 'One-Arm Douglas', who once laid up my brother Jack for a week as the result of caning. I did not hear what was the offence he had committed, but I expect my father approved the punishment, his argument being, 'If you behave yourself and do your work, you do not get the stick.' Douglas's method was to shove the boy by means of his one arm between his legs, back to front, hold him with his knees and apply the medicine.'

'The staff on my arrival and during my time was Mr Amoss, Mr Grice, Mr Herbie Giraud, Mr Pender and Miss Brown. The school was composed of an equal number of uptowners and beach boys and as it was situated about half-way down Wilde's Score, the Score often formed a battle ground, we Beach boys trying to chase the up-towners into the High Street (uphill all the way) and they in their turn trying to run us down to Whapload Road. This went on for a long time, until Gaffer Amoss feared it was getting too rough and that was a battle neither side of us won.'

George Osborne was born in 1911 and was a Wilde's School pupil between the ages of eight and 14, leaving in 1925. "I never lived on the Beach but there were too many at the Church Road School, and so I went to Wilde's School. Amoss was headmaster then. When he came to school he had a cane up his sleeve. The teachers in my time were Mr Watson, Mr Regis, Mr Boswell, Mr Snelling and Amoss. My teacher was Mr Watson. During the school teachers' strike in 1923, we went to the camp at Oulton for 2/6d a week to be taught and we still had school every day!"

During the strike, a Mr Brown took temporary charge of the school and in the mid-1920s, the long and strict reign of Mr Amoss finally ended when he presumably retired and was replaced by Charles Phillips, a keen cricketer. He stayed until 1936 when Wilde's became a mixed school and Miss F Quintrell became headmistress. Benny Knights was born in 1909 and, like many of his generation, can clearly remember the notorious Mr Amoss. "He was a sod he was," "recalls Benny, "I got three on each hand for fighting in the playground. He used to have a cane up his coat sleeve, and if you were marching into school he used to just slash you across the legs if you were out of step!"

Charles Ellis also has less than affectionate memories. "Old Amoss, I was glad when I got away from him. I saw him one morning give thirty-six boys three cuts of the cane on each hand, he went through the lot and he never raised a sweat... There was this one time when Amoss met his match though, and that was old Maud Wilson. She was a West Indian, about 16 stone and built like Frank Bruno, with arms like tree trunks. Although she had a heart of gold, that old girl, she didn't stand no nonsense. She had a boy called Tommy. One day he'd done something wrong at school which upset Amoss and he came in there and he took Tommy out of the classroom. In the passage was a coffin-shaped box with a lid and all the waste paper used to go in there, and he put Tommy across it and all the boys in the class heard him. We counted the strokes. 28 strokes. But Amoss made one mistake. When he finished, he let go of Tommy's collar, and he ran home. The next thing up came Maud. She'd got on a pair of men's leather sea boots and her apron and her sleeves rolled up. She came storming up there. Lynn Regis and Phillips were the masters there then and Phillips stood at the top of the steps at Wilde's School and all Maud said to him was, 'Where's Amoss?' and before he could answer she pushed him out of the way, and he went straight down, flat on his back. And she looked in every class room, every cupboard, and behind every wall and desk. Do you know what the old beggar had done? Down the playground there was a little classroom on Whapload Road (which later became the Hiker's Rest) and there was a long narrow passage down there, and he went down and hid behind that old stove. He must have seen her coming and realised what he'd done. She went through that school like a cyclone, I've never seen anything like it, she was absolutely boiling, steam coming out of her ears. All she could say was, 'Where's Amoss? WHERE'S AMOSS?' And I do believe to this day, if she had caught Amoss at that time she would have killed him. She would. Of course, she couldn't find him so she went home and she must have cooled off. She was like a man gone mad though. I've never seen a woman like it!"

Edward Capps-Jenner remembered Amoss more fondly in the early years of his tenure, having been taught by him from 1894 to 1901. Writing in the 1960s, 'I left Wilde's when I was 13 years old and I am glad that I was decent enough, years afterwards, to tell Mr Amoss that I reckoned I owed a lot to him and what I principally owed was not what he was able to knock into my head during the short time in which he had me: which was the Three Rs plus a little drawing, Geography and a few other elementary subjects; but the clear knowledge that I was an ignorant little object, that there was much knowledge and wisdom (not always the same thing) in the world and that I should, if I had good sense, spend the remainder of my life trying to acquire some of it. I began with this idea but should not like to estimate with what degree of success I pursued it.'

Charles Oldman was at Wilde's School during Mr Phillips' tenure as headmaster and although he was only there a year he recalls that discipline was strict, but that not all punishment came in the form of the cane. "The school had an allotment near St. Margaret's School and if you were a bad boy, you got put on allotment detail and spent all day weeding!" Charles especially remembers playing Wilde's cricket, a game unique to Wilde's School. "We used to have a sloping playground and we played cricket on there, with stumps in the four corners, and if you were facing the bowler bowling downhill, you knew it!"

"I used to play Wilde's cricket," Leonard Boyce recalls. "Because the school was built in the Score the playground was on a slope at the back of the school, and we used to have stumps in four corners and four batsmen and fielders in the middle and bowl from end to end. This game was mainly Mr Regis's doing, he was very keen on sport. He was eventually chairman of Lowestoft Town Football Club." Mr Boyce can also remember playing standard cricket. "Phillips was headmaster in my day, and he was captain of Lowestoft cricket team. He used to march us up to Corton Road playing fields once a week in the summer, and most of the time we spent bowling to him, give him practice for Saturday. I always remember he used to put his pads on and say, 'I'll show you how to bat, boys!'"

Leonard went to Wilde's School in 1926, after going to Arnold Street School and St. Margaret's. "It wasn't a very large school and I can remember the names of the teachers.

The headmaster was Mr Phillips, the senior teacher was Mr Lynn Regis, a very nice man, then there was Mr Taylor but I was never taught by him, a Mr Bull and Mr Boswell. I don't think there were any more down there, but they all ruled with a rod of iron and they were all good teachers. I finished up with Mr Regis in what they used to call the top class, which amounted to the class you were in before you left school at 14. I was very fond of Mr Regis, he was strict but very fair and he used to stand very straight, a very proud man he was. He'd been in the army in the First World War, and he used to tell us tales about that in school. He used to have a stick, two or three feet long, and though I never saw him hit anyone with it, he used to smash it upon the desk if anyone was misbehaving or anything like that."

"At Wilde's School I saw several children who came to school with no shoes or socks on, just bare feet, and he used to speak about it did Mr Regis, but he never pursued it because he knew the poor devils didn't have any money to buy them. And though some of the children were a bit rough and ready, he had them under his thumb, he was a very good teacher."

In 1924 Wilde's Score School was inspected by the School Medical Officer, Mr W Stott in his annual report of schools in Lowestoft. The equipment in the school was described as unsatisfactory – 'Old type of six-seater desks with no back rests. The blackboards are in a very bad condition'. Although the toilets had 'recently been done up and repaired' and there was a 'good concrete well-drained playground', Mr Stott is damning about one particular classroom. 'I have reported on this school during the year, particularly with regard to the temporary building abutting the Whapload Road, which is being used as a class room for

The image has a label reading: 162. Wilde's School, Looking W. 12/5/43.

(Left) Wilde's School pupils in 1923 during the teachers' strike when they were being taught at the St Margaret's Institute. Pictured to the right of the back row, is the notorious Mr Amoss who was feared by a generation of schoolchildren from The Grit.

(Above) A wartime 'stereo' photo showing two almost identical images which would have created a 3D effect when seen with a stereoscope. Looking towards Wilde's Score, the view shows the damage caused by the air raid on 12th May 1943. The gable end of Wilde's School can be seen standing amongst the rubble but the school would never open again.

Standard I boys; but up to the present time nothing has been done to rectify matters. The room in question is most unsuitable in almost every sense of the word, as a class room. It is overbuilt so there is no skyline to be seen through any of the windows, and the lighting and ventilation are both deficient.'

This particular room had its own name amongst the pupils and was recalled by George Osborne. "In my day the 'Bottle Shed' was more or less for the first class and then you came up into the main building. I remember the toilets were outside in the playground. In the main building, where the three classes were, on the end wall it said '1788'. Underneath was a clock and then there were these three nails on the wall with brass discs hanging from them and if you wanted to go to the toilet you had to take one of these with you. If there wasn't one there, you couldn't go, you had to wait for someone with a brass disc to come back."

Charles Ellis also spoke of the Bottle Shed, "That held about 20 children and the kids used to stand around a big cast iron stove which had a chimney through the roof. In the 1930s the school didn't use it any more and it became Walter Larke's billiard room and was called the Hiker's Rest." Perhaps Stott's report was responsible for the Bottle Shed's demise after all!

In the mid-1930s Wilde's School became a mixed school with Mr Phillips leaving the post of headmaster and Miss Quintrell taking over. Joy Pearce remembers, "I went to Arnold Street School first, then I went to Wilde's Score School where Mr Boswell was my teacher. Then the war came along and I had a break from school as my grandmother wouldn't let me be evacuated so I stopped at home."

Wilde's School closed at the start of the Second World War and never re-opened. Most of the school's buildings were destroyed during an air raid, but the remaining Victorian structure was leased to the newly established John Wilde Club in 1948, which was a sort of social club. Members refurbished the building and during the works found the original date slab which was inscribed '1788'. The club moved from these premises at the end of the 1970s and on 8th February 1980 the building was bought by Birds Eye Foods and used for their personnel training rooms and later as a store room for staff archives. In 1995 Birds Eye asked Waveney District Council if they wanted the property, and the Lowestoft Civic Society were approached to see if they could find a use for the old building. Refurbishment work began to turn the building into the Heritage Centre it is today.

The history of Wilde's School shows links with Annott's school, the oldest in the town and established in the 1500s with money bequeathed by Thomas Annott. Originally situated in the Town Close next to St. Margaret's Church, in 1674 this building became so dilapidated that the school moved to the Town Chamber over the Corn Cross. In the first half of the 19th century, Annott's School moved to a building east of Flint House, which we suppose was at the top end of Wilde's Score, where pupils received instruction under John Salmon and Samuel Chambers. This building was enlarged in 1843.

In 1872, with both schools in Wilde's Score, it was suggested that they should be amalgamated and move to Beccles Road in Oulton Broad, presumably on land that was part of John Wilde's bequest. However the idea never came to fruition, and in 1883 Annott's School was moved from Wilde's Score and united with the National School in Mariners Score, although the Annott name was retained until the last years of the 19th century, when it became known as Mariners Score School. It seems there had been a school in Mariners Score since the mid-1800s. This appears to have been established by the Rev F Cunningham who in 1830 started building the first of his three schools in the north of the town. One of these was the Great Girls' School in Mariners Score, and it seems likely that this was the Mariners Score School referred to in the 1902 *Kelly's Directory* as being built in 1846 for 182 children.

In 1877 the Boys' National School also moved to Mariners Score, from their building which would become the Convalescent Home opposite Belle Vue Park (now Abigail Court) and presumably joined with the girls' school already there. Now this became known as St. Margaret's National School. In 1883 the National School was amalgamated with Annott's, who moved from Wilde's Score. With Mr E Atkins as master and Miss Hubbard as mistress, this newly combined school took the name of Annott's. By 1901 it had simply become known as Mariners Score School and had 181 pupils with Mr Atkins remaining the Head. There was also Christ Church Infants School, which was situated at the bottom of Herring Fishery Score in premises which were built in 1892, currently part of Christ Church Hall.

Edward Capps-Jenner wrote of his schooldays on the Beach Village in the late 1890s, "My first school was the Christ Church Mixed Infants, which was then held in the Christ Church Parish Schoolroom, used also for Sunday School and all parochial meetings. After I was about seven years old I graduated to Wilde's School in Wilde's Score, on neutral ground between the Beach and up-town."

A vivid portrait of Christ Church Infants from 1908 is drawn in the *Borough of Lowestoft Education Committee Annual Report*. Situated at the bottom of the Score near the Church, the school is described as 'Quite open on the south side but surrounded by buildings in the other three. Poor neighbourhood. A one storey building.' The inspection was done in note form. Heating was supplied by 'two stoves in the main room and open fire-places in two classrooms. There were a few old desks without backs but the majority have them. A gallery at one end is too high, otherwise the equipment is good.' The toilets were less than satisfactory, 'Three trough closets flushed three times during school hours. There is a separate one for teachers but it is never used as it is not suitable. Urinal without flush, smells very badly in summer. Two wash basins in a very dirty condition.' However the general cleanliness at Christ Church Infants was acceptable – 'The school was swept down every night and scrubbed out three times a year.' There were 71 children inspected (37 boys, 34 girls), two were absent on day of inspection. Their age was between three and nine years old. 10% of boys and 7% of girls were described as having poor clothing. Four of the boys were described as having a 'dull' mental state. The report goes on to state, 'There is no playground, only a small yard of about 32 square yards, paved all over. Well arranged for light but classrooms too small for present purpose, being re-arranged.'

The Mariners Score School was also inspected as part of the report. 'There are no windows in the north end of school. The level of Score on the outside is higher than the floor of the School. There is a small unpaved playground for boys but none for girls. The latter play on the pickling plots on the Denes which are partly paved.' The school's equipment is criticised; 'All old fashioned desks without backs, seven in a row, 50 to 60 years old, cannot do with duals or singles, not sufficient room. The tops of the desks are very rough, they were either made without a plane or the soft wood has worn away, probably the latter, children's hands are protected by pieces of millboard when writing.'

Mr Atkins was Head of Mariners Score School until 1914 when the schools in the area were re-organised. In 1914 Christ Church Infants, with Mr Atkins as master, moved into the new Whapload Road Council School which had just been built and would later become the Central School when the schools were re-structured again in 1919. It was then that this new school was upgraded and the infants school moved from here into the old Mariners Score School building, becoming known as Mariners Score Infants, under the headship of Miss Ethel Strickland. In 1974, Beatrice Hardingham, one of the teachers at this school, wrote a letter to the *Lowestoft Journal* which included some interesting details of the time she spent working there. 'Miss Strickland, Miss Hook and I all taught in the same long room in that school (there were about 100 children). Our classes were separated by a curtain, and two shoulder-high screens. The youngest children occupied the small room at the rear of the building and their teacher was Miss Walker. We went to Mariners Score School supposedly for three years, but remained there 15 years until it was finally closed in 1934.

Miss Strickland was transferred to Morton Road School, Miss Hook to Lovewell Road School and I went to Lovewell Road Junior School. In spite of working in such difficult conditions, we had some happy and amusing times.'

The local *Annual Report of the School Medical Officer* in 1924 continues to paint a picture of Mariners Score School at this time. It seems the school has updated some of its equipment since 1908 with the old fashioned desks now gone. Mr W Stott reports, 'There are modern dual desks. Tables and chairs for babies. Sanitary Conveniences – five WC's and urinal all satisfactory, situated in the playground.' There are now two cloakrooms but, 'pegs arranged round the walls which are damp. This arrangement is not good.' His final remarks throw doubt on the use of this building for a school not for its condition but for the landlords. 'As this building is used three times weekly by the Plymouth Brethren as a Meeting Hall, on this account alone, is most unsatisfactory for the purpose of a school, especially for an Infants' School. Fresh accommodation should be found as soon as ever practicable for these children.' However, Mariners Score School remained open until the Second World War and was recalled by the generation who grew up between the wars.

Ruby Timberley went to the school in the late 1920s and early 1930s, "My brothers, sister and myself were all born in the Beach Village, and lived there until about 1941. We all attended Mariners Score School as infants. We had teachers who were strict, kind and dedicated. We could all read and write by the age of six years and could repeat most of the tables. At the age of eight years we moved to other schools. We had prayers at the beginning of the day and before we went home in the afternoon. We also sang the hymn, 'Now the day is over.' We had a good grounding and were disciplined."

"I went to school at Mariners Score," recalls Ron James. "Miss Strickland was the headmistress and she was something strict! One of the things we used to do on the way to school was after the Scots girls had filled the barrels with herring. They'd put the brine in and just tap the cork in because after a while the fish soaked up the brine so they used to fill up before they shipped them to Russia or wherever. Before they put the bungs tight in, we'd run along there to school and kick the barrels and if you weren't quick enough the brine would go all over you or the boy running behind you. When you went into school at Mariners Score, those tortoise stoves, they used to get red hot and if you sat near them after you did that, you would really stink of fish! And Miss Strickland would come along and she used to clip you across the lug and tell you to go home and change! Of course, you had nothing to change into!"

Charles Oldman remembers, "I was about three years old when we left my mother's parents and rented a cottage, if you could call it that, in a block called Scarle's Buildings, which was at the back of Mariners Score School. If you went down Mariners Score you came to the school and there was a little gate and a passageway, and you turned left and there was a row of cottages which as I said ran parallel with the Score and you also approached them from the bottom where now Waveney Tyres are. In fact, nothing remains there now … I was four years and five months when I went to Mariners Score School which was out of the cottage, just up the passage and you were there. There were only three classes there

and three teachers. Miss Strickland, who was the headmistress, and Miss Hook and Miss Hardingham. Mariners Score School was like a primary school. After I was about seven and a half I went up to St. Margaret's School and from there I went for about a year to Wilde's School ... when I was ten and a half I got a scholarship to Lowestoft Central School."

Lowestoft Central School was opened in 1919 in the former Whapload Road School which had been built in 1914 at a cost of £6,800. 300 pupils were admitted to the new school, entrance to which was by scholarship only. Mr T H Adams MBE was the only headmaster of the school for its 30-year history, during which time it gained an excellent reputation. The pupils were proud to wear their uniforms and display the yellow and black badge. Known as 'Plummy', the nickname derived from one of the town's mayors of the same name who was a greengrocer, Mr Adams was well thought of by his pupils and everyone who can recall him seems to hold him in high regard. He was considered to be both a good headmaster and a kind and generous man too. Although Jack Rose never went to Central School, he has his own recollection of Plummy Adams. When Jack was a young boy, his back gate opened out into Herring Fishery Score and he often sat on the back step watching the older children going to school. "Sitting there with my backside out of my trousers, clothes torn and dirty through playing in the fish yards, perhaps you would think no-one would have time for this ragamuffin. However, Mr Adams always stopped and asked, 'How's my little man today?'" Jack didn't know who he was until several years later but it always stuck in his mind, those words and kind attention meaning a lot to a youngster in those days.

Among the first teachers at Central School in 1919 were Miss Cecily Rhodes, the senior mistress, Miss Ethel Howden, Miss Rose Monk, Miss Alison Penzer, Mr Percy Blake, Mr C W E Todd, Mr Fred Wales and Mr Fred Moore. Charles Oldman can remember some of the later teachers at the Central School, "Mr Wilkin was the history and maths teacher, the art master was Arthur Gooch, Miss Spadham was an English teacher, Miss Gibson

(Above left) Mariners Score School was an uninviting factory-like building, thought to have been built in 1846. In 1925 the school had 120 pupils, with one small classroom and one large hall, divided by a curtain to split the classes up.

(Above right) Built in 1914, Central School was next door to Christ Church Hall (pictured left). Charles Oldman remembers, "It had two floors with long corridors, classrooms each side, a big hall down the bottom and on the top floor on the left was the headmaster. There were about 12 classrooms."

(Above) The Central School was bombed on 13th June 1941 at 3.45am. At the time the building was providing accommodation for servicemen, and 14 soldiers and a civilian were killed, one body being blown up as far as Ayers' pigeon loft at the rear of 104 High Street.

was music, Herbie Bushell was geography, Oscar Outlaw was woodwork and metalwork, and 'Fiddler' Moore (he used to play the violin) he was the science teacher. When I was at Central School the tuck shop of the school was Squire's shop."

"Central School had two floors with long corridors, classrooms each side, a big hall down the bottom, and on the top floor on the left was the headmaster. There were about 12 classrooms there. The teachers taught their subject throughout the school, like Wilkin would be taking maths and history but he would be teaching forms three, four, five and six. You had a form classroom but for every lesson there would an allotted classroom. So if you had English, you went to the English classroom. The teachers didn't move, you went to them... I should have stayed at Central School until I was 15, it was one of the conditions of the school, so when I was 14 I had to go before the full Education Committee in the town to get released from school because I had a job lined up."

Charles Ellis remembers, "I was 12 when I left Wilde's. I won a scholarship to the Central School and I was there until about 1932... The Central School was the first to serve school dinners. Miss Grieg used to cook the meal and it was sold to some of the pupils, the boys from Lound and places like that. The rest of them as I remember used to go down Hammond's fish and chip shop."

All the schools on The Grit closed at the beginning of the war because of the evacuation. Initially, Central School was used by servicemen as accommodation during the hostilities but during an air raid on 13th June 1941 at 3.45 a.m. the school received a direct hit and 14 servicemen and one civilian were killed. Although the Central School was destroyed, three separate classrooms along Herring Fishery Score, the science laboratory, the woodwork room and the cookery room survived and after the war became part of the Navigation School. Many of the former pupils of the Central School perished during this war too. Charles Ellis continues, "There were 32 boys in my class. Times were bad in the 1930s, and there was no work and Mr Adams told us that the Royal Air Force were recruiting for air crews. You had to pass an entrance exam but at least it would be a career and about 20 of the 32 volunteered for the Royal Air Force. There was so many of them that they allowed a room to be put aside at Central School and they took the exam there. They all passed I think and, of course, when the war broke out, they were all trained air crew, and if I look back at my class, 16 were killed in the Air Force."

After the war, none of the schools in the Beach Village re-opened, the buildings being either demolished or put to a variety of other uses. The children were sent up into the town for their schooling, and another part of The Grit's sense of community and independence was lost.

Class 1, Mariner's Score School in 1924. In 2018 this photo was posted on the Beach Village Facebook page, which yielded many of the children's names. (Back row) Ethel Strickland, Ada Jones, Daisy Howlett, Jack Aldred, unknown, Doug Bellinger, unknown, George Dalley, Rita Turner, Maud Nunn, Beatrice Hardingham. (Middle row) Jessie Bullen, William Haylock, Mary Smith, Eileen Cullum, Annie Blyth, Danny Dyer, Willie Butcher, unknown, Ivy Harness. (Front row) Harrod, Hazel Disney, Ivan Hull, unknown, Ivy Beard, Jimmy Bullen, unknown, unknown, Winney Utting.

8. THE MOST EASTERLY PARISH

Not that there shall be wrecks, but if there are, that they may be on our beach.
THE BEACHMEN'S PRAYER

"We went morning, afternoon and evening to Christ Church," says Hazel Boardley, "and at 8 o'clock used to have an open air meeting down there. I was a teenager then, and we had a little old organ, which we called Wheezy-Anna, and we all used to gather round this lamp-post. As soon as they heard the music all the cottage doors would open and the ladies would all come out and lean on their doorposts and listen to our meeting. And that was called the 'hallelujah' lamp-post."

Although situated, as *Crowe's Handbook* puts it, 'among that class of inhabitants who are generally least disposed to go in quest of religious instruction', there were always places of worship in the fishing village. One of the earliest of these was a Primitive Methodist chapel which could be found near the bottom of Denny's Score (now Wilde's Score) in the early 1800s, and there was also a Ranters Chapel situated in the area where Coleman Square was later built.

The North Beach Bethel was in East Street at the bottom of Rant Score East, between Whapload Road and the gasworks. It was also known as the 'Little Bethel' to avoid confusion with the 'bigger' Bethel in Battery Green Road, officially opened as the Seamen's and Fishermen's Bethel in February 1899. This is still standing and in 2012 was converted into *The Players Theatre*. The North Beach Bethel was on The Grit and established in the early 1900s. This owed much to the persistence and efforts of Mr Alexander Gaviller Boyd who purchased the property, entirely at his own cost, at the north end of East Street for the site of the Bethel. There were difficulties initially in obtaining the old cooperage building that stood there and had been let to J Grieve & Son, but apparently as soon as they heard what the purpose of Mr Boyd's purchase was, 'they came forward with the greatest kindness and accepted space found for them on another part of the property.' The site was cleared and the cornerstone laid on 10th July 1902. 200 people attended the opening service on 4th September 1902 and the North Beach Bethel continued until the Second World War, Mrs Boyd becoming Superintendent after her husband's death in 1922. The stone scroll erected in his memory can now be found outside *The Players Theatre* on Battery Green Road.

The plans for Christ Church were drawn up during a religious revival by the Rev Francis Cunningham shortly before his death on 13th August 1863. Cunningham was the rector of Pakefield from 1815 to 1855 and vicar of Lowestoft between 1830 and 1860, and it was he who started a collection for the construction of the church and the endowment of the new vicarage at the end of 1862, with the Bishop of the Diocese among the first of the contributors. Christ Church was built for the ever-increasing residents of the Beach Village, giving them their own minister and church and establishing a parish of their own.

(Below left) Christ Church opened on 12th February 1869 and was originally called the Cunningham Memorial Beachmen's Church for the Beachmen and Fishermen of Lowestoft.

(Below right) The Hallelujah lamp-post on the junction of Anguish Street and Wilde's Street where parishoiners from Christ Church gathered for open air meetings.

(Bottom left) The North Beach Bethel was in East Street at the bottom of Rant Score, between Whapload Road and the gasworks. Carved in the stone over the door – 'Christ Jesus came into the world to save sinners', with 'Ever reconciled to God' underneath.

(Bottom right) The Primitive Methodist Chapel on Whapload Road was built by 1863 and closed when a new chapel was built in St. Peter's Street in 1876. During the First World War the old building was put to use as a soup kitchen and later, in the 1950s, as a sanitation store by Birds Eye before it was demolished in January 1968.

(Right) Mr Alexander Gaviller Boyd who established the North Beach Bethel in 1902.

3,000 people attended the stone-laying ceremony which was a festive occasion. The weather was said to have been 'splendidly fierce' and the scaffolding, flagstaffs and the houses displayed a 'profusion of flags and banners'. This stone was placed at the south-east corner of the tower and had the following inscription which is now illegible:

This First Stone
of
Christ Church Lowestoft
Erected to the Glory of God and in the memory of the
Rev. Francis Cunningham M.A., R.D.
Was laid on 4th day of May by the Rev. Williams Nottridge Ripley, M.A.
W. Oldham Chambers   *Jackson & Rounce*
Builders   *Architect*

The new church, built in the Early English style and originally seating about 460, opened on 12th February 1869 and was called the 'Cunningham Memorial Beachmen's Church for the Beachmen and Fishermen of Lowestoft'. The first incumbent was the Rev E J Barnes (1867-1878) who before the Church was opened gave Bible classes and started a Sunday School in his front room for young lads. The Rev Barnes soon became involved in community life in the Beach Village and if the maroons were fired to call out the lifeboat during a service, everyone including the vicar left the church to help launch the lifeboat, continuing the service on their return.

The villagers signed a pledge to 'follow the Lord's example and be present at the services in our Father's House on His day unless prevented by good reason that could be conscientiously given to our Lord and Saviour, the Head of the Church'. To encourage the residents further the church wardens were instructed that the hiring of 'sittings' (the reserving of pews) should be exclusive to inhabitants of the Beach Village and the rent kept low.

When the church opened in 1869 it was chronically short of money and unable to raise £500 for the consecration. 30 years later, when Christ Church still hadn't been able to scrape the money together, the Bishop agreed to waive this requirement. The western aisles and the church organ were not added to the church until later, and the clock was installed on 15th June 1901 when a generous parishioner, Mr Slipper Barnes, who lived in Old Nelson Street, paid £120 for the timepiece. However, due to the church's precarious finances, it was unable to pay for the upkeep of the clock and the town council agreed to take over maintenance costs and responsibilities. A Mr J Bonsall was appointed to wind and regulate it for the sum of £4 a year, although there was some difficulty handing it over as a public clock since it had been a private gift. This was overcome by drawing up an agreement under which the council had the right of entry to the church. The council was also granted the right to light, wind and repair the clock and have done so until the 1990s, when they decided that public clocks were not so important given that wrist-watches were so widely worn.

(Left to right)
E J Barnes
1867 - 1878
J Lancaster
1878 - 1883
E W S Kingdom
1883 - 1890
D Dickson
1890 - 1912

Born in 1887, Edward Capps-Jenner – whose father William was the Lowestoft lifeboat coxswain (1883-1901) – recalls how Christ Church was a big part of his family's life. 'My parents were married in Christ Church. I was baptised there, confirmed there, married there and my two children were baptised there. All our lives centered around the Church. My mother was Sunday School teacher and school caretaker for many years. I was successively choir-boy, organ blower, Sunday School teacher, scoutmaster, sidesman and secretary of the Parochial Church Council.'

Edward continues, 'In those days whole families attended services regularly, occupying reserved pews. My father-in-law Robert William Benstead was a Post Office telegraphist and clerk and wore a high top-hat and tail coat, with rolled umbrella, every Sunday and escorted his family of six children to church. My wife and I met at a Church children's concert when we were 12; at least that was when I first realised what a very nice little girl she was. After courting her, and being married to her (on 23rd June 1913 by Rev A Hewitt) for a total of 56 years, I realised that in one thing at least, I had learned wisdom. She was a Sunday School teacher, pianist and many other helpful things during most of our time at the church. Our religion was very strict in those early days, evangelical and sabbatarian and church attendance was a must. I was often at Communion Service at 8am, Sunday School at 10am, Morning Service at 11am, School at 2.30pm, Evening Service at 6.30pm and every Wednesday at 7.30pm. For good measure there was a monthly afternoon Children's Service and during autumn and winter, a monthly Men's Service. During Holy Week, every evening except Sunday after evening service, I and/or my scouts worked the projector. Later we had a 'Scouts' Own' meeting in the church every Sunday afternoon, in lieu of the boys attending Sunday School. There was thus not much temptation to break the Sabbath day by frivolity. I kept all this up during the lifetime of my mother, largely I am afraid, in deference to her wishes and prayers.'

Edward confirms that during the heyday of the fishing village in the early 1900s, church-going was not a regular occurence for many on The Grit. 'I am afraid the adult Beach population did not themselves attend church very much, but on the first Sunday after a funeral, a whole family would parade in deep mourning. My father used to say there were Beach people who attended church twice in every year, once in the last hour of the old year and once in the first hour of the new (ie Watch Night Service!).'

Christ Church always tried to relieve the poverty of the surrounding community, such as in February 1895 when in one week between 5,000 and 6,000 free breakfasts were provided for hungry children in its school room (which had opened in 1892) at the cost of one pound per 200 children.

As school caretaker, Edward Capps-Jenner's mother Harriet was responsible for organising these breakfasts. 'The church on the Beach did good work, and my mother got through a lot of labour for very little pay in running free breakfasts for children during hard times, and a canteen during the Home Fishing [autumn herring fishing season] for fish workers in the Mission Room, which belonged to the John Wilde Trust, and stood at the bottom of Wilde's Score, near the school playground.'

The free breakfasts would have been one of many initiatives introduced by the Rev David Dickson, vicar from 1891 up to 1912 when he died aged 55. Edward Capps-Jenner remembered the Rev. Dickson. 'I owe a very great deal to his interest and help. He was very anxious to get the fishermen into the church and made several special efforts to do this. One of them was to purchase an old square-stern smack, named *John and Sarah*, renamed by him *Good Hope*. I can just remember meetings in her, but she was almost unused, although drawn up in the middle of the beach, between the shods. *Good Hope* finished her life as a stable and by being washed over twice onto her broadside by sea floods.'

Edward realised the difficulty of the Rev Dickson's quest. 'The Beachmen were very clannish, and the only way to influence them as a whole would have been to get among them in their own shods. But in their shods they smoked, drank beer and played cards! Subsequent attempts to form Mens' Clubs in connection with the Mens' Service proved failures too, and I was the last member in attendance, chiefly, be it confessed, because I opened and closed the room.'

Church attendance was certainly another aspect of life on The Grit which was boosted by the autumn herring fishing. Edward explains, 'We Christ Church people also made a practice of attending, after Sunday evening service during the Home Fishing, a special service run by and for Scottish people in the Marina Theatre when our people did a bit of singing and David Dickson would sometimes give the address.'

'The attendance at the church was, in those days, sometimes very considerable and I have known the building, seating about 600, so full – e.g. at the first Sunday in the month Mens' Service when police, army volunteers, fire brigade and lifeboat crew attended – that extra flap-seats at the end of the pews had to be pulled out for use. I fear they have not been so un-shipped for many years.'

One of the happiest times in Christ Church's history was in March 1921, when a religious revival began in Lowestoft under the preaching of the Rev A Douglas Brown from Balham,

(Left to right)
A Hewitt
1912 – 1918
J Hayes
1918 – 1923
J A G Ainley
1923 – 1928
E Morris-Jones
1928 – 1933

London. The first meetings were at London Road Baptist Church and at the Fishermen's Bethel, Battery Green, both of which were packed for every service. After the first week it was decided to hold afternoon Bible readings at Christ Church. The first one filled the Parish Room, the next one filled the church, and so it continued for three weeks, including Easter week and on Good Friday, in spite of services in other churches, Christ Church was more crowded than ever. On those afternoons the trams were full of people carrying bibles, and the conductor would call out, 'Get off here for Christ Church,' as they reached Old Nelson Street.

The vicar of Christ Church at the time, Rev John Hayes, wrote about this experience in March 1921, saying, 'I want to take you into my church one Wednesday evening. At a quarter to seven the church is full, it is 'bung' full, and I have to go up into the pulpit and say to the people, 'My friends, I want those of you who love the Lord Jesus to go out. I want you to go into the Parish Hall and pray.' They got up and went, here and there all over the church; they passed into the Parish Hall, some 200 of them gathered there, and they held a prayer meeting. Then I had to say to the young men, 'I want you to get up and sit on the floor at the front': and we had to get people into that church packed in that way, and in the vestry. In the Parish Hall they were praying; there was a sister praying for her sister who was in the church, and at the close of the service that sister came to me and said, "I want to talk to you". On the following Tuesday evening that sister was led to Christ in my study in answer to the prayer offered in the Parish Hall.'

Two of Christ Church's longest serving parishioners were Matthew and Hazel Boardley who both grew up on the Beach, and were married in the church in 1939. Matthew was born in 1916 and lived more or less next door to the church, at 1 Jubilee Terrace. From the age of three he was in the Sunday School class, moving on to the Boys' Brigade and becoming a Sunday School teacher. "I missed out on the choir though," explains Matthew, "because I couldn't stand the stiff shirt collars you had to wear!" In 1956 Matthew became the first

(Left) Christ Church, circa 1910. Edward Capps-Jenner wrote, 'The adult Beach population did not attend church very much... Our congregation and church officers were made up chiefly of up-towners.'

(Below) On 22nd June 1907 the *Lowestoft Journal* reported, 'On Thursday afternoon the children of Christ Church Sunday School had their annual treat. Headed by the Salvation Army band and accompanied by the Rev D Dickson, they went to Gunton Old Hall – a happy band – and had a jolly time.'

CHRIST CHURCH SUNDAY SCHOOL JUNE 1907

Beach boy to be made churchwarden, although this was on a temporary basis, a 'temporary' period which lasted 23 years until he retired in May 1979 and was succeeded by Derek Bacon.

Hazel was born in 1918 and lived opposite the *Rising Sun* public house and she too went to Christ Church from an early age. "My mother was a Methodist but sent us to Christ Church because it was the best Sunday School... Up in the High Street, Porter had a bakers shop and a cake shop but behind, running down into Crown Score, there was this wide stretch of garden – apple trees, flowers and all sorts – and we used to hire this at Christ Church for a tennis club... Then there was the Sunday School treat. They used Pretty's coal carts as Mr Pretty was a Superintendent at the Sunday School. Mostly we used to go to Boardley's Meadow, which was to do with the other side of Matthew's family. The meadow was at Normanshurst, where the fire station is now, but we also went to Hopton and Beccles, places like that."

Edward Capps-Jenner came from an earlier generation than the Boardley's. Sunday School at Christ Church was a big part of his childhood in the 1890s and early 1900s. 'Our congregation and church officers were made up chiefly of up-towners. However the Beach mothers took tremendous delight in seeing that their children attended Sunday School, and the annual Sunday School treat was a great affair of clean starched pinafores and 'Sunday clothes'. We were preceded on foot by a band (at one time our own Boys' Brigade No.1 Company Fife and Drum), followed by the entire school on foot, except the infants who were carried in horse-drawn vehicles such as coal-carts, millers' wagons, and other trade vehicles, specially scrubbed for the job. At first we went to Pope's Farm in Norwich Road and in later years to the Old Hall, Gunton and Miss Clurland's grounds at Normanston. It was an honour to be one of the six boys who carried the School Banner, much like a Trade Union Banner.'

Ruby Timberley went to Sunday School at Christ Church in the 1920s. "We were christened when we were babies in long clothes. When we were about three or four years old we started to attend Sunday School. Our teacher at this early age was a Miss Spurgeon, who was related to Mr Spurgeon, the coxswain of the lifeboat at that time. The room where we were taught was very bare. There was a wooden floor, no mats, and there were two long forms down the middle on which we all sat, our feet not touching the floor. We were not allowed to speak unless spoken to. If we did not pay attention to what Miss Spurgeon was trying to teach us she would lift us up and bang our bottoms on the form."

Ron James also remembers Miss Spurgeon, "I used to go to Sunday School there and Albert Spurgeon, the coxswain of the lifeboat, had a sister who used to be the Sunday School teacher. She weighed about 16 stone and if you didn't behave yourself or you got caught talking she used to shake you up and down."

A generation after Edward Capps-Jenner, Ruby's memories are remarkably similar. "One Sunday afternoon each summer all the Sunday School children marched along Whapload Road followed by the Boys' Brigade Band and the Christ Church banner on the occasion of our Sunday School anniversary. Of course, we always had what was called the Sunday

 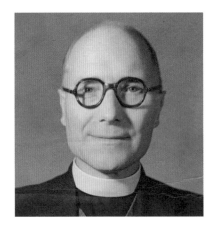 

(Left to right)
T Bragg
1934 - 1937
V L Treanor
1937 - 1946
H Sutton
1946 - 1952

School treat. This took place on a Thursday afternoon which at that time was early closing day and some of the teachers worked in shops. The venue in the 1920s was the Crown Meadow. The older children and teachers, also helpers, walked behind the church banner but the infants were transported in Mr J Pretty's coal carts. Mr O Pretty was our Sunday School Superintendent so he made sure that the carts were scrubbed out, with clean sacks put on the seats. It was a great occasion for us – the highlight of our summer. We were all dressed in our Sunday best and some of us had buttonholes of sweet-peas provided by aunties. Mums and grannies came to wave us off as the band started up. We were so excited that we could have been in a Rolls-Royce. Mums and grannies joined us later and joined in the fun, games and races, and of course, tea with two kinds of slab cake. There was always someone with a large tin of sweets which were thrown into the air for us to scramble for. We all went home tired out!"

"I can remember the Sunday School treats," says Mrs Jessie Hitter, 'They used Pretty's coal-carts, scrubbed out with clean sacks on the floor and all the kids used to get in there. We used to go as far as Carlton and think we were right out in the country. We played games in a field and had our tea which was potted meat sandwiches and a little bit of cake and we used to run round the field and have about threepence to spend which was a lot of money in those days. We used to buy flowers for our mothers but they'd be dead before we got them home. We'd have a ha'penny cornet. Our mothers used to come and see us off in the cart with our nice little frocks and hats."

Many of the Beach children joined the 'Young Harvesters' Club' which was held above Christ Church school room. Mrs Wright was the lady in charge in the 1920s, and there were magic lantern shows once a week and other events. The North Beach Bethel also ran a Sunday School, and this too proved popular. In 1912 the Bethel's Sunday School had 15 teachers and a Superintendent, and about 125 children attended each Sunday, and 110 of these earned prizes.

(Left to right)
P E Street
1952 – 1957
R H Smith
1957 – 1967
E P Rudman
1967 – 1973

Born in 1947, Sheila Rogers was part of the post-war generation and lived at 34 Old Nelson Street in Bow House. "My mother's family all came from the Beach. She was Edith Armes before she was married. And I went to Christ Church as a baby." Sheila would attend Christ Church for the next 66 years and remembers Sundays when she was growing up in the 1950s. "I used to go to the Brownies at the Church and when my brother was young they also had Life Boys and Boys' Brigades, cubs and scouts."

The Bethel also catered for the younger generation. "I went to Sunday School in the Little Bethel," says John 'Rhubarb' Gurney, "There was Sister Nell and Mr Wylie, they were the teachers. Of course, a lot of the boys would only turn up when the treats were on, but they didn't seem to mind."

Amongst Jean Mitchell's earliest recollections are, "Going to Sunday School at the Little Bethel where Sister Nell and Gwenny Nunn taught us our scriptures. We used to have Sunday School treats and once a year if you had a very good attendance you received a prize. Every week you received a small printed text."

"I went to the Little Bethel's Sunday School," says Charlie Ellis. "You had a blue card and every time you went you got a stamp, which was a little star, and if you got 52 stars you were given a book to keep, something like *Treasure Island*. You were something proud of that! I had three or four prizes."

Ros Parker was born in 1924. "I remember my mother taking me to the anniversary services in the Bethel when I was little. They used to be wonderful, all the concerts they put on. My parents, they talked about when they were younger down on Whapload Road. They used to go to the Bethel church, that's where they met one another."

The North Beach Bethel closed at the beginning of the Second World War and never re-opened. Christ Church however is still standing, having not only survived the war and the demolition of its surrounding parish, but also the flood which engulfed the area on the night of 31st January 1953. "There had been floods before," explains Matthew Boardley, "but the

1953 flood was different, a wall of water swept down Whapload Road. If Christ Church had a door facing north when that flood water came down, we'd have had a lot more water in the church. The way Christ Church was built meant that it didn't affect it much. Most of it was in the aisles and we could just sweep it out."

The Rev Peter Street was the vicar at the time, and was having a bath that evening at the vicarage when the phone rang. 'It was around 10.30pm,' he told Royal Flaxman for his book *Wall of Water* in 1993. 'I answered the phone and it was the police with disturbing news. "Your church is under water. You'd better come quick!" I made a hasty finish to my bath and arrived at the church shortly before 11pm to find that the church was indeed under water.' That night the Rev. Street was one of many who worked tirelessly against the flood, with the vicarage opening its doors to 24 people left homeless by the sudden surge of water. By morning Rev Street was tired and filthy, and while he was standing on the back of a lorry travelling up the High Street he began to see members of his congregation walking to the church completely unaware of any flood. 'I was quite surprised when I realised it was already time for morning service, and there was even more surprise on their faces at seeing their vicar standing on the back of a lorry, as black as a coalman!'

With around 8% of the Church's parish flooded, immediate action was necessary and the next day Christ Church Hall was opened to provide food and clothing for flood victims. The Rev Peter Street remembers, 'Through the agony and damage caused to many homes we were able to bring Christian help to many people. Some of the fisher folk and members of the congregation also gave many hours of their time. The flood brought people together in the weeks following as never before.'

In 1967 there were proposals put forward to close Christ Church and amalgamate with St. Peter's Church in the town. Although Christ Church had lost most of its parish by this time, the church's congregation was growing due to an influx of people from a wider area. "The congregation now come from all over the place," says Hazel Boardley. "We haven't got a parish like we used to have, our parish is up the town now. The church is now in the middle of an industrial area. We all descend in cars, we come from all over." As a result it was St. Peter's Church which was closed and demolished, and its organ relocated in Christ Church.

By the mid-1990s Matthew and Hazel Boardley's long involvement with Christ Church was only surpassed by George Francis who was the church's longest serving parishioner. George, who was also the church verger for nearly 40 years, was born and bred on The Grit. "My father worked in a fish-house, he was a 'smoker', then he went and worked for Jewson's. We lived at 5 Rant Score East, near Binks' Bakery and I went to Wilde's School, it was called Wilde's Endowed then if you please! When I left school I was a cooper at Sayer and Holloway for a time till I left there and went to Jewson's until my retirement. But I left the Beach when I got married and moved up into the town to Crown Street. Christ Church has been my life though, really. I was a choir-boy, Sunday School teacher, Bible class leader, officer in the Boys' Brigade. I got married there, and was verger there for nearly 40 years. My wife was a Sunday School teacher there too. I've been at Christ Church since I was three years old and I am now 90! Yes, it's been my life."

(Top) A fresh community spirit was born out of the desperation of the 1953 flood. Gus Jensen remarked, 'People were coming down with ordinary clothes on, no rubber boots, and wading in waist-deep to piggy-back others out or take in hot tea and sandwiches. They didn't seem to bother how wet they got as long as they could be of some help.'

(Bottom) The following day Christ Church Hall was open, providing food and clothing for victims of the flood. The Rev Peter Street, fresh from his daring rescues of the night before, can be seen at the back of the hall, wearing overcoat and cap, overseeing the sorting of clothes.

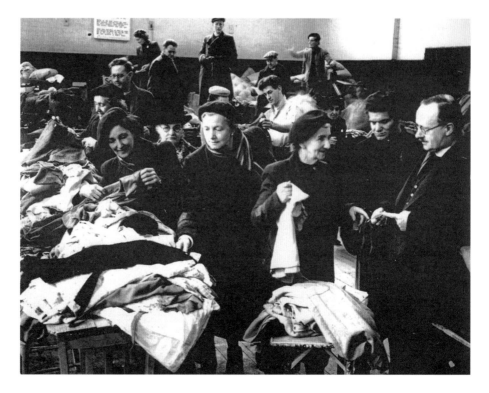

(Left to right)
P J Bye
1973 – 1980
R J Payn
1981 – 1992
P Moon
1994 – 2004
M Payne 2005 –

In 2019 one of Christ Church's longest serving parishoners is now Pam Lord, who was church organist for 70 years. "I started when I was about 20 and I am 90 now!" Pam comes from a Lowestoft family and her mother's brother was Frank Coleby who opened the long-running sports shop in the town. As a young woman she was living in Leiston where her father was a pharmacist and it was in Knodishall Church where she first started playing the organ. When her father died suddenly at the age of 47, the family had to move quickly back to Lowestoft, although Pam remained in Leiston where she was training to be a pharmacist herself. She would however soon relocate to the town when she got a job as a trainee dispenser at W H Cole & Son which was near the Post Office in London Road North.

Pam says, "When I came to Christ Church in 1949, where the police station is now, there was Boothroyds, a grocer's shop. Mr Boothroyd's son Billy was in the boy's brigade and he used to bang the drum!" She continues, "When I arrived Mr Weller was the organist and choirmaster. He had a walrus moustache, I can see him now. He was very strict with our young choirboys... he used to go along at choir practice and he had a ruler and he'd go along and say, 'Come on, top A! Top B!' Poor man, he suffered a lot. He wasn't well and eventually he started coming out only occasionally and so Harry Sutton would say to me, 'On the organ, Pam.' So I used to play. And gradually that became permanent. I eventually did take over when I was about twenty-one."

Pam also provided musical accompaniment to the open air meetings around the hallelujah lamp-post. She recalls, "I used to play a harmonium which was foot-powered in those days. It had a little flap and you'd press it up and down with your foot to make a sound. And we had a service and sang hymns under that lamp-post."

Pam fondly remembers the Scots fisher girls. "You'd see them walking up and down Whapload Road, always with folded arms. A lot of them were Christians, very godly women but I don't think we ever drew them into the Church. Many of them were Salvationists, so I think they went there, also the Bethel of course, on Battery Green. That was in its heyday, because it was for the fishermen and that was where they went."

The current Vicar of Christ Church is Rev Matthew Payne, an admirer of Pam's commitment to the Church and dedication to her faith. "The point here is that Pam is by no means just the organist. She's done so much in the life of the Church over many years and is far more than simply playing the music. She's been Brown Owl and leader of the Women's Fellowship. If you play five hymns in the morning and five in the evening, that's 10 per Sunday. And if there are 52 Sundays in a year and you only have a couple of weeks holiday that's 500 hymns in a year. In 70 years that comes to 35,000 hymns! That's without funerals and weddings."

Matthew arrived in Lowestoft in the summer of 2005 to succeed Phil Moon who left the previous year to become vicar of Bishop Hannington, Hove. Matthew grew up in Tonbridge, Kent and had a curacy for four years in Sussex near Arundel. He says, "I think Lowestoft is an interesting town. It's got huge assets such as the beach and the sea. It also has great need of new investment. With the Gulliver wind turbine which was put up just before I arrived here – late 2004/early 2005 – and the Orbis Energy Centre, we have been blessed to see some of the renewable energy businesses come this way."

"Christ Church's congregation is drawn from people all across Lowestoft and the surrounding area. Community is much more fluid now, with more networks and huge mobility. It's quite common for people not to know their next door neighbours very well, but now know people they meet in the gym or on the bus or in the hospital. Our social networks are very different."

"We've got an eclectic mix of people from all sorts of different backgrounds, a lovely mixture. In the last 10 years we've had a tremendous number of other nationalities join the Church and what was once a very local white working class fishing community church is now quite remarkable for having a dozen nationalities here. Which is not what you'd expect in little Lowestoft, even if you might in London. It really began with a Jamaican family 12 years ago, and we welcomed them. There are Nigerians, Sri Lankans, a Dutch lady, an American woman, South Africans – and we welcome this. From a Christian point of view it's a visible reminder that the message of Christianity is for the whole world, it's international."

"We have a lot of contact with children and mums and toddlers, and have a group that meets in the church hall three mornings a week, called Shrimps. We have contact with 50 non-church families every week, where young parents can come in, sit in a hall and chat and have somewhere on a rainy day where kids can run around. It is a ministry of support and care for the community in a small way. We need to be thoughtful, wise, relevant. Hold fast on to what you believe but explain it in fresh ways. That's the challenge."

Christ Church is the most prominent remaining link to The Grit. How did the Church survive the social changes of the 1960s? Pam says, "I think Christ Church has been tremendously blessed by the fact that there have been people who have constantly prayed for its outreach and cared for people. There has always been a group – sometimes small, sometimes large. People who have been cared for and looked after, whether there's a vicar there or not. We've had some wonderful curates over the years, and also leaders. George Francis and his wife, Gladys – bless her heart – she was a lovely lady and she's never mentioned anywhere.

A 1990s view of the most easterly parish, with Christ Church standing between the police station, the Birds Eye factory and a car showroom.

She used to have me up to dinner every day when I was at work. People like that, doing little things. She used to come to Women's Fellowships. She was one of those people, like so many others, who did little jobs that nobody knew about. And I think it's those people behind the scenes, who deserve to be mentioned as much if not more than me. They used to pray, they used to give their money, their time, cooking and looking after people."

Pam continues, "And in a way, you could say that stemmed from the 1953 flood. Because people looked after one another then. And from that was born a group of people who cared for people. You think of The Bethel on Battery Green, what it is now, a theatre. I've been in there when it was a church, when it was packed. I had a girls' choir and we used to go and sing there on special occasions. It would be packed full. But that's gone now, you see. I think it is this group of people who have prayed and given of their lives for others. And that happens in the world, outside the church buildings."

"I would put it down to prayer. I am a great believer in prayer, I really am. I often told my Women's Fellowship, I pray about everything and anything. I mean, even if I lose my keys or my purse, I'll say, 'Lord, please what have I done with my purse, what have I done with my keys?' But suddenly after a few minutes that comes to light. People say, ah that's a load of rubbish. I don't think so! And I think there are others in the Church who believe it as much as I do. And that has carried that Church through. In Harry Sutton's time, this hallway used to be full on a Tuesday night at a prayer meeting. In Peter Bye's time they'd be 60 or 70 people come to these prayer meetings. And I think it's that which has kept this Church going."

9. THE VILLAGE SHOPS

I lived on Whapload Road, at 2 Canary Cottages, next door to Mr Burwood's grocery shop. He sold almost all and everything in that tiny cramped shop, and had a slate where you paid for items when you had the money.
JOHN DAY

The shops on The Grit were humble affairs, small, family-run businesses, but they gave the area an independence because almost any item could be purchased from these shops, from muffins to paraffin. There was no need to go uptown; the Beach was a self-contained community.

"Milk came to the doorstep like it does today," says Ruby Timberley, "but it was sold from a big milk churn on the back of a pony and trap." This was delivered by Joseph Flertey who was the milkman on the Beach and had premises at 89 Whapload Road. You could also buy milk elsewhere on the Beach, as Ruby recalls, "There was a dairy (milk only) at the bottom of Old Nelson Street owned by two sisters, the Misses Bishop. Their milk was in large china bowls covered with net cloths, you took you mother's jug to buy milk."

Leonard Adams also remembers Joseph Flertey. "He would come up Maltsters Score and ask us lads to look after his float while he went round the houses. When he came back he would ask one of us to take a few bottles down to the shop and he would give us a ha'penny. This went on for months and we thought we were helping until I heard my mother thanking him. It was just a way of him helping us lads as when he came up the score we was only 20 yards off the dairy shop."

In the late 1920s when Joseph Flertey moved away from the Beach to premises in the town, his old shop was acquired by Godfrey 'Maggot' Girling. "I had my first barber's on the Beach Village where old Flertey's dairy used to be," explains Godfrey. "I rented it for about six bob a week, something like that. This was in the days when I used to charge fourpence or threepence for boys. I was there three or four years till I moved to 8 Whapload Road, near Fletcher's bicycle shop, where I was for about five years until I joined up in January 1940."

Godfrey had begun his career as a barber at the age of 11, working in Crown Street as a lather boy at Albert Hawk's. He went from there to Jack Blowers in Commercial Road for four years. He recalls, "He used to go for his dinner at one o'clock, and he wouldn't come back until four. There was me going like hell, it was a busy shop, and so I say to him, 'Look here Jack, I do all the work, I want a ten bob a week rise.' He say, 'I can't afford that,' so I say, 'All right, I'm packing up Saturday night and going to start up on the Beach.' I had it all planned and that's when I went down there, the last day in the old year, 1929."

Like most of the shops on the Beach Village, one of Godfrey's busiest times was during the autumn herring season, "I went down there one Saturday morning during the fishing time.

The south end of Whapload Road in the early 1900s. The single storey building on the left is the Bishop sisters' grocery shop, next door to brother John's ironmongery with the ship lamp-makers sign. Over the road, on the corner of Hamilton Road, is Hughes Dining Rooms which subsequently became the Corner Cafe and, later, Alan Delf's shop.

Quarter to eight I started working and I didn't finish there till ten past nine in the evening, and I didn't have a drink or anything, didn't stop. When I counted my money up, do you know how much I took? 34 shillings and ninepence! I thought to myself, that doesn't seem very much, but then I sat and thought, them poor buggers who work for Boardley [haulage business] only get 34 bob a week. I earned that in one day so I couldn't complain, could I?"

When Godfrey used to ask his customers, 'Do you want anything on your head?' he often used to get the reply, 'Shove some Yarmouth oil on.' This puzzled him as he'd never heard of Yarmouth oil, so one day he asked one of his customers and was told it related to the fishing. It seems that the old fishermen used to wear leather boots and to soften theirs the Lowestoft men used oil. However, the Yarmouth men used to tow their boots behind their boats when steaming, so what Yarmouth oil amounted to was water."

Some people couldn't afford haircuts though, and many children had to make do with a pudding basin over the head for Mum or Dad to cut round. "Times were very hard for most families and also for some tradesmen. Money was very short," recalls Ruby Timberley, "and the tradesmen needed your custom and in most cases went out to get it. I remember a Mr Gray who had a bakehouse on Whapload Road, quite near the church. It may have been him who came round on Sunday mornings selling hot muffins in time for breakfast. He always looked as if he had been in a flour bag himself. He would cook cakes or joints for families. Another man came round ringing a bell on Sunday afternoons selling freshly boiled shrimps."

"The butcher and baker came delivering on trade bikes with a little front wheel," recalls John Day, "and they carried a wickerwork basket and all goods for sale were inside the basket. A man who sharpened knives and grass shears also visited now and again. As did a chap selling paraffin from a huge drum drawn by a horse. 'Tinks' or Romanies also did running repairs during the year and fixed kettles and enamel basins and sold clothes pegs, washing cloths and wooden utensils."

"Between the wars my father George kept a shoe repair shop on the Beach at 8 Anguish Street," remembers John Buck. "It was a house converted into a shop with two rooms downstairs. He used to mend the shoes in one room and in the other room he had a big finishing machine. You used to open the door, go in, and he had a counter along one side and the finishing machine for polishing the shoes on the other. My father was in the army during the First World War and his old tin hat hung up in the shop for years. In the room upstairs he kept racing pigeons – you had to deal in all sorts of things in those days. Sometimes he'd get a litter of dogs and they'd be in a tiny little room upstairs too! It must have been in 1940 when my father gave up the shoe shop and he never went back to shoe repairing."

"My uncle was a shoemaker too," John continues. "He was Frank Bunn, or 'Ditto' as he was known, and he used to live next door to us in Vigilant Cottages where he worked in his front room. Ditto's wife and my mother were sisters. Then there was another man who used to mend shoes by the name of Fred Lilley. He had no legs and went about on a little board with four wheels... We lived in four different places on the Beach, Vigilant Cottages, the *Rising Sun*, Jubilee Terrace and then just past Mrs Gibbs' later shop, in a little row of houses which are still there, at 287 Whapload Road. I can remember a Mrs Clark who was in that shop before Mrs Gibbs, and she used to sell a few sweets."

Another regular sight around the Beach in the 1930s was Walter Larke who, in the summer months, used to drive around on a motor-bike with a sidecar, selling ice-cream. Walter also ran a billiard room, known as the Hiker's Rest, which was a youth club situated in a building which had originally belonged to Wilde's School and known as the 'Bottle Shed'. Alan Doy recalls, "Walter Larke was married to my mother's sister, so he was my uncle. He lived in those cottages opposite the Almshouses. In the Second World War, Walter went into the Merchant Navy and got torpedoed. He survived and came out of the Navy and joined his family who had moved up to the Midlands. He died a short while later though, he never came back to the Beach."

"Cook's the butchers, they were on the Beach," remembers Ann Smith (née Wigg). "He used to bring his cattle down the Ravine and along Whapload Road, and there was always quite a do when they got to the place where they were going to be slaughtered. When they used to scoot, so did we!"

Historian Hugh Lees, who did much to record the streets and houses on The Grit, notes that Cook's shop at 87 Whapload Road on the corner of Spurgeon Score had been a butcher's shop for many years. 'In the year 1863 one William Scarf was there. Charles Goldsmith had it for a while, after which Samuel Howard ran it. In 1892 William Richard Boggis took over

(Left) There were many bakeries on the Beach, and one of the earliest known was the Noah's Ark Bakery, located in East Street and shown here in the 1890s.

(Right) The long-established butcher's shop on the corner of Spurgeon Score and Whapload Road was run by Sidney Cook from 1907 to 1934.

the business and was there until 1907. From that time Sidney Cook had it and was the last of his trade to occupy the shop until 1934. By 1936 it had become a confectioner's.'

This butcher's shop is also recalled by Lydia Cullen (née Hammond). "Sometimes cows came along Whapload Road to Cook's, who had an abattoir at the side of their shop. The wall ran along the side of Maltsters Score and once, when several of the children stood there watching them coming along the road, one started to go wild and run away. It was a bit frightening but I think they could smell the abattoir. We all used to climb on the wall and see the poor cows tied up for slaughtering."

There were several bakeries on the Beach Village, and one of the earliest of these was a place called The Hut or Noah's Ark Bakery, which stood on the west side of East Street where Ayers' net store would later be. In the 1920 there had been William Gray's bake-house, situated at 40 & 42 Whapload Road, while Arthur Maurice Binks had a bakery at 11 & 12 Rant Score East, which was taken over by Eric Stanbridge in the mid-1930s. There was also Waller's Bakery at 60 Whapload Road, premises which had once been used as the North Beach Post Office. After the Second World War this became Bingham's, who already had another shop in Lowestoft, established in the early 1930s. "Bingham's Bakery had a window onto Whapload Road," recalls Michael Duncan, "which was painted up to a height which prevented pedestrians seeing in as they walked past. My friends and I would help each other to climb onto the window sill and gaze into the bakery where we could see the big ovens, the work bench and the baker pulling out the long trays containing pastries of all shapes and sizes from the ovens. On many occasions, he would pass to us all the off-cuts from the cakes and sponges instead of throwing them away."

Jack Moore also has mouth-watering memories of Bingham's. "When they finished with the cakes that day which they didn't sell, we used to go to the bakery and we'd get what we called a penny bag of stalies – a big brown bag of yesterday's cakes. They weren't all those cream cakes you get now. They usually had lots of currants in. But we didn't go short of food or nothing. You only needed a penny and you could get a big bag of them."

Before the Second World War, there was a refreshment stall on the sea wall which was run by Mrs Violet Eva Collins. Mrs Collins was a member of the Cook family, who had business connections with The Grit in the days when the north beach was as popular as the South Beach, and the Cooks opened chalets on the sea wall for bathers. There were also cafés in the Beach Village. One was the Corner Café belonging to Mrs Bond, who was known as 'Blondie', which after the Second World War became Mrs Delf's shop. There was also the Kumfy Kafe on the corner of Rant Score East and Anguish Street which was run by Ron and Doris James in the early 1950s. Doris recalls, "We opened the Kafe in 1951. The place used to be a pub called the *Flowing Bowl* and we took it over. We had it as rooms and we turned the bar into a café. There were some people living in what had been the smoke room and when they moved we took it over to open a fish shop, but the fish and chip shop was only open one night when we all came down with flu, and before we had recovered we were flooded out in the '53 floods! We lost everything that night, and never opened again. All the tables and chairs were washed away and found near the Sparrows Nest." Fortunately, Ron and Doris were one of the only businesses on The Grit to have insurance against sea flood and were compensated.

(Top right) 60 Whapload Road was on the corner of Salter Street and had been a bakery since the 1930s. Originally opening as Wallers, this became Bingham's after the Second World War. In the 1960s it was bought by Birds Eye who used the premises as a laundry.

(Right) A Beach resident jauntily dressed for the Lowestoft carnival in the early 1920s. In the background is 60 Whapload Road in the days when it was the North Beach Post Office.

Despite the short time that the Kumfy Kafe was on the Beach, Mr and Mrs James were real locals who knew the Gritsters' ways. Ron remembers, "When we were down there all the Scots girls and fishermen were still about, and Doris was dead crafty. She used to make hot coconut buns and work it so that they came out of the oven at 11 o'clock, piping hot, and these big hairy-chested Scotsmen used to buy them by the dozen. You couldn't keep up with them!"

Opposite the *Rising Sun* public house was Harry Hammond's fish and chip shop, in premises that had once been another public house, the *Fishermen's Arms*. His daughter Lydia Cullen was born in 3 Jubilee Terrace, but the family moved when her father bought the empty public house and converted it. She recalls, "It was a fairly large place. I expect many people from the Beach Village remember how we also used to sell shrimps, winkles, mussels and crabs, boiled in the copper at the back of the house. It was a very busy time in my young life, and many people would know my sister Lily who used to serve in the fish shop. I am sure she must have been the fastest server in the Lowestoft area! The children used to call out to her and say, 'One penny of chips and a few scraps please'."

Lenny Norman was a regular at Hammond's. "I remember we used to get 'one and one' – a penny of fish, a penny of chips, tuppence that would be. Sometimes if you were lucky he'd give you two fish, it all depended how he was, whether he had plenty of fish." Hammond's was also a favourite place for the Central School boys as Charles Ellis recalls, "Some of the boys would have fish and chip dinners and there'd be about 30 or 40 boys dash round as soon as school finished and Lily used to say, 'Now, all behave yourselves and you'll all get served!' There would be about 30 or 40 fish and a bloody great stack of chips and it would be good grub. It was wholesome food. You had a dab or a plaice, a good helping of chips, you had a good meal."

Past Hammond's, on the corner of Spurgeon Score, was Wilson's Confectioner's. Ronny Wilson recalls, "We lived in 4 East Street. My mother took up a business at the bottom of Spurgeon's Score, a sweet business in a shop that used to be Cook's the butchers." In Anguish Street at No. 12 was Moss's sweet shop, a favourite with all the kids. Colin Dixon remembers it well. "Moss's sweet shop always had a cat in the window. Amongst the displays of sweets, there was always this cat. In those days we never bothered about it but now I would think again." Ronny Wilson also remembers Moss's. "She had a little hole in her front-window, and we used to put a little piece of wire through and pull the jelly-babies out."

"I was sometimes given a ha'penny on Saturdays," Eric Horne recalls from his 1930s childhood, "and would spend a long time in Gibbs' deciding whether to buy two chocolate novelties at a farthing each or spend the whole ha'penny on a marshmallow wafer."

Sheila Rogers belonged to the post-war generation visiting Delf's, Bishop's and Grieve's shop for her childhood supply of sweets. "On Sunday my family all went to Christ Church in the morning, but in the afternoon my Mum, Dad, my brother and I used to go for a walk down Hamilton Road and around the fish market, and then we'd stop at Delf's and buy a bar of chocolate which had six pieces on it. It was a bar of Fry's creams with different coloured fruits. We had a piece each walking down Hamilton Road and then on the way back John and I had the other two pieces."

"Sometimes we used to go to Bishops too. Just after the War we were still on rations for sweets and the people who were in the other flat at Bow House would save their sweet tokens for me and I'd take them around to Miss Bishop and she'd give me a little bag of sweets for my token. There was also a shop at the bottom of Christ Church Score, Mr Grieve, he used to keep that. When we came out of Brownies we'd go across there and buy something out of his shop and sit on his windowsill and eat it."

Mr Grieve had taken over a long established business at 67 Whapload Road in the 1950s which had dated back to the 1870s when John Gooderham had first opened a shop there. Cyril Provart, Mr H Hatcher and Willie Boothroyd had been amongst the shopkeepers there between the wars. Certainly Boothroyd's, Burwood's, Delf's, Squire's and Gibbs' were the best-remembered grocery shops on the Beach, but these establishments did not usually confine themselves to groceries: they would try to sell everything and anything that people wanted. Benjamin Burwood's shop was at 28 Whapload Road, near to the *Rising Sun* public house, and was listed in *Kelly's Directory* as a 'shopkeeper and confectioner'. However, as Ruby Timberley recalls, he sold a far wider variety of goods. "It was a little shop that sold almost every grocery, plus paraffin oil and candles. Since in the 1920s most houses had only oil lamps and candles as lighting, they did quite well."

Colin Dixon lived with his grandmother in Wilde's Street. "I used to go to Squire's shop quite a lot. I didn't have far to go. You'd go in there and there would always be a smell of paraffin. It was a general shop. On the counter there would be a very large bacon slicer. There would be cheese. But you could also get a gallon of paraffin and she would go out and get it from the back where the tank was. You'd buy a gas mantle – we didn't have electrictity we had gas. Mantles were a common thing to buy then. And you could telephone from there! Because the people on the beach didn't have telephones. But the shop did and there was little notice up on the wall just above the entrance which said 'you may telephone from here'. And I can remember going in there for my Grandmother once to get someone on the phone and I said to Mrs Squire, 'I want to phone number something-or-other' and I had to give her tuppence and she took me through the back to the telephone. And when I looked it was one of those phones which were stuck on the wall. And I was only a little lad. So I said, 'I'm sorry Mrs Squire I can't reach.' And she got me a lemonade box to stand on."

David Waterman grew up in the 1950s living just outside the Beach Village in Old Nelson Street although his grandparents lived in Whapload Road. His family's 'local' shop was Alan Delf's on the corner of Hamilton Road. "I used to do a paper-round for old Delfie. I used to deliver right up to Waveney Road. Then I used to cut across the fish market, delivering newspapers to the fish merchants then I'd come back to Alan's, and pick up the next load he'd have waiting for me. Then I'd go up Old Nelson Street then down Herring Fishery Score and then deliver to the Beach Village. The two favourite papers there were the *Daily Mirror* and the *Daily Sketch* but the *Mirror* was the most popular."

Michael Duncan's family bought their groceries from another of these Beach Village shops. "We obtained our groceries from Arthur 'Gibbies' shop and even after we moved to a new home he continued to deliver my mother's weekly order on a Friday night, in a car that made him seem like a millionaire in our eyes."

The original Gibbs' shop was situated at 106-108 Whapload Road, opposite the Eagle Brewery. The shop opened in 1931 and was run by Nellie Gibbs and later by her son Arthur and his wife Iris. Iris recalls, "My late husband Arthur was born at Yarmouth in 1917 and he came to the Beach at 14 when his mother, Nellie Annie, opened a little shop in the building that used to be the *Dutch Hoy* public house, where Birds Eye's offices are now. Arthur joined up at the outbreak of war but became a Japanese prisoner of war and didn't come home in 1945. We eventually married in 1949."

The shop was bombed during the Second World War and the Gibbs moved to 283 Whapload Road. "We lived there too," Iris continues, "but later we bought a cottage near Arthur's mum when she got too old to be on her own. We were here during the 1953 floods, didn't have time to save anything, and it was about three months before we could open again."

"When my husband died in January 1994 I decided to carry on. Arthur used to deliver three nights a week, but I can't drive so when he died that had to stop. Since the houses were pulled down our customers have mostly been workmen, there are no locals these days. Now and again someone will pop in who I haven't seen for years, and it's always nice to see old friends again. They're amazed that I'm still here but I am, open from seven to five every weekday!" Iris Gibbs died in 2008 and 283 Whapload Road was soon demolished. Opened in 1931, Gibbs' had remained in business well into the 21st century but after more than 70 years of trading, the last original shop on The Grit was gone.

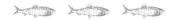

(Opposite) Filled rolls made while you wait! Iris and Arthur Gibbs behind the counter and (above) their shop in the mid-1980s.

(Right) Iris Gibbs standing in the shop doorway in 1997 when it was still open, 7am to 5pm every weekday.

(Opposite left) In August 1931 the German Graf Zeppelin embarked on a round Britain flight as part of a peacetime goodwill visit. Passing over the Beach Village, curious locals left their houses in Coleman Square and Benjamin Burwood's grocery shop (right) to view the spectacle.

(Opposite bottom left) Squire's Ness Point Stores, on the corner of Wilde's Street. In the 1920s Walter Emery ran this grocery shop but it was taken over by Frederick Squire in the 1930s.

(Above right) There had been a grocery shop on the corner of Herring Fishery Score since as far back as 1874 when John Gooderham was proprietor. In the 1950s the shopkeeper was Willie Boothroyd but by the end of the decade the business was taken over by the Grieve family.

(Right) After the Second World War, Delf's grocery shop was established on the corner of Whapload Road and Hamilton Road in premises known as Kent House, formerly occupied by the Corner Cafe. Popular shopkeeper Alan Delf is standing at the door.

SHOPS ON THE BEACH c.1925

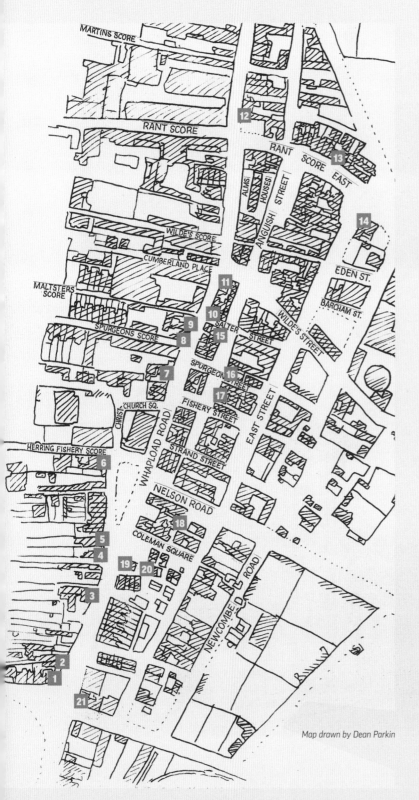

Map drawn by Dean Parkin

1. The Bishop sisters' shop was at 1 Whapload Road, and although the business was listed in the local directory as a confectioners it also sold other general grocery items, such as milk.

2. Their brother John Bishop had an ironmongery business at No.3 Whapload Road, which later moved to London Road North. Another brother, Tom, then had the premises as a fishing tackle shop.

3. Pretty Son & Co, were decorators, situated at 25 Whapload Road. In 1934 Godfrey Girling the barber moved from 89 Whapload Road into these premises and remained there until 1940.

4. James T Day was a basketmaker. Known locally as 'Jasper' he worked there but lived at 1 Nelson Road for many years.

5. Leslie Charles Peachman was selling bicycles from this site in 1925 but later had East Garage there.

6. In 1925 Cyril Provart was a grocer at 67 Whapload Road in a shop which had been used for this purpose for many years. In 1874 John Gooderham ran a similar establishment there, while Provart's predecessor was Mr H G Hatcher. In the 1930s the shop was taken over by Willie Boothroyd and in the 1950s Mr Grieve ran the business.

7. Hammond's fish and shop shop was situated near to Jubilee Terrace in a building which had formerly been the *Fishermen's Arms* public house.

8. Cook's the butchers could be found at 87 Whapload Road. By 1936 these premises were converted into a sweet shop which was run by Mrs Wilson, Ronny's mother.

9. Next door to Cook's was Joseph Flertey's dairy at 89 Whapload Road, In 1930 Godfrey Girling had his first barbers shop there.

10. 60 Whapload Road was vacant in 1925 but had previously been the North Beach Post Office. In the 1930s Waller's converted the building into a bakery and after the Second World War Bingham's could be found there.

11. Walter Emery had two grocery shops in the town in 1925, one in Mariner Street and the other on the Beach at 72 Whapload Road. In the 1930s this was taken over by Frederick Squire who ran the shop for the next 30 years.

12. Mrs Nellie Gibbs first opened a shop in the Beach Village in these premises at 106-108 Whapload Road, formerly the *Dutch Hoy* public house. Bombed during the Second World War, the Gibbs moved to 283 Whapload Road (off the map, northwards) and the shop closed in the early 2000s.

13. At 11 & 12 Rant Score East was Arthur Maurice Binks' Bakery which was taken over by Eric Stanbridge in the mid-1930s. This property was destroyed by bombing in the Second World War.

14. In 1925 this property was the *Flowing Bowl* public house but in the 1930s it became Thurston's dairy. After the Second World War the building housed the Kumfy Kafe until the flood in 1953.

15. Wilson's fried fish shop was situated at 15–17 Anguish Street.

16. Many people remember Mrs Moss who had a sweet shop at 13 Anguish Street until the mid-1930s. In the 1950s the shop was taken over by John & Paula Price.

17. George Buck was a shoe repairer who had his shop at 8 Anguish Street for many years until he took over the *Rising Sun* in 1940.

18. Another baker, William Gray, had his premises at 40–42 Whapload Road.

19. Benjamin Burwood's general shop was next door to Canary Cottages at 28 Whapload Road.

20. Frank 'Ditto' Bunn was another shoe repairer on the Beach who worked from his front room at 1 Vigilant Cottages.

21. In the early 1900s this was Hughes Dining Rooms but by the mid-1930s these premises were the Corner Café, run by Mrs Bond. After the Second World War Alan Delf had his shop here.

10. FISHING FROM THE BEACH

The Beach Village consisted of two lots of people: those that went to sea in the drifters, and the rest of them that worked in the kipper houses all over the village. I suppose everybody relied on the drifters and what they produced.
CHARLES ELLIS

"Most of my family worked on the Beach," recalls Harry Harper. "My grandad was originally a fisherman, but then came ashore and worked for Boardley's who carted the herring. My nanny worked for Dick Ayers in the fish-house, my aunt Becky served in Flertey's shop on the Beach, and my aunt Nora worked in the steam laundry. My father and two uncles who lived with us were all fishermen. My wife was a Scots fisher girl. I met her when she came down to Lowestoft in 1947 for the herring. She came down from Fraserburgh."

After the Second World War, the over-exploitation of the shoals resulted in dwindling catches and by the mid-1960s the home fishing voyage ceased altogether. The contrast was stark for many Gritsters who vividly recalled how the fishing village came to life every autumn with the arrival of the Scottish fishing fleet and the fisher girls.

The fishermen would purchase provisions and supplies from the local shops and pubs, while the Scots girls and coopers would take board and lodgings on The Grit, benefitting many families and helping them to make ends meet. "Every September prior to the herring season," Ruby Timberley recalls, "the Scots girls would arrive at lodgings which had already been arranged for them by the firm they worked for. The men would go round the Beach Village seeking lodgings so that two or three could share. They needed to be as close as possible to the pickling plots, near to Hamilton Dock where the drifters landed the herring. The girls duly arrived with their large wooden boxes with all they would need whilst away from home. These came by lorry from their fishing-boats."

"These 'girls' as we called them – though some were middle-aged – worked very hard in bitter weather, early and late. It gave the people who took them into their homes a few pounds to help stock up with coal or buy their children some clothes for the winter. These Scots girls were a jolly lot. They didn't work on Sundays, but went to church or chapel. If during the week, owing to the weather, there was no fish for a couple of hours, they were not idle but got out the jerseys they were knitting for their men folk."

"They would walk through the town in twos and threes, knitting and talking as they went. To us children it sounded like a foreign language! We missed them when they left because some of us would go to watch them working, their fingers wrapped round with rags to prevent the knives they used so skilfully from cutting them. Some would gut herrings and some would pack the herring in barrels between layers of salt. The coopers put on the lid, knocked in wooden nails and then they were ready for export to Russia."

"We used to take in lodgers from Scotland, up to three at a time during the herring season," says Michael Duncan, "and conditions were fairly cramped then as we only had three bedrooms, and no bathroom. The fisher girls were very nice in their attitude and hard working, but my sister and I used to have great difficulty in understanding them. They used to go to work early after a breakfast of porridge sprinkled with salt and return home late afternoon ready for tea. I remember how they always had bandages on their fingers and how prominent the smell of fish was when they came home."

Lydia Cullen remembers, "My mother, Mrs Hammond, used to take in six girls. We had a large room at the side of our shop which, of course, was an old pub. My Mum used to clear and clean the room. There was just an old fireplace and an electric light bulb and a cupboard where they stored some of their food as they cooked for themselves. A couple of days before they moved in the Scottish men would bring six great wooden trunks with their clothing and bedding and blankets into this room and they were put around the walls. This was their seating and also their beds. I think I was 9 or 10 years old when I used to take mugs of hot tea down to the pickling plots where the girls were working, gutting the herring. I used to have to walk through Boardley's horse and cart shed. I think the old horses used to know me because when they saw me their heads used to lie hanging out of their sheds thinking I would bring them food. It was a lovely time because the Scots were very friendly."

Rose Sansom (née Durrant) remembers, "The Scots girls would come down from the north of Scotland and work on the herring fishing (when the silver darlings swam this way in September to December). They would 'lay' toys in the shops (put money down to keep them) and when the settling up came at the end of the season, they would collect them, and take them down to their ship for the return journey back to Scotland. They did this with a barrel of grapes and a case of oranges and apples they purchased from my father, who was a wholesale fruit merchant in the town."

The Scots girls had a canteen hut built on the pickling plots where Eric Horne's mother had a job, cooking and cleaning. He can remember, "On Saturdays and at other times I helped out by collecting the dirty cups and became known by the girls as the 'Wee Bairn'. For lunch they ate Scotch broth which my mother prepared on a huge cooking range which had to be hot first thing in the morning. The eating area was kept warm by an old tortoise combustion stove. The girls loved their jam doughnuts and iced buns which were delivered in great long trays from the local bakery."

"A perk of my mother's job was being given a large enamel jug of any left-over broth each day, together with a sheep's head, which had presumably flavoured the broth. Wrapped in newspaper the sheep's head was thrown over the high wall of a derelict building on the way home, but we all enjoyed the broth for evening meal."

(Overleaf) The Scots fisher girls were hard working and fast at their job. The herring were sprinkled with salt and tipped into big wooden troughs known as 'farlins' (farlanes). Working in threes, the girls gutted the fish – some as fast as 60 herring a minute – which were sorted and packed head to tail in barrels, layered with salt. Every full barrel was covered and left for 10 days then topped up with more fish to be tightly packed.

"Nurse Rae arrived with the Scots girls to keep them in check and to look after any injuries they suffered while gutting the herring. She was somewhat old but efficient and quite strict. She was always the last to leave the hut in the evening and on the way up Rant Score to her digs, she would pop the key though our letter-box for my mother to open up the next morning. One morning my mother arrived to find the hut broken into – goodness knows what they hoped to find!"

Leonard Boyce lived with his grandparents at the *East of England* public house on Whapload Road. He remembers, "When the fisher girls were doing their gutting they used these old acetylene lamps or flares, and of course the smoke used to pour off these things and the whole area was full of smoke. But how those women worked in the weather, the snow even, they'd still be gutting herrings. These horse-drawn carts used to come with loads of fish which were tipped in the troughs and fast as they could gut them they'd fill them up. It was remarkable."

"My grandmother took four of them in, these Scots fisher girls, staying with us at the pub. I think she gave them one bedroom and I had to move into my aunt's room, we only had three bedrooms I believe. They always used to have bandages on every finger to protect themselves instead of gloves. When they used to come in from the other side of the road where they'd been gutting they had great heavy boots on, oil skins down to their ankles, perhaps a scarf round the head. They used to come in, and they'd stand out in the yard and take all their gear off. Of course, they couldn't come indoors like that, stinking of fish, herring

(Above) The pickling plots were to the north of the Beach Village, near to Crown Score until the mid-1920s. Surrounded by huge piles of barrels, this was where the fisher girls packed the herring, each barrel containing around 600 fish.

(Above) In the 1930s the pickling plots moved to a site in Hamilton Road. Each barrel was made locally by coopers who played a vital role in keeping the herring moving. Once there were dozens of coopers in Lowestoft; by the late 1960s there were only three.

all over their boots, but no matter how cold it was or how wet it was, they'd take everything off outside and put it in the shed and then they'd come in and go straight through to their room. We had the same four girls for about three years, they came about October and went home just before Christmas."

"I can also remember how they used to load up the 'Klondikes' as they were called, the ships from Russia which used to come in to pick up the barrels of herring. The horses and carts used to stand on the road for hours and hours waiting to go on the fish market to load the fish, queued up from the old trawl market, Waveney Road, right round as far as Battery Green, queuing to load up the ships. Hours they used to stand! The horses used to stand there and sleep and the drivers did and all, I reckon!"

Many of the children from the Beach Village would visit the curing yards to try to scrounge a few herring and, though the yard foreman sometimes chased them away, one way of getting free fish was to cheek the Scots girls who would then throw one or two herrings at them. The girls would be told off for doing this but they retaliated with a few well-chosen words and the foreman would usually beat a hasty retreat. What he didn't know was that as the Scots girls threw the herrings at the children, they would give them a wink, knowing they would be taking them home to tea!

Sometimes though fish would be simply given away. Myrtle Porter (née Durrant) remembers, "When I was a girl, all the fisher girls used to gut the fish and pack the barrels outside the front of our house in Newcombe Road. We faced the pickling plots and we used to go and watch them and they used to give us bucket-loads of fish. We had a lot of fish!"

In October 1936 the Scots girls went on strike over their pay, demanding an extra two pence a barrel, and two and sixpence extra lodging allowance. Meetings were held on Battery Green, which in those days was a stretch of grassland, and it was here that tempers rose and some colourful language was spoken as the girls fought for their rights.

During this strike, some of the girls carried on working and had to be protected by the police, as words flew – along with one or two gutting knives. The strike ended when the drifters were brought almost to a standstill and the Herring Board were forced to relent, although the girls never got the lodging allowance they asked for.

By this time the Scottish fleet had considerably reduced in size, and the following year herring catches on the home voyage were just a third of the 1913 level. Most of the European market for herring had collapsed and the silver shoals had become rarer and unpredictable, all resulting in hardship for the fishermen between the wars. Money had always been scarce in fishing families. Even in the decade before the First World War when the herring industry was at its height, it wasn't the fishermen who made the profit, but the skippers and the boat owners.

"Dad was a chief engineer on the drifters," recalls Bert Prettyman. "and after the home fishing season he would have to go on the beach and pick stones. I can remember taking a flask of tea down to him. When you think, he was a chief engineer with all the papers to prove it, and these time-served men had to go on the beach and pick up stones. It must have been very degrading but it was all to give us something to eat."

"At the age of 13 my Dad stowed away on a trawler," Yvonne Scriggins adds, "which gave him the taste for the sea. After that he became a fisherman sailing the fishing smacks and trawlers. In the 1920s work was very depressed so if there was no fishing he had to look elsewhere. He would perhaps hear of a job but that would mean standing in line with many more men, so he could be queuing from approximately two o'clock in the morning to stand a chance of a job. Many a time he would comb the beach for coal or wood washed ashore; with a wife and eight children, they needed any work that brought in money. While combing the beach one day (during the war) he came across an unexploded bomb. Having notified the authorities, they offered him work filling sandbags and then repairing the sea wall. He did other jobs such as washing down the floor of the fish market – there was always a chance he would get free fish. He sold papers and if he sold 12 he would be paid threepence. When he was fishing he would be away for weeks fishing in the North Sea, Aberdeen, North Shields or wherever the fish were. My Dad's life was a struggle."

Many times fishermen could be away for a week or 10 days and when they returned to shore have nothing to show for the journey. With the long periods away fishing, or just chasing work around the country, family life was difficult. John Day's father was one such fisherman. "His name was Bobbie Day, a small balding man who had a taste for rum when coming off fishing trips. But off-season he would travel round Britain trying to get a job, on any ship, as a cook. He died at 35 and the sad thing was, because he was never really in my young life, I didn't notice his passing. He simply didn't return from a fishing trip."

Norma Wilson's father was Vernil Tuck, who was a lifeboatman for many years. She recalls, "Because my Dad was a fisherman he used to go away for quite a while and when he came home my eldest sister used to cry because she didn't know who he was. Then my Mum said, 'I'm not putting up with this,' so that's why he gave up the sea, to get a job on the land."

Michael Duncan lived in Wilde's Street next to the *Gas House Tavern*. He recalls, "My father was a fisherman in drifters and spent many years on the *Adel* and the *Tritona* and like many others doing the same job, was away from home for much of my childhood. On his rare occasions at home I can remember being taken for walks along the Denes towards Sparrows Nest, trying my best to jump up to and swing off the goalposts they used to hang the nets from. I can remember holding his hand which was big and strong but above all the skin was dry, taut and so hard, caused by sheer hard work."

Fishing or a related job was in many cases all The Grit had to offer. The only way of bettering your lot was to become a skipper, as fishermen tended to leave the Beach Village when they became skippers. Despite this, some boys still wanted to go to sea. Leonard Boyce was one such boy, his grandfather, Lenny Tripp, having been a fisherman. "I crazed him to go out on one of these boats, the *Christmas Daisy* it was called. 'All right, boy,' he said, 'they're going out to test the compass, you can go out for a few hours.' So we went out near the Claremont Pier and I was sick as a toad. I think I was in bed for two days after, I was really bad I was. The cook kept coming and asking if I wanted tea and all sorts of things, and it really stunk, with that smell of oil and whatever, and of course they were rolling the boat

During hard times in the fishing industry some fishermen were forced to find alternative low-paid work, such as picking up stones on the north beach for which they were paid by the bucket-load. The flints they collected were then split by stone breakers and used for making roads.

HOSANNA

about to test this compass on the top of the wheelhouse. Anyway, I had enough of that and I never went to sea any more in all my life. I've never been on the water since."

The hard life of fishing offered little security and the risks were all too regularly illustrated. "In 1930 when I was just two years old, my father was lost at sea," recalls Eric Horne, "he was on a fishing vessel working the cod ground. Although a cooper by trade, he was no stranger to the sea, having served in the Navy in the Great War, and if work was scarce it had to be taken where it could be found. My mother was left a widow with three young boys to raise on her own. I was the youngest, Ernest was five, and Fred was nine."

"The widows's pension, (known, I recall, as the Lloyd George pension) of just ten shillings a week did not go very far. Whatever work came along had to be taken. Charring (housework for the better off) brought in two shillings a day, while other jobs included making or repairing fishing nets and peeling onions for pickling at a house down Old Nelson Street. For this job we all gave a hand at home, washing hundreds of salvaged jam jars which my brothers and I then delivered to the pickling house in a barrow made from a sugar-box and old pram wheels. From the pension of ten shillings a week, my mother had to pay four shillings and sixpence rent for our four-roomed terraced cottage at 4 Rant Score, which was owned by a Mr Beamish."

(Above left) The *Hosanna* was a steam drifter built in 1930 and requisitioned for War service in 1939, for minesweeping in Milford Haven. By the early 1950s she was fishing from Fleetwood, then re-registered at Lowestoft in 1960 and converted into a motor trawler before being broken up and sold for spares in 1975.

(Above Left) A steam drifter and a sailing trawler, known as a 'smack', leaving the harbour for the fishing grounds in 1910.

(Above) The *Young Duke* was a diesel trawler built in 1953 for Small & Co. by Richards, a long-established Lowestoft shipbuilder whose origins date back to 1876.

(Left) Steam drifters racing away from the port – always great competition to reach the fishing grounds first.

(Left) Herring being unloaded from the boat by fishermen using quarter-cran baskets. One cran equalled 1,320 fish.

(Below left) Fishermen at the fish market emptying their catch into cases ready for export to Germany. In the bumper year of 1913 when 536,400 crans of herring were landed at Lowestoft, 87% of the catch were cured and pickled and exported to Germany and Russia. Herring exports stopped after the First World War.

(Right) Swinging the catch ashore. At busy times the fish market was crowded when up to 300 drifters could be in port, each with a crew of 10 men.

(Below right) In 1950 metal boxes replaced the wooden ones. Easier to clean, they were also taken to sea and sometimes, if the fishermen hadn't caught enough to return to port, they would pack the fish into the boxes and stay out another night.

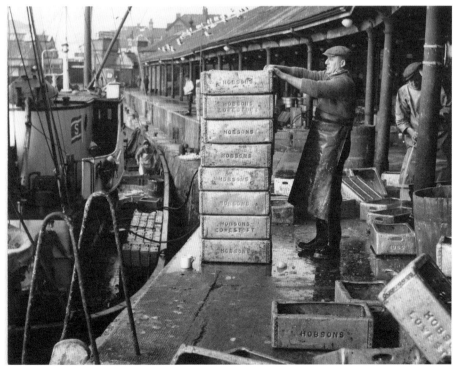

Sayer & Holloway girls, 1920 (Back row) left to right, Violet Clark, Violet Keith, Jessie Hitter (née Harper), Connie Hugman, Emma Pickess, Mrs Hemsby, Lilly Harper. (Front row) Gladys Falkner, Annie Johnson, Bessie Bowler, Clara Gurney, Eve Osborne, Emma Sturman.

Yvonne Scriggins' mother Hilda May Gurney, who died in July 1983, also had a family heavily involved with the fishing industry. Born in Lowestoft in 1910, Hilda had two brothers Ernest and Jack, also a sister Clara. Yvonne recalls how, "Jack, the youngest, was on board a fishing smack when it was run down by a liner. No-one survived and Jack was only 17 or 18 years old when he drowned... My mother's father William John Gurney also had a bad accident at sea and lost an eye plus other injuries. Sadly, he died at the age of 45. Nan ran a fish shop on the Beach, but Nan being Nan would never be rich as she was always nipping into the *Gas House Tavern* for a drink!"

"Many men lost their lives at sea," Yvonne continues. "While he was on the trawlers my Dad did all the cooking and he could always cook a good meal but he had a very bad accident at sea which resulted in him losing a finger, plus badly damaging his arm which prevented him from working for quite a while. Compensation took a long while coming through and involved his being checked by different doctors. He received £200 which at that time was good. On the occasions when the fishing catch was good they were paid out in sovereigns. Whenever he got paid, he and the rest of the crew would head for the nearest pub although, having said that, he always made sure his family had food on the table, and clothes. Even when Dad was old, the sea was still in his blood and he often talked about the boats he sailed in – *Peaceful*, *Bonny Lass*, *Antelope* and the *Consolidated*."

11. A HOME FOR INDUSTRY

Really, you have to be pleased with the industrial estate that's down there now because of all the labour that it brings to the town.
HAZEL BOARDLEY

The Grit has always been an industrial area, although at one time most of the industries to be found there related to fishing. "There were a lot of beating chambers where many young girls were employed mending nets," Lydia Cullen recalls. "There was always a smell of tanning and when they were finished they were hung over poles on the Denes, and there are still some poles standing there. It was quite an exciting time because it was very busy and full of activity. My sister Stella was a good one for mending nets."

Herring nets were made at Beeton's Sunrise Net Works in East Street and tanned for strength in the net yards, while the net stores housed the fishing gear between trips. An essential part of each store were the beating chambers where the nets were repaired by a team of beatsters. Before the nets were tanned or 'barked' in the tan copper, they would be checked by ransackers, and it was this whole process that provided many jobs for the people of the Beach Village.

At the start of the 20th century, a beatster's wage was eight or nine shillings a week, although apprentices received nothing for the first year and only two and sixpence a week during their second year. Due to the large amount of nets that needed to be mended, many were repaired at home as well as in the chambers. Women would work in the evening by oil lamp and in every house where a beatster lived you could find a beatster's hook, which was a big staple, driven into the woodwork around the window or into the door-frame for this purpose. During the 1920s and 30s women working on the trawl nets was common practice. "I remember an aunt of mine did this," says Ruby Timberley. "The owner sent the bales of twine by horse and cart to houses. My sister and I filled spools for our aunt, so that she could carry on working away at her net without stopping. She started by casting on with a loop on a hook above the sitting room door. These nets became very heavy and the horse and cart would collect the finished nets."

Ros Parker was born in 1924 to parents who both came from the Beach Village. Her father George Stanford Clark was a boot and shoe repairer and she started her own working life on The Grit. "I left school when I was 14 years and eight months and went to learn to mend the nets down Whapload Road in Hastings House. I was getting three pounds a week. I was mending the nets but you did more work cleaning up than anything else. I was just an apprentice you see. Lighting the fires and seeing everything was in order. You learnt to mend the nets. I would have done it for three years but it stopped when the war came. There were five or six of us working in Hastings House but they had places all up and down Whapload Road and they hung them out to dry opposite Sparrows Nest on the net posts.

(Right) Men cleaning and tarring a sail ready for use near the net-drying racks. Dating from the late 1800s, these posts were still being used after the closure of the herring fishery with trawl-nets being hung there in the 1970s.

(Below) Beatsters mending drift nets on the Denes in the early 1900s. Across the centre of the photograph are cotton strands used for net mending. Having been dipped in linseed oil, the cotton was draped over the posts with a wooden pole laid along the bottom to keep it taut.

(Left) Alfred Breach working at Beeton's Sunrise Networks in East Street. Although beatsters were usually women, men also did the work and were paid more to do the same job.

(Below left) October 1947, Beatsters at work in the Shoals, a net store situated at the bottom of Lighthouse Score. From left to right: Rita Sharman, Flo Balls, Cissy Freestone, Vina Harris, Ernie Woolner, Edna Fiske, Gerty Woolner, Doris Willgoss, Pauline Harris and Kitty Waller.

(Opposite bottom) In the 1950s exhibitions were sometimes held on the trawlers. Summer visitors were welcomed aboard, shown around the vessel and given a demonstration of net mending in one of the holds.

(Below) Beeton's Sunrise Networks in East Street, one of the many suppliers and repairers of nets in the town.

And my sister, when she left school, she went to make the nets at Gourock Ropeworks and I did some of the work there with her during the war. We made camouflage nets then for covering the tanks. We made those nets at home, in our back bedroom."

Gowing's Ropeworks operated on The Grit for over a century. Their ropewalk was established in 1790 and was a quarter of a mile long, running parallel to the north end of Whapload Road. The ropery buildings could be found facing the 'hanging gardens' of the High Street, and consisted of a winding room, dressing chambers, tar-house, rope store and offices. At one time in this area there was also a twine ground, where men would spin the big ropes which were used for trawl warps, tow ropes and cables. Towards the end of the 19th century Gowing closed, due to a slump in fishing, the arrival of wire ropes, and the effect of the big roperies at Gourock, Belfast and Edinburgh. Gowing's property was bought in 1887 by the Lord of the Manor, Mr R H Reeve, and was then acquired with the rest of the Denes by the council when Reeve died four years later. The ropery buildings were then demolished, but the walk remains to this day as a roadway between the posts and nets on which Lowestoft fishermen still have the right to dry their nets. Other minor ropemakers in the Beach Village were Mr S S Francis and Mr S Saunders, both with premises on Whapload Road.

Boat building was also prevalent on the Beach. In 1785 Thomas Johnson obtained a permit from the Lord of the Manor to build a shed on the waste or beach, 'abutting on the Whapload Way'. The small plot of land rented was 40ft x 20ft and was on the corner of (what

would become) Whapload Road and Rant Score East where a shed was built, probably for stores, and a saw-pit. Barcham's yard was in this same area, Barcham being the builder of the *Frances Ann* lifeboat in 1807 which is recorded as having cost £200. The exact site of the yard is unknown, but in May 1838 the Lowestoft Paving Committee inspected the end of the town drain 'on the Beach near Mr Barcham's boatbuilding yard', and recommended that such drain be lengthened the full width of the intended road.' So wherever the drain and the intended road met nearby was Barcham's yard.

One short-lived and ill-fated venture that has almost slipped from memory was the salt factory, which was built near Ness Point in the late 1920s. Lenny Norman recalls, "They started to build a salt factory. They were going to refine the salt from the sea but that never worked. That was on the pickling plots in the 1920s and stood there empty for years and years... When the Scots girls used to come here, they built a little hut where they used to go and have their tea, and this was alongside the salt factory"

Charles Ellis can also remember this. "The salt factory was just to the right of Ness Point, as near to the sea as they could get. It was there in the late 1920s. I lived in Scarle's Buildings and as you walked up the road, it was dead opposite, near Ness Point itself. There was a high wall around the factory, which had a great big chimney. Inside there were these huge trays made of steel and underneath were the furnaces. Those huge trays were where they put the salt water which was pumped straight from Ness Point. The water was heated to get the salt out. The idea was that they could use it for the curing of herring but something went wrong, they never thought it out. What they didn't realise was that when they pumped in all this water, there would also be a certain amount of sand amongst so they were getting sand in their salt, and there was no way they could separate it. So whoever built that factory must have lost a lot of money."

Richard Ayers' Fish Merchants & Curers had premises near to the Steam Laundry on the east side of Whapload Road. Established in 1870 by George Thomas Ayers, the company later added some stables, which were converted into garages when motor vehicles replaced horses. At the beginning of the 20th century the firm was known as Ayers Brothers Ltd, but by the early 1920s had become Richard Ayers Ltd, and although the building was damaged by a bomb blast during the Second World War, the company continued until 1953. These premises were taken on by the Belfast Ropework Company until 1968 when they sold to Birds Eye Foods who then cleared the site in March 1969 to build their offices.

Clifford Arthur Gouldby's company was another firm of fish merchants and curers to be found on the Beach. Gouldby's had premises on the west side of Whapload Road, abutting on to Scarle's Buildings, and had a fleet of lorries delivering freshly-landed Lowestoft fish to customers over a wide area. The Gouldby family had long been associated with buying and selling fish in Lowestoft, and by the 1950s the fleet comprised refrigerated lorries which were something of a rarity in those days.

Some of the most familiar lorries – and before that carts – on the Beach were those belonging to the Boardleys. Billy Keith remembers, "They used to run up and down Whapload Road to the fish market, and take all the fish in carts up to the north quay to be lowered into the boats and taken away. And there'd be carts all along Commercial Road, waiting and they were just going round in a continuous circle, back and forth all these horses and carts. Boardleys also used to supply the horses for the [lifeboat] rocket teams."

Jack Moore recalls, "Boardley's had horse carts and they had stables scattered all over the Beach. They had some up Wilde Score East, they had some down past the *Gas House Tavern,* stables all over the place. Us kids, when the fishing was on, and they had to take all the fish boxes to the Scots girls, what they were taking to dump in their trough, we used to jump on the back and get a ride all the way down Whapload Road, on the back of the wagon."

The Boardley Brothers hauling contractors were established in the second half of the 19th century. "They started off as the Boardley Brothers," Matthew Boardley explains. "This was my grandfather and his brothers, but then they had a difference of opinion and they broke apart into two businesses. There was A & S Boardley and M Boardley, who was my grandfather. They had premises nearly next door to each other, both off East Street. They both did the same work and were in competition with each other. My father took over from his father, and when he died in 1943, the business on our side of the family all finished. I was at Coventry then, before I left to serve in India, but my mother didn't want me to take on the business."

The premises of A & S Boardley were in Nelson Road, just off East Street, and were founded by Arthur and Samuel Boardley who began trading with horse-drawn vehicles in the mid-1890s, their work mainly being carting herrings. In the 1920s lorries were added to their fleet of vehicles and eventually the business was taken over by Samuel's son Ronnie. By this time the fleet was completely mechanised and they continued operations until 1968.

Conrad Smith's grandfather was a haulage contractor who was taken over by the Boardleys. "His name was Edward 'Lump' Ellis," Conrad remembers. "When he was delivering the Klondike boxes opposite Birds Eye he would sometimes stop for a little drink, but it was all right because if he had too much they would lay him on the cart and the horse would take him home! My mother's uncle was Jack Gooderham. He was a coal merchant and had a place at the bottom of Rant Score."

The three gas holders which once dominated the skyline on The Grit were part of the gasworks. The town's first gasworks – built in 1837 by Mr James Malam at a cost of £2,500 – included a gas holder with a capacity of 8,000 cubit feet. This began as only a modest enterprise, with the whole gas holder holding only £2 worth of gas, and it was from here that the gas was supplied for the first lamps in Lowestoft's streets. In 1852 a new company was formed who bought the gasworks for £8,000 with the objective of supplying gas for the lighting of the town on a more permanent basis. A major expansion got underway and the service was improved, and in 1864 the first gas main was put down across the harbour to take supplies to the south of the town. For nearly a century Lowestoft continued to make its own gas supply, until 1963 when the town began to take gas from the 'grid', when coal gas gave way to natural gas from the North Sea. In 1964 the old hundred-foot chimney at the works was demolished and in 1975 the two older gas holders which had served the town since 1882 and 1904 respectively, were pulled down, leaving just the newer one, built in 1965 with a capacity of a million cubic feet.

Ness Point Works, situated on the corner of Maltsters Score, was the home of Rist's Wire & Cables. Leonard Boyce worked there before the Second World War and says, "When I left school I had a couple of herring boy jobs, and then I got a job at Rist's, where I met my wife and we married in 1939. I was there when war broke out when I was 23 and I had a

(Above left) Matthew Boardley Senior (1889-1943) took over his father's haulage company which had been established when the original Boardley Brothers company split up at the end of the 19th century.

(Above) Matthew Boardley Senior taking the reins of one of his carts, with his son Matthew by his side.

(Above) Ronnie Boardley with some of his lorries at the rear of his haulage business in the Beach Village. Before the Second World War, when Arthur and Sam Boardley ran this company, horse and carts had been used for all the haulage work.

reserved occupation at first. They were doing government work, cables for aircraft and things and so they were evacuated because of the invasion scare. They moved to Nuneaton in June 1940 and we went with them, and worked there until I was called up in 1942. Then I found out that I had an ear problem that kept me on home service in England which was lucky for me really because I might not have been here now. Pals that I trained with who went to Italy all got killed."

On the corner of Rant Score was Youngman & Preston's Eagle Brewery. Established around 1856 as Youngman & Son, it was not until around 1870 that Preston became a partner. In 1919 the company was absorbed by Lacons of Great Yarmouth, and the Eagle Brewery was sold to Charrington & Co. Ltd. After the Second World War it was acquired by Birds Eye, and was demolished in September 1958, to make way for new developments. One of the two stone eagles, once the symbol of Youngman and Preston's, was broken whilst being removed, but the other was saved and is displayed over the entrance to the Birds Eye Cafeteria on Whapload Road.

Another long-standing business on The Grit was the Steam Laundry. Their premises on Whapload Road, opposite Crown Score, were built in the late 1880s and the construction met with a great deal of opposition from local boat-owners who insisted that the land was part of their net-drying grounds and there should be no enclosure on the Denes. But the building went ahead and in the early 1900s the company were advertising themselves as 'noted lace curtain cleaners'. The laundry remained in business beyond the clearances of the 1960s, the building surrounded now by Birds Eye factories. In the 1990s the laundry finally closed to the public, now solely providing cleaning services for Birds Eye. That too closed and in the early 2000s the building was partially demolished and has been left derelict.

(Right) The Lowestoft Steam Laundry on Whapload Road was built in the late 1880s. Jack Rose worked there as a van boy in 1940, from 8am until 7pm for nine shillings and sixpence a week.

(Opposite below) Inside the Lowestoft gasworks in the 1930s. John Day lived nearby and remembers, "My father would ask me to go down with a metal wheelbarrow and see Charlie near the furnace and he'd put coke, the residue from huge ovens that produced the gas, straight from the furnace into the wheelbarrow and that'd light our fire."

(Right) An early motorised delivery vehicle, circa 1900, belonging to the Youngman and Preston Company who had offices at 69 High Street and Grosvenor House in Lowestoft.

(Below right) The yard of the Eagle Brewery situated on the north side of Rant Score. Owned by Youngman and Preston, it closed after the First World War.

(Left) In the 1950s Palfrey & Webb, the builders, were one of many businesses on the Beach Village unrelated to the fishing industry but attracted to the area by cheap properties with plenty of storage space. Their premises at 150 Whapload Road had been William Westgate's net store in the 1930s.

(Below) The Belfast Rope Company was once the largest rope factory in the world, with a net store on Whapload Road next to the expanding Birds Eye factories. The Lowestoft net store closed in 1968 and was demolished in 1969. The company itself was dissolved in 1979.

Birds Eye was certainly a modest venture when it first arrived on The Grit. "I can remember Birds Eye opening in 1949," says Brian Springer. "They used to just come in the summer for the pea season. Never had no freezers or nothing. They'd hire the freezers from Lowestoft Ice Company, who were opposite the *Rising Sun*. They used to have blokes walking with an electric barrow backwards and forwards to the factory, taking peas to the freezers. All day, 12-hour shifts doing that! Then Birds Eye started buying lots of little buildings around the town for storage, not just on the Beach Village."

That small depot soon grew into a complete production unit by 1952 and that same year the company invested £70,000 to build the plant required for freezing peas. In subsequent decades the Birds Eye factory along Whapload Road went from strength to strength. To meet increasing demand, the massive Steakhouse building was added in the mid-1980s, and in 1988 the company's entire vegetable packing operation was transferred here, in addition to a third potato line the following year. The development of the factory continued into the 1990s: following an £18 million investment, Denes IV was opened in 1993 with three lines running 24 hours a day, seven days a week. The factory had five main production buildings over an area of some 31 acres and had around 1,500 employees.

In 2019 the company celebrated the 70th anniversary of its arrival in Lowestoft and now has a state-of-the-art modern food plant, which was the focus of a behind the scenes BBC television documentary, *Inside the Factory*, presented by Gregg Wallace. The programme followed the production of frozen waffles with Gregg describing how, "The frozen potato frames are picked up off the belt individually by six pairs of robot arms and placed into groups of 10. The robot arms can locate each one via a scanner which takes a photo of every single waffle."

Greg concluded the documentary, "This is an enormous food processing plant, basically making mountains of mashed potato that they form into waffle shapes. What really astounds me is how few people there are making them. This means that the responsibility for millions of families' waffles are in the hands of just a few workers here in this factory in Lowestoft."

In this very place over a hundred years earlier on one day – 12th October 1913 – nearly 8,000 fishermen caught 10 million herring which were processed by thousands of fisher girls in a year when 466 million herring were exported to Germany and Russia. Now, over a century later, just 'a few workers' produce a million waffles every 24 hours – 750 every minute – each weighing 68g and exactly 15mm thick to be sent all over the UK (the biggest fans are in the Republic of Ireland!) and as far afield as Malta and Cyrpus. It's easy to see what those numbers mean in terms of employment and also how in the 21st century these very few workers are no longer required to live next door to the factory. Community spirit is no longer the product of people living and working together in the same place.

(Above) In the 1950s Birds Eye began to expand across the Beach Village, utilising many of the existing properties and, by the 1960s, employed 1,400 workers at peak periods. (Above) They built onto the front of Wilde's Cottage to create their first personnel office.

(Left) By 1980 Birds Eye was the biggest frozen food company in the world with Lowestoft home to the main vegetable processing factory. Following a merger in 1981 the company became Birds Eye Walls until 2004 when they reverted to the Birds Eye name.

(Above) Birds Eye's cold store was built close to Ness Point and opened in 1958 to keep up with increasing demand and could store up to 20,000 tons of fish. In the 1960s the Birds Eye factories across the country and in Lowestoft were booming.

(Bottom) The 'runner bean snippers' at Birds Eye in 1959. In December 1960 Prince Phillip visited the expanding factory and was shown kipper filleting and sprouts being cleaned, graded and packed. Having wisely brought his duffel coat he was also shown the new cold storage area of the factory.

(Above) Looking towards Squire's shop in Whapload Road in 1950. On the right, the Gooderham's coal merchants and the Eagle Brewery at the foot of Rant Score would be demolished in 1958.

(Right) The same view in 1960. The area had started to transform into what would become the Beach Village Industrial Estate. Around Squire's shop (left) new buildings for Birds Eye's main factory, fish and dinner lines appeared.

12. THE THIRSTY BREED

All those pubs down there got a living because there were such a lot of people on the Beach.
LENNY 'WINKY' NORMAN

In 1900, when the price of beer varied from one to one and a half pence a pint, there were 13 pubs and beer-houses on The Grit. Fishermen were a thirsty breed and at a time when the population of the Beach Village itself was over 2,500, their number swelled every autumn from the influx of fishermen for the herring season – more than enough to fill these public houses.

The smaller beer houses were actually no more than front rooms. These came about because in the middle of the 19th century anyone assessed for the poor rate was entitled to a licence to sell beer. The cost of the licence was two pounds and two shillings a year and the result was a boom in beer houses. 'Much evil resulted' says a contemporary report and finally in 1860 the Justices Licence was introduced.

Drink was a problem in some cases, and to try to combat its allure, the Church of England Temperance Society opened five coffee houses in Lowestoft in 1879, two of which – The Lifeboat Tavern and The Tea Pot – were situated in Whapload Road. The Lifeboat Tavern was on the south side to the south of Christ Church, and was actually a residence which had been turned into a temperance house. In one of its bay windows there was a sign which said, 'A public-house without the drink, where men can sit, talk, read and think. And sober home return.'

Jack Moore, born in 1929, lived at 66 East Street, next door to his grandfather's pub, the *Flowing Bowl.* "My mother was from a Grit family. Before her father had the *Flowing Bowl,* he had another pub, the *Fishermen's Arms.* And people think that because there were 13 pubs on the Beach that they were all drunkards – they weren't. They used to go in the pub, one pint of beer and sit and play dominoes all night. They never used to drink a lot 'cos they never had the money."

Drinking was often part of the fishermen's life though. Lenny Norman's late brother, Bob 'Umshi' Norman told a local newspaper in September 1966, 'Every drifter started the season with beer. The crew used to have two gallons of beer and bread and cheese for fitting out and I used to take it down to the boats with a nanny goat and cart. Then there was hot stout to be taken over, day and night, to the women working in the smoke houses.'

The Norman family pub was the *Suffolk Fishery Tavern* in Anguish Street. Lenny Norman was born above the pub in 1921, by which time his parents had been running the tavern for about four years although his father had originally been a fisherman and his mother a braider. Lenny recalls, "They used to open at five o'clock in the morning in the fishing time for the drivers of the carts and for rum and beverages up to breakfast for the herring workers. At that time my mother used to take some Scots people in, coopers, and they came down from Wick, employed by the McCormacks, and she was paid at the end of the season when they went home. The money was then five shillings a head allowance to feed them on, and there used to be about six of them in there including the main cooper at the time… In the pub we had a 'snug'. The women used to come in there, sometimes early in the morning, when all their husbands had gone to work. Come in with a jug and fill it up with beer to take home."

When Lenny was six, his family gave up the pub due to his mother's ill health. "So we had to move," he explains. "We'd had the pub for about 10 years when Walter Strange took it over. He became landlord, but as far as I can remember that didn't stay open long after we left." Indeed, in 1927 the pub was de-licensed and closed.

The names of the Beach Village pubs came from many sources, with the *Dutch Hoy* and the *Fishermen's Arms* from the fishing industry, and the *Princess Royal* named after an Old Company yawl. The *Inkerman Arms* and *Balaclava* commemorated British battles which had been fought abroad, while the *East of England* and the *Rising Sun* referred to the geographical location, the latter also becoming known as the 'Japanese Embassy'! (Japan's national flag has long been known as 'the rising sun').

The *Princess Royal* was situated on the corner of Nelson Road and East Street and was run for many years by Mr Wilfred George Jones who was landlord when the premises were modernised in the late 1920s. The pub had been in this family for 90 years when they left in the early 1930s to take on a newly built pub, the *Norman Warrior* in Oulton Road in the town. Wilfred died on 4th February 1933 aged 56, leaving a wife, two daughters and a son, Billy, who were all well-known locally. The younger daughter, Ada, born on 30th December 1916, can still remember the old pub on The Grit. "Our living quarters were in an old adjoining building, but years ago there was a club room above the pub where the old fishermen used to sit and talk."

In the early 1900s the *Princess Royal* was the home of one of the town's best fund-raisers for the Royal National Lifeboat Institution. This was Spot the dog who had been trained by Wilfred Jones to do various begging tricks and for these he was given money which was deposited in the lifeboat collecting box. In 1908 it seems that this little fox terrier collected more money than was contained in all the other lifeboat collecting boxes in the town added together! As a result the Institution presented the dog with a silver collar suitably inscribed. Spot's death in 1910 was reported in a local newspaper, which stated, 'The honourable secretary told the annual meeting of the Royal National Lifeboat Institution about the death of our canine friend at the *Princess Royal*. This dog has provided a considerable sum to the Institution through collection boxes. Although Mr Jones is training another dog to replace our late friend, it will be some time before it is as accomplished as the other helper.' The dog was given a fitting burial, 'enclosed in a handsome coffin with brass fittings.'

Leonard Boyce lived with his grandparents who ran the *East of England* which was on Whapload Road. What follows is part of Leonard's detailed account of his childhood experiences of the pub. "I wasn't born on the Beach, I was born in Tennyson Road.

(Above)
The *Princess Royal* was on the corner of Nelson Road and East Street. Here we see the pub before it was modernised in the early 1920s, with the landlord Wilfred Jones (second from left) with daughter Ada. Also in the picture is Spot the dog, the town's best fund-raiser for the Royal National Lifeboat Institution.

(Left) By the end of the 1920s the exterior of the *Princess Royal* had been refurbished. Landlord and landlady Mr & Mrs Jones stand proudly outside.

(Right) Wilfred Jones (centre, near trophies) pictured with the victorious *Princess Royal* darts team in 1929.

(Below) A line-up of regular patrons of the *Princess Royal*, circa 1920. Posing for photographs was thirsty work and Wilfrod, with sleeves rolled up, looks ready to return behind the bar to provide liquid refreshment.

(Far left) The *Flowing Bowl* was a long-established pub on the corner of Rant Score East and East Street and was open from the early 1860s until 1932. Landlord John Lewis Burwood, with his daughter Renee is pictured outside the pub in the early 1900s.

(Left) Leonard Tripp was the landlord of the *East of England* public house and had a long association with the place. After the pub closed in 1934, the Ness Point Angling Club took over the building and he became manager until he died in 1941.

(Bellow) The *East of England* was the most northern pub in the Beach Village. Leonard Boyce said, 'There was one long bar and a small smoke-room at the back. They would throw sawdust down on the wooden floor and there were a couple of spittoons there too.'

My father was killed in the First World War and my mother remarried, in 1922 I think it was. I was about six years old and my step-father was one who didn't want step-children and so my grandparents took me and brought me up and that's how I came to get on the Beach. It was about 1923-4 I went down there and I was brought up in a pub called the *East of England*, which was the last pub before you got to Sparrows Nest. My grandfather was Leonard Tripp, a boat owner who made a bit of money from the fishing during the First World War and then he took this pub, moving from Old Nelson Street, and I went with them."

"I was never allowed in the pub. If I stuck my head round the door, it would be, 'Boy! Out of there!' That was my grandfather. He was very strict in some ways but a nice old boy really. My dear old grandmother was stone deaf from birth, she never heard anything. I did used to have a nose in the bar to see what was going on at times, especially if he wasn't there, and I remember the beer was drawn out of a wooden tap, not pumps or anything like that. They were busy though, and it was surprising in the summer how many visitors would stroll down there and come and sit in the backyard, where we had round tables."

"At the back of the *East of England* was a long garden, a terrifically long garden, and there used to be a couple of brothers, called Miles, who made twine in this yard, I think they paid my grandfather for using the yard. They used to wrap it round their waists and go backwards right from the top of the yard to the bottom, making this twine, and some youngsters sat at the top spinning a wheel and I used to help out with that sometimes. I got sixpence or a shilling a week if I helped them."

"Our sitting room was behind the bar, with just this glass partition separating it. I could see through the frosted glass though, what was going on. The pub itself was like a lot of those pubs down Whapload Road, you wouldn't call them pubs today. There was one long bar and a small smoke-room at the back. They would throw sawdust down on the wooden floor and there were a couple of spittoons there too. The Miles brothers, who used to do the twine spinning, as soon as they finished, their first call was the pub and one of them acted as a bouncer, he used to get his beer free I think. He stood up in the corner and he was ever such a big fella, and if there was any trouble he'd throw them out."

"The pub was quite busy in the 1920s, especially during the fishing time, because you had all the Scots down here using the pub. Very often they'd have fights in the road, especially on Saturday nights. The Scots lads would come in, mix with our lot, and get drunk and finish up outside, eleven o'clock at night, and I used to peek through the window and see this lot fighting, and down would come the police, on their bicycles in them days, two or three of them trying to sort 'em out."

Leonard remembers his grandfather getting into brawls. "There'd be an argument and they'd get outside fighting. One night he got mixed up in this and he came in with the knee out of his trousers, blood on the side of his face, and he was a-swearing. Of course, his poor old lady would get worried and upset in the back sitting-room, knowing what was going on. She used to go upstairs to the bedroom and look out of the front bedroom window. I would be in there with her..."

Like any pub, the *East of England* had its regulars, men who spent many a long hour in an atmosphere thick with smoke from pipes and cigarettes, telling yarns over a pint. Leonard continues, "Some of them old chaps who used to come in that pub had their names engraved on the seats, had little bits of wood with their names on! About half a dozen of 'em like that. And very often they'd come in that pub dinner-time on a Saturday and wouldn't go out until about ten or eleven at night. They never went home to dinner, just sat there drinking and playing cards."

"One regular character that sticks in my mind is Happy Welham, him and his donkey. He was a peculiar looking man, great big nose and sort of hunched up. He used to live in Lighthouse Score and he'd come out of there, along Whapload Road with his donkey and cart and little dog, get as far as the *East of England* and stop. Into the pub he'd come, and sit there for a time, and I can't ever remember seeing him over-drinking, but he was always very happy – as they called him."

"I remember my grandfather used to have this big slate where they put the fishermen's debts down, especially the Scotsmen. They used to come in there and drink all the voyage, when they were in from the sea, and always put it down on the slate and they always used to pay up before they went home near Christmas. I don't ever remember him complaining that any of them had let him down."

"Things went all wrong in the 1930s, but he kept on there until he died. During that period he had a big net store on the east side of Whapload Road. Nearly opposite the pub was a big net chamber run by a firm called Westgate, and a little further along was my grandfather's, it was isolated, it stood all alone on the Denes. It was a big place with two storeys. It had a tanning copper for the nets, and I can remember the women going up there mending the nets. A whole row of them would stand mending the nets. I used to have a rare old time running about the net chamber."

"I remember many of the old pubs down there although I was too young to go into them. The brewers for the *East of England* were Morse's who were in Crown Street, and that's where he used to get his beer from. I think Morse's owned the pub and when they finished, the pub finished but somehow it was kept open as the Denes Fishing Industry Club and we just carried on and the old man was manager of that till he died in 1941."

Brian Springer, born in 1941, recalls another pub – long closed but still very much in evidence in the 1960s. "That was only a little old place at the bottom of Christ Church Score, near that corner where the police station is now. And if that rained and you were walking along Whapload Road and then the sun came out, you could still see the name on the gable end – the *Mayfly Inn* – but only when it rained!"

Perhaps the two best known Beach Village pubs were the *Gas House Tavern* and the *Rising Sun*. Alice Coleman, formerly Mrs Brady, kept the *Gas House Tavern* for about four years from the late 1940s. "We were friendly with the people who kept the pub, their name was Kemp, and when they told us they were leaving they suggested we put in for it, so we did. When I went down there Gus Jensen was in the *Rising Sun*, and me in the *Gas House Tavern*, and I believe there was one further along, the *Dutch Hoy*, but that closed down, and then there was the *East of England*, which was a club by then, and that's all the pubs there were down there by that time."

"The *Gas House Tavern* was my first pub. When we took it there were two little cottages on the side of the pub and my husband and a gang pulled them down and we made a little beer garden there. We lived upstairs but the kitchen was downstairs until after the flood. We were right opposite the old gasworks and we used to make a good living from them as their workers would pop over for a pint or two every day. I made tea and rolls twice a day for the Birds Eye people, and the shoe factory, and old Daisy Dinks was a regular."

"It was an interesting pub," Alice continues, "and people down there were the salt of the earth. Tough as nails they were. If it hadn't been for the flood [1953] I think I would have stopped there, but every time the wind got up I used to get frightened. I'll never forget that gale that blew that night. I stood there washing the glasses at the sink and I saw this water bubbling through and I thought, crikey, the blinking drain is overflowing. 'Course, when we looked out the bar door, the sea was coming up the road, you've never seen anything like it! And there was me, putting my foot over the drain to try and stop the water. Harry Burgess, he was coxswain of the lifeboat, he came down in a little rowing-boat. He said, 'Alice, I've come to take you up mine.' And I looked out the door and I said, 'Not on your Nelly! I can't swim', so my husband and I went upstairs till they got the water out. You ought to have seen the muck the flood left behind. It took us ages and ages to get rid of that, although we had a lot of help. We had a bogey stove in the middle of the bar, run by coke, and because the people round our area couldn't get any cooking done I had a big saucepan on there, and made saucepans of pea soup. I had the *Gas House Tavern* for about four years, but after the flood I couldn't settle. Whenever it was windy I used to get nervous, so when the *Blue Anchor* in the High Street came on the market I went for that. I think Billy Brown had it for a time after us."

John and Evelyn Baldry were licensees during the 1960s. John recalls, "We used to live at 51 East Street which was right near the Bethel. We were ten years in the cottage before we took over the *Gas House Tavern* in 1962. Russell and Queenie Kemp had it before Alice [Coleman], and then Billy and Emma Brown took it over for a while, and we had it from 1962 to 1966. After us Keith Reid had it till it closed. We lived upstairs where there was a large lounge and three bedrooms and a bathroom. There was a backyard beer garden."

Evelyn remembers, "We had a good four years in there. It was during the time that the fishermen used to wear their coloured suits. It was a good family pub too. Fishermen and families. Tony Jensen, John Catchpole, who's now the coxswain of the lifeboat, Peter Gibbons, who was another lifeboat coxswain, they all used the *Gas House*. The crew of the Pioneer, the ship that went down, they all used to be regulars. We were there in the *Gas House Tavern* when that happened. It was terrible."

John continues, "Alfie Hall, Dick Hall, Jamie Lake, all used to come in. 'Umshi' Norman, he was a regular too. Then there were the 'ladies' of the Beach, Daisy Dinks and Maudy Linder, they were always in. Sonny Pickess, he used to help us to serve in the bar; Jean

(Right) Outside the *Gas House Tavern* in the early 1950s. (Left to right) 'Darby' James, 'Young Darby' James, unknown, Alice Brady, Fred Brady, unknown.

(Below) In the late 1940s the Landlubbers versus Fishermen darts match drew a crowd at the *Gas House Tavern*.

(Left) At the darts match the Fishermen's team came dressed for the occasion in sou'westers and oilskins. (Top left) Billy Ayers, Ted Boon, Sadie Springer. (With dart) 'Young Darby' James, (sitting) Bob Prettyman, Georgie Prettyman, 'Lemon' James, (front) 'Dough' Clark.

(Below) The *Gas House Tavern* was situated in Wilde's Street. Landlady Alice Coleman said, "We were right opposite the old gasworks and we used to make a good living from them as their workers would pop over for a pint or two every day. I made tea and rolls twice a day for the Birds Eye people, and the shoe factory, and old Daisy Dinks was a regular."

Keable used to wipe the glasses. Sometimes when the fisher boys didn't want to go to sea they wouldn't go in the bar for a drink in case the ship's husband came after them, so they went in the room at the back. Christmas time when Birds Eye knocked off you couldn't move in there, the bar was so full. A horse and dray visited the pub every summer, as publicity for Stewart and Patterson pubs."

Evelyn adds, "Sometimes I used to have to go out the back door, and round to the side door in the pub, because I couldn't get through, we were so busy, people were all in the passageway."

The *Rising Sun* stood opposite the Herring Industry Cold Store on Whapload Road and was the last surviving pub on The Grit, closing 4th November 1968. "The *Rising Sun* was in my uncle's family for forty years," says Ron James, who after the Second World War opened the Kumfy Kafe in premises which had once been occupied by the *Flowing Bowl* pub. "My uncle was a Burwood, and in 1940 he took his own life. He was so traumatised by the Second World War starting; he'd been through the first one and he was so scared of doing it again, then the pub came out of the family and he took his own life."

"It was a lovely pub," Ron recalls. "Uncle Jimmy was awarded the cleanest pub in Lowestoft around 1937 and when I was a little boy I used to have the job of wheeling a barrow down the beach and filling it up with sand which was for throwing on his bar floor. Every morning he used to be up before six, sweep all the sand up, put fresh sand down, then he used to go outside and wash down and polish the wall which was red tiles up to the window-sills, and then he'd scrub the pavement. That was a lovely pub, that was."

"I can remember they used to have what they called a 'Didlem' Club. That was about a penny or tuppence a week, and they used to have a 'do' at Christmas in the Smoke Room and of course no little children were allowed but being as it was my uncle, he used to let me go behind the bar, sit on a stool and listen to them. They used to have an accordion player and the old boys used to get drunk and dance on the table."

The Burwood name had a long association with the *Rising Sun*, one of its first landlords being James Burwood. By 1863 the pub had been taken over by Bob Hook and by 1883 had passed to Robert Carver Butcher. In 1896 the pub returned to the Burwood family, with George Henry Burwood becoming landlord in 1902, succeeded by Ron James' uncle, James William Burwood, in 1913.

In 1940 Burwood was succeeded by George Buck, who had run a shoe repair shop on the Beach for many years. His son John recalls, "My Dad had the *Rising Sun* after Jimmy Burwood. Burwood died shortly after, I can remember he went to live in my aunt's old house, at the back of Vigilant Cottages. It was there where he killed himself, cut his throat. Before he took the pub on, my Dad had run a shoe repair shop in Anguish Street since two or three years after the First World War. He had the *Rising Sun* for a couple of years at the start of the Second World War and then Alfred Tungate had it and then Gussie Jensen took it after him."

"The *Rising Sun* became too much for my Dad at the time. You see, although he was in his forties and had been in the First World War, he had to register for service. By trade he was a shipwright, so he registered and had to go and work in Richards shipyard. So he was

(Right) The *Rising Sun* was on Whapload road, near to Spurgeon Score. After the Second World War it was also known as the 'Japanese embassy' because of Japan's 'rising sun' national flag.

(Bottom right) In the *Rising Sun*, (back row) 'Twee' Swan, Johnny Rose, Billy Thorpe, Jack Saunders, unknown, Billy Capps Jenner, Mr Tuck (Hon. R.N.L.I. Sec.) (second row) Hilda Burgess, Florrie Tuck, Mrs Saunders, Vernil Tuck, Harry Burgess, Tommy Knott, Bob Capps Jenner. One of the main features of this pub was the 'model cabin' which had shelves decorated with model boats visible at the top of the picture.

running the pub and working at the shipyard. Then he had to do fire spotting at night-times and although my mother and aunt helped, it was all a bit too much for him, so he packed the pub in. But not for long; he had the *Greyhound* and then the *Triangle* after that."

By 1952 Gus Jensen had become landlord of the *Rising Sun*, but in 1955 the tenancy passed to George 'Bloater' Nicholson. Bloater's daughter, Mrs Edna Mortensen, recalls, "My father took over the pub in February 1955. He was a trawler skipper before that. He'd been at sea since he was 14. I only lived down there a year, but I was down there every day after we moved. I had two brothers, Fred and John. There were four bedrooms over the pub, absolutely freezing cold, no central heating or anything. We weren't there during the 1953 flood but all around the pub, especially in the front room, whenever we had the slightest bit of damp you could see where the water had come up to on the walls. Salt would come out of the walls. Of course, it had been treated, the brewery did all sorts of treatments, but they couldn't stop this salt coming out. All round the cellar walls too. The building was never the same again."

"Dad used to let all the Scottish fishermen in on Sunday mornings at ten o'clock. You weren't supposed to but they all used the back-gate, and the bar was quite full by 10.30am, they all liked the whisky! In October and November all the smoke houses round there used to smell of kipper smoke. I didn't mind that, I thought it was lovely! I used to like living down there. My Dad kept his hand in at fishing, sharing a boat with the landlord of the *Belvedere*. He still went herring fishing and long-shoring in October with a friend of his, and my husband looked after the pub at night-times and my mother would have it during the day."

"There was a fireplace in the bar which I think someone bought when they pulled the pub down. That fire was so stoked up in the winter that you couldn't get near it after a while. There were some carvings of dogs' heads on the wall too, but one of the main features of the pub at this time was the 'model cabin' which had a magnificent layout of model boats which were made by Leonard Carr (known as Len), who was a local fish packer."

"The models of the boats were there when my Dad took over the pub from the previous tenant who was Gus Jensen," explains Mrs Mortensen. "You used to have to put a penny in the slot and the room went dark and all the ships lit up. It was a real feature of that pub. I think my Dad sold them when he left, to a pub in Orford." The models represented boats that had sailed out of Lowestoft since 1900, from the old drifters to the steam trawlers of the First World War and between the Wars, to the modern diesel trawlers. There was also a model of the *Girl Pat* which Skipper Osborne of Lowestoft made famous with his round-the-world exploits. There were models of boats lost at sea and models of both the Ministry of Agriculture and Fisheries research ship and the Naval Protection vessels."

"There was also a lovely clock on the wall," continues Mrs Mortensen, "a big old wall clock, and it was the sun coming up over the water, the rising sun. I don't know what happened to that. He used to have jars of whelks and cockles on the bar. The *Rising Sun* was on the site of what is now Karpet Kingdom."

Perhaps one of the biggest nights at the *Rising Sun* was on 4th February 1956, when the pub was visited by the BBC television programme, *Saturday Night Out*, said to have been

(Above left) 'Bloater' Nicholson and his wife Jessie had the Rising Sun from February 1955 until September 1966.

(Above right) 'Bloater' in the front room of the *Rising Sun*, with the fishermen's wives who were interviewed by Robert Beatty on *Saturday Night Out*. (Left to right) 'Bloater' Nicholson, Mrs E. Cook, Mrs Reader, Joan Soloman and Mrs Randlesome.

the first live broadcast from Lowestoft. Three cameras were positioned on the premises: one covering the street, alley and bar through the window; another behind the bar, covering the bar room; and a third was used to film some of the fishermen's wives in the lounge.

Mrs Mortensen kept a copy of the working script used during the filming. "I can remember Robert Beatty coming down and making his *Saturday Night Out* programme from the pub. The picture was taken of some wives sitting in our front room, talking to their husbands at sea via the radio. They had a fishermen's waveband then that they could talk on. My father is on the left. It was broadcast live and the pub was packed out that night. My husband and I, we couldn't get in the bar it was so crowded, we had to go up and look in Morling's window, to see it on television!"

The 40-minute programme began with Robert Beatty standing on a wet pavement in front of a plain brick wall on which was pasted an old and torn Fishermen's Week poster, announcing, "Welcome again to *Saturday Night Out*. Tonight we are with the fishermen of Lowestoft – a famous old fishing port in East Anglia where the sea has provided the main means of livelihood for hundreds of years." Then there were a few shots of wet cobblestones and a cat eating fish-heads, two old fishermen coming down an alley together, then a shot of the trawler *Lowestoft Lady*, while Beatty gave a brief description of the town and its fishing. The programme then switched to the interior of the pub with Beatty inviting the viewers to, 'Come into the smoke room of the *Rising Sun*, in the original old Lowestoft fishing village and meet some of these fisherfolk.'

Beatty then interviewed 'Bluey' Last, Mrs Last, Alonzo Mewse and Leonard Carr, the model maker, at one table before moving over to Barney Smith, 'Tosher' Moore, and

(Left) The last night of the Rising Sun 4th November 1968. David Waterman remembers, "Not all the people there that night were regulars. A lot of them came up from the town. Although you can spot a few Beach boys – there's Donny Cole (centre, in the white shirt, smiling at the camera) and in the crowd there's Ashley Gardiner and Roy Benstead. And Reggie Reynolds is behind the bar, arms up in the air!"

(Below) Alan Youngman has fond memories of Reggie and his wife Eileen, both pictured busy at work behind the bar. "At about two in the morning Reggie used to say, 'Go home to your wives or some other buggers'. His wife Eileen was lovely. At the end of each night we all used to sing to her, *Goodnight Eileen*. Sometimes you'd have an all-night drinking session there and she'd cook you breakfast, eggs and bacon at six in the morning!"

Billy Thorpe at another table, drinking and chatting while Bloater Nicholson served. Also featured on the show were the wives of the crew of the Lowestoft Lady – the skipper's wife Mrs Reader, the mate's wife Mrs Soloman, Mrs Randlesome, wife of a deckhand, and Mrs Cook – who had gathered in the lounge for a 'staged' conversation with their husbands on the trawler waveband and an interview with Robert Beatty. What then followed was a piece shot on the deck of the Lowestoft trawler, with Bob Danvers Walker on board describing the conditions and work of a fisherman.

The programme ended with Beatty at the quayside with some fishermen's wives waiting for a sister ship of the *Lowestoft Lady* to come into harbour. As the crew and relatives walked away down the quayside, Beatty and the skipper of the boat together with his wife went to a waiting car and Beatty asked, "Is there anything you would like to say to our viewers before we go for a well-earned drink at the *Rising Sun,* skipper?" To which the scripted reply was, "Yes. We're all very glad to have had you at Lowestoft and I hope that you people at home have enjoyed seeing something of what it takes to go and get good fresh fish to you. To any youngster who's interested – if you are prepared to work and know in your heart that you want to fish – come and join us and welcome."

Mrs Mortensen remembers, "We got a telegram later, from Peter Webber and Robert Beatty at the BBC saying, 'Magnificent show, congratulations and thanks to our trawlermen, it was really great, the offshore sequences were fine'."

Bloater Nicholson ran the *Rising Sun* for nearly 12 years before he made the decision to retire. On 15th September 1966, Bloater spoke to the *Eastern Evening News*, at a time when the *Gas House Tavern* had only just closed, and he had witnessed the decline of the Beach Village. "There are no locals left now," said Bloater, "it's all passing trade – people working down here, lorry drivers and that sort." He admitted he would be glad when the area was cleaned up. "You get all sorts in empty houses, old ones and youngsters and no-one knows what they get up to."

The *Rising Sun* was taken over by Reg Reynolds and kept open for a further two years until 4th November 1968 when the pub enjoyed a memorable last night. Trevor Collis, who worked at the fish market during this time, well remembers this occasion. "The place was packed. They really drank the place dry that night. One chap had to go to work at six in the morning and only got an hour's sleep! Another chap was really drinking and there were so many people that when he wanted to go to the toilet, they lifted him over their heads and he was passed along by the crowd. Every other record was the Animals' old song, *House of the Rising Sun,* or *Those Were the Days* by Mary Hopkin. There was a Japanese flag outside. Those certainly were the days."

(Left) Arthur Howell (left), Harry Howell (front) and Alfred Whybrow (front right) park their family Ford Anglia outside the *Rising Sun* in the early 1960s.

(Below) Looking down Whapload Road towards the *Rising Sun* pub in the late 1960s.

(Opposite) The *Dutch Hoy* could be found at 47 Whapload Road opposite the Eagle Brewery and was named after a type of cargo boat with origins in Holland. The pub was established by 1853 and kept by Isaac Capps, then later run by the Yallop family. In 1931 these premises became Nellie Gibbs' grocery shop until the building was bombed during the War.

(Left) In the early 1920s Edward Capps-Jenner lived at No 65 Whapload Road, next door to Hatcher's shop. He wrote, 'No 65 had had been a pub, the *Mayfly Inn*, the name being painted on the wall above the door and still visible, if you knew it was there, until it was demolished in 1972.'

(Top) The *Sailor's Return* was situated at 24 Anguish Street and was recorded as far back as 1855 when it was kept by Mrs Elizabeth Capps and William Burwood Capps. In 1927 the building was converted into a dairy by Joseph Flertey who moved there from his previous premises at 89 Whapload Road.

(Bottom) The *Waggon and Horses*, 48 Whapload Road, was on the corner of Rant Score East and next door to the *Dutch Hoy*. In the 1870s the pub was run by Martha Pye, a widow, whose grandson was well-known beachman Harris Allerton who lived there when he was a boy. The pub was still trading in 1906 although it closed before the First World War.

THE UNLUCKY THIRTEEN

I down it in one
in the Rising Sun

Have two halves after
in The Balaclava

Best ale and joyful
in The Princess Royal

Four sheets to the wind
in the East of England

Sink five rums
in the Inkermun

Fell for Jessie's charms
in the Fisherman's Arms

It's 'woss he having?'
at the Gas House Tavern

They say 'he wunt learn'
in the Sailors Return

All braggin & curses
in the Waggon & 'Orses

Drunk too much m'boy
in the ol'Dutch Hoy

Mud in your eye
in the ol'Mayfly

And in the Flowing Bowl?
Blotto! Out cold.

Then it comes back to me
in the Suffolk Fishery

Shoulda been home for m'tea
sometime yesterdee.

So, I have another one so,
in the Rising Sun...
(faster)

DEAN PARKIN
from *PEARLS FROM THE GRIT* (2018)

PUBLIC HOUSES ON THE GRIT

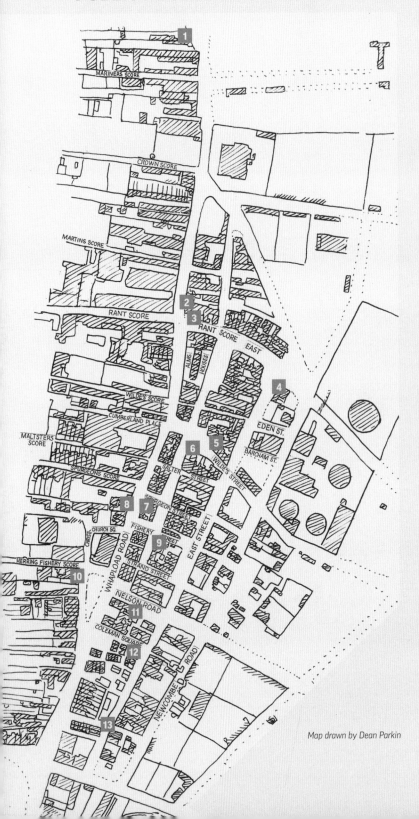

Map drawn by Dean Parkin

Here's the list of the thirteen public houses which were located in the Beach Village based on original research by Jack Rose and Ivan Bunn.

1. *East of England Tavern* stood in Whapload Road opposite the present-day Birds Eye coldstore. It was first recorded in 1879 – demolished in 1967.

2. The first record of the *Dutch Hoy* was in 1853. This pub stood opposite the old Eagle Brewery where the Birds Eye office now is.

3. *Waggon and Horses* was next door to the *Dutch Hoy*. First Recorded in 1840 it was still trading in 1960.

4. *Flowing Bowl* was situated on the corner of East Street, and can be found recorded in 1863. It remained as a pub until 1932 when it became a working men's social club. After the war the premises became the Kumfy Kafe.

5. *Gas House Tavern* stood in Wilde's Street, close to Cumberland Square. The earliest record of it dates from 1855 and it was one of the last two pubs left on the Beach Village until it closed in September 1966 and was later demolished.

6. *Sailors Return* was on the corner of Anguish Street and Wilde's Street and was there by 1855. In 1927 this was converted into Joseph Flertey's dairy.

7. The *Rising Sun* stood opposite Herring Industry Cold Store on Whapload Road. This was the last surviving pub on the Beach Village and closed its doors for the last time on 4th November 1968.

8. The *Fishermen's Arms* was situated opposite the *Rising Sun* and had been established by 1840, continuing until 1922. The premises were then used by Hammond's fish and chip shop until 1938 before finally being demolished after the Second World War.

9. *Suffolk Fishery Tavern* was in Anguish Street. This pub was de-licensed in 1927.

10. *Mayfly Inn* was next to the shop at the bottom of Herring Fishery Score. In 1865 a William Alexander lived here who described himself as 'beer retailer and hairdresser'.

11. The *Princess Royal* was on the corner of Nelson Road and East Street, It was completely renovated in 1927 before closing in the early 1930s.

12. The exact location of the *Inkerman Arms* isn't known. It is thought to have been situated in the area where the Inkerman Cottages are believed to have stood, on a site which became part of Beeton's Net Works.

13. *Balaclava* probably stood close to the *Inkerman Arms*, on the site of Reynolds & Hurrens Fish House.

Another public house, although not strictly speaking in the Beach Village, could be located near by. *The Canteen* is thought to have been Bow House in Old Nelson Street, and was last recorded back in the 1820s. This was so called because it served the soldiers who manned the fort opposite during the 18th century.

13. BEACH LIFE

You wonder now how you lived there. I can remember sitting around the table for dinner, and I had to sit in one particular corner because I was the smallest one and that corner was only big enough to hold me.
BERT PRETTYMAN

I n 1954 Jean Mitchell had her first daughter at her mother's house, at 19 Wilde's Street, "Although we had no bathroom, and outside water and toilet, I had her at home. We had no sterilising units for bottles or fridges to keep food fresh, yet food poisoning, or unhealthy babies, we hardly heard of. You sterilised the teats of the bottles in cups of boiling water."

You could be born on The Grit, and die there too, as up to the Second World War the Beach Village had both a midwife and an undertaker. "We had a lovely midwife," recalls Lydia Cullen, "I don't know whether she had any medical certificates but she was very busy bringing a lot of babies into the village. She always wore a great big white apron. She was a very plump woman and very kind and meticulous in her work. Her name was Mrs Osborne." "She was known as Granny Osborne," said her son 'Bimbo'. "She went about with her white apron and was at the birth of many of the babies on the Beach."

"If we were ill," remembers Jessie Hitter, "Mother used to give us syrup of figs or liquorice powder, dose us up with that. You used to have to pay for a doctor in those days, a pound every time he came." These were known as club doctors who, in the 1930s, charged two pence a week which covered you in case of illness, and one pound for the doctor to call. However, the Beach Village had its own cure for anyone with breathing difficulties. "People who found it hard to breathe used to come down to the Beach a lot, sometimes from abroad," remembers Ronny Wilson. "They came to smell those gasworks and that was supposed to make them breathe a lot better. They thought it would help to clear the chest."

According to Edward Capps-Jenner, in the early 1900s Gritsters had a particular way of showing that a residents was seriously unwell. "When a person was dangerously ill, straw was strewn on the road in front of the house and those adjoining to deaden the noise of the traffic. We boys knew that it meant we must also deaden our noise. My father [the coxswain] died of pneumonia and heart failure on 10th February 1901 after ten days of illness. His coffin was carried by boatowners into Christ Church for the funeral service."

When any resident was struck with illness it wasn't long before everyone on The Grit knew about it. In a small community, where everyone knew each other, births would be widely celebrated, while a death could cause the whole Village to grieve, such as the tragic case of Ronny Wilson's brother, Victor, who drowned in December 1927 when he was just 11 years old. Ronny recalls, "My brother and the boy Lark got drowned skating on a pond at the bottom of Fir Lane in Oulton Broad. My father told him not to go skating, but he got his skates and went."

(Opposite left) Sarah Jane Osborne was the Beach Village midwife. She had seven children herself and was known as Granny Osborne. She died on 3rd September 1953 at the age of 81.

(Opposite right) The Hammond family at the rear of their house in Jubilee Terrace. (Back row) Mrs Jane Hammond, Mr Harry Hammond, Charlie Miller, Jack Barber, Jane Hammond. (Middle row) Clifford Hammond, Alice Hammond, Mrs May Miller (née Hammond) with daughter May on her lap, Mrs Anna Barber (née Hammond) with son Lennie on her lap, Harry Hammond (Junior). (Front row) Lily Hammond, Lydia Hammond (now Cullen), Stella Hammond.

Lydia Cullen recalls another similarly sad incident, "I remember two young lads aged about 17 and 18, their name was Cracknell, and they lived near Christ Church. One afternoon they were riding about on their motorbikes and they had an accident. One was coming out of the car park at Battery Green and the other was going in. They collided and both were killed. It was a very tragic thing and I think the whole village mourned for a time."

Jack Moore remembers, "Flo Smith was very well known by the all the Beach people and did a particular service when someone died – she laid them out. That meant she washed and dressed them, ready for laying out in a coffin, so the family and friends could come in and pay their last respects. People like Mrs Smith helped make the Beach a self-contained place."

The Grit had its own undertakers, the Adams Bros, situated in Cumberland Place. "They were carpenters and undertakers," says Leonard Adams, whose grandfather and uncle ran this business. "On the 10 inch rafters that held the floor of the loft he would write in chalk all the nine day wonders that happened – wrecks, floods, etc – for all to see. His brother Richard

(Dick) was a bit of a lad in his young days, but he married a Salvationist who changed him and he finished up as a preacher at the Mission Hall in Chapel Street. As the people on the Beach were poor, most of the funerals were processed by the charity board (parish), so funerals that came their way were only about one every fortnight, although when they retired in 1931 they still had oak planks that had been bought by people for future coffins."

"I was born in 1919, at 13 Spurgeon Score," he continues. "My grandfather, with his son and war-widowed daughter, lived next door at No.11, my grandmother having died before I was born. My father was a carpenter, my mother was in service, and I had an elder brother. My father died when I was four years old… We were not allowed in the workshop when they had a coffin to rush through, but we did see enough through the window – how they cut and steamed the sides to bend them, boiled the pitch and rolled it inside as soil proofing,

Cumberland Place was a row of four houses recalled by Bob Wigg who lived at No 3, located on the west side of Whapload Road between Maltster's Score and Wilde's Score.

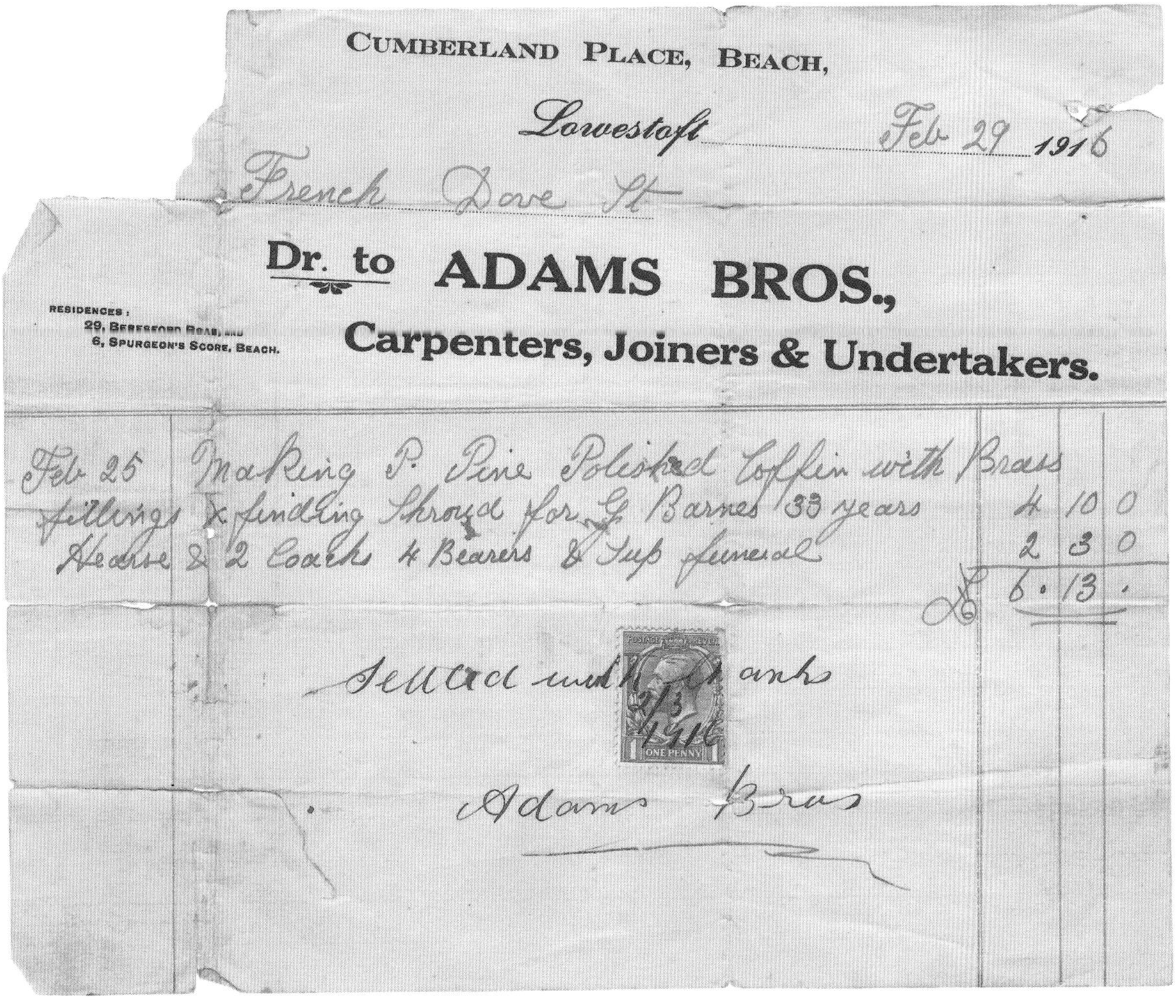

CUMBERLAND PLACE, BEACH,

Lowestoft Feb 29 1916

French Dove St

RESIDENCES:
29, BERESFORD ROAD, and
6, SPURGEON'S SCORE, BEACH.

Dr. to ADAMS BROS.,
Carpenters, Joiners & Undertakers.

Feb 25 Making P. Pine Polished Coffin with Brass
fittings & finding Shroud for G. Barnes 33 years   4 10 0
Hearse & 2 Coach 4 Bearers & Sup funeral   2 3 0
                                                  £ 6 . 13 .

settled with thanks
1916
Adams Bros

According to this Adams Bros. invoice from 1916, the price of a funeral was £6 and 13 shillings.

and filled the cushions with sawdust. We would be given the job of taking the plate to be written by Mr Rose in Police Station Road, and we would take a barrow with the stools to put the coffin on in the house if it was a long way from the yard. The hearse and horse were rented from Watling's in Clapham Road. We knew when they had been paid for a funeral – Grandad would look through his pockets to see if he has an odd ha'penny, the workshop would close, Uncle Dick would find a job at his Mission Hall, and Grandad would go to the *Gas House Tavern* or lifeboat shod and come back the worse for wear."

Fishermen were lost at sea every year – it was a risk they all faced – but the Beach community was strong and families stuck together. "My father's brother was going to be my mother's husband," says Lenny Norman, "but he was lost at sea so my Dad took over and married her instead. That's how it was then."

"There were three cottages in Spurgeon Score which had 70 young children between the three houses!" Mrs Rose Sansom tells us. "All the men went to sea. The man in the middle house was lost at sea and between the three houses they brought up these 70 children. This will tell you what Beach people were like. They were the salt of the earth. Generous-hearted and kind. The front door could be left unlocked all night without fear."

Large families would be crammed into small houses and one such example is illustrated by the Rose family who lived in Barcham Square off East Street. In the late 1800s this was home to two adults and 14 children, as a result of premature deaths and re-marriage. James Rose and Harriet Cone had married on 20th December 1858 and had four children – John William, Michael James, Emma Elizabeth and Henry George – but Harriet died on 4th October 1874 and James Rose remarried. His new wife was Ellen Ann Sheppard, née Reynolds, herself a widow with four children by her first marriage. They had a further six children together – Edward Francis, Celia Annie, Ellen Louisa, James Richard, Harry and Charles Samuel. The girls slept in one bedroom, full of straw, and the boys in another. On Friday night the old straw was burnt and replaced with a new load.

Mrs Jessie Hitter recalls, "We used to sleep tops and bottoms, with these big families. At the most there were three bedrooms in the houses on the Beach, and we were lucky because we had three. When we lived opposite Christ Church, the house had an attic and my mother got two beds up in the attic and all the younger boys used to sleep in one and all the girls in the other. My two brothers that went to sea were in one bedroom and my mother and father in the other one."

Benny Wilson lived near Ness Point Works, the premises of Rist's Wire and Cables, on Whapload Road. "In our family there were four girls and five boys. The house had four rooms, two up, two down." His brother George continues, "Four girls and five boys, we were sleeping head to toe, but that didn't mean a thing in those days."

"Our house was, for a family of four, small to say the least," says John Day, who was born in 1943 and brought up at 2 Canary Cottages, Whapload Road. "Even as a pre-teenager, I could lay on my back and my head would touch one wall while my toes reached the other wall and I could spring on the bed springs and touch the ceiling."

Yvonne Scriggins says, "My parents were married in 1926… they had eight children and as the Second World War approached, money, jobs and houses were scarce. With eight children to feed and clothe it was a struggle to say the least. Home for them was a two-bedroom house on Whapload Road."

Jean Mitchell came from a family with many Beach Village connections and was one of the last to leave the area in the 1960s. "I was born in 1933 and was nearly six when my father died at the age of 29 years and my mother and I, with my older sister and young brother, moved to the Beach. My mother was Jenny Prettyman and we lived with her family at 55 East Street, next to the Little Bethel. She had married my Dad, Henry Keable, in December 1928. All my uncles were fisherman – my mother's brothers Bob, Charlie, and Jack Prettyman – and all lived at 55 East Street till they married. Her sister May married

(Above) The Woodrow family who lived in Spurgeon Score and had 23 children.

(Right) The sisters Rose Sansom and Myrtle Porter lived in the house at the far end of this row in Newcombe Road. On the left is Albert Spurgeon's shod; at the end of the street is the shod belonging to Harris Allerton.

Sadie Springer and her sister Edie married 'Oxo' Coleman... First we lived at East Street next to the *Flowing Bowl*. Then, just after war broke out, we moved to 19 Wilde's Street. The house had three bedrooms, two downstairs room and a large wash house with a coal-fired copper and one cold tap with a bucket under it, no sink. We had an outside loo. Our house in Wilde's Street was very damp, with lots of mice, and flying ants in the hot months."

Jack Moore was born in 1929 at 66 East Street. "When people say they come from the Beach, I always ask them if they were born there. I mean lots of people came after the war, but I didn't class them as Beach people. I thought and I still do, that you have to be born in a place to claim the name of it. And like I say, I am a Beach boy and I was born there." Jack certainly came from an old 'Grit' family. "My Mum used to work in Rant Score at the box factory there, where they made the fish boxes. The brewery was one side, the box factory was the other side. My Dad was a fisherman, called Boono Moore. His father was a fisherman, his name was Sam."

"No 66 was a comfortable little house," Jack continues. "We used to say it was the most easterly house in England! That had three bedrooms, two bedrooms on the second floor, then they had an attic bedroom too. And when my Mum used to take in the fisher girls every year when the fishing season started, she used to take in three and they had the other bedroom and my brothers and I moved into the attic which was a great big bedroom. And that overlooked the sea, you could see right down the gasworks gap there and then right out to sea. And from there I used to watch the battles of the MLs and MTBs [motor launches and motor torpedo boats] and when the convoys went past. You could see it all from there."

Eric Horne spent his 1930s childhood at 4 Rant Score. "There were six houses in the terrace, with another two or three joined at a right angle. The kitchen had a cooking range (also used for heating), a brick copper with a fire underneath, and a double gas ring for hot water or cooking. Outside in the yard was the only tap, and the ancient lavatory. An old sink of sorts sat on bricks but was unplumbed and never used. Opposite the back door was the coal shed and mother's giant mangle."

Edward Capp-Jenner speaks for an earlier generation, having been born in 1887 and able to remember the Beach Village before the First World War. He wrote, 'In my youth none of the cottages on the Beach had WCs but were served by middens (a dungheap) and the scavenger's cart. This, although we were the nearest settlement to the Ness Point Sewer Outfall. It was usual for a row of cottages to share a water-tap in the yard. Often frozen in winter, of course, and thawed out by the first tenant needing water in the morning. It was firmly believed that to thaw a tap with hot water bursted the pipe.'

"I was born at 8 Rant Score East next door to the Jensens," recalls Joy Pearce. "Ours was a bit of a weird old house. It had a yellow stone sink just inside the kitchen door, and there was a cooking range in the kitchen. It had a little open fire in the living room. There were three rooms, and the front door opened onto the pavement."

Sheila Maye tells of the house where her father, William Almond, used to live. "William was born on 11th May 1908 and in 1912 the family moved to 3 Coleman Square. The house was tiny, two small rooms up and two down, with an outside lavatory. There was the luxury of gas light in the downstairs front room, but the rest of the stone-floored house was lit by candles and paraffin lamps. The small kitchen had an open coal fire, with an oven set in a wall beside it. All the family cooking was done there, including the twice-weekly bread making."

Billy Keith was born at 2 Cook's Buildings, "...near to Sayer & Holloway's fish-house on Whapload Road," he said. "The house had two down and four upstairs, but the bathroom where we had to wash was outside. In the winter we'd get the bath inside the house. We had a tap outside and a tap inside, but all the washing was done outside... I had four brothers and two sisters. My mother worked in a fish-house and my father was Scottish. He came from Peterhead and was the foreman in a smoker, Sayer & Holloway, and from there he went to Mummery's and then Arthur Easto. When I was about seven I had a mastoid, and Lowestoft's new ambulance came to get me. But they couldn't get me down the staircase, it was too narrow, so they had to take me out of the window."

Harriette 'Elly' Ellis (née MacKinnon) lived next door to the Keiths. She recalls, "I lived in Cook's Buildings. The Pitchers lived in one house, the Keiths the next one, and we were next door, and then there was the Francis family. Next to them were the Boardleys. I had two sisters and one brother. My father's family came from Fraserburgh in Scotland. He died when he was 37, and then my Mum married again. My grandfather lived in Cook's Buildings, and my grandmother's maiden name was Cook, the buildings belonging to her family. I used to take the rent down to them."

Benny Knights, born in 1909, lived in Nobb's Buildings, a row of 12 cottages along Whapload Road, near the Gourock ropeworks. Benny recalls, "We didn't pay any rent for 16 or 17 years because we lived in a condemned house. We had no back door, no sink. If you wanted to go to the toilet you'd have to go 20 yards across the road."

"We never used to bother to lock the door," remembers Leonard Boyce. "A lot of those little cottages were only tiny places, more like dolls' houses some of them. Broken-down places, very, very poor. Sometimes they never even bothered to shut the door, you could see right through."

As a child in the 1920s, Charles Oldman lived in Scarle's Buildings which were at the back of Mariners Score and ran parallel to it. These were a row of 15 cottages which were condemned by the council in 1935. "You wonder how you survived in a place like that," Charles says, "My mother's brother lived next door and at the back of each house where the stairs went up was a little window where they could talk to each other. There was a hole down between them, but you couldn't get out, it was all dark because of this building at the back, which was a fish-house, and the window used to blow rubbish down there, and you had to lower someone down to get it."

Dennis Leach also lived in Scarle's Buildings. "My family moved down there when I was four. We lived right on the corner, near the net store. There was another opening half way along Crown Score. There were a lot of cottages joined together, but for some reason ours was on its own. The one nearest to us, what we called our neighbours, housed Dick Songhurst and his family. You went straight out of our living room into the opening. There was a little kitchen behind and you went up some narrow little stairs to the two bedrooms. Our windows looked out into the net store. Now and again, if we were short of coal, we used to go and pinch the coal from the net store."

Other residents in Scarle's Buildings were the Ellis family. Charles remembers, "Scarle's Buildings was dead opposite the Steam Laundry. You only had one door into the house, which was at the back, and Gouldby's fish-yard was at the back of the row. You went to the door and down the yard, 30 or 40 yards, and there was a brick shed with a copper in it and that was where the washing was done. Let's face it, Scarle's Buildings were slums, there was no doubt about it. They were damp, you had a tap down the yard, lavatory down the yard, no electricity… I can remember old Harry Green lived next door, he lived alone but I tell you why I remember him, he had an alarm clock on a piece of rope instead of a watch. He used to carry this blasted thing about. For a time 'Puggy' Utting lived in Scarle's Buildings. He was a tramp really… a rag and bone man. He lived in the house but it wasn't much of a house. In this day and age it wouldn't be tolerated."

John Buck recalls, "We were all like a clan down there, we lived in groups, my aunts were in a large circle more or less. We lived in Vigilant Cottages which were just off the south end of Whapload Road. Just in our row of cottages we were all related. My uncle, Frank Bunn, lived at No 1, I lived in the middle with my Mum, Dad and one brother and two sisters, and my grandfather John Rose and my granny lived in No 3. My grandad was Jack Rose's grandfather's brother so, you see, my mother was a Rose. I think my granny had seven girls and one boy. Later on they moved from Vigilant Cottages to the Almshouses."

"After my father come out from the *Rising Sun* we went and lived in Jubilee Terrace for a little while. Boardleys lived in one near the church, we moved into the middle one and the Gowers were on the other end, next to Hammond's fish shop. We lived in four places on the Beach: Vigilant Cottages, the *Rising Sun*, Jubilee Terrace and in the row of cottages past Gibbs' later shop."

The Tucks lived at 27 Wilde's Street. Beryl Clover remembers, "You can't believe now that we could ever have lived there. Eight terraced houses were there, how they all fitted in I'll never know… This house had four rooms, the tap was in the yard, the toilet was outside, and we had a wash house where we had to do our washing. There was no water or electric indoors, we had gaslight."

"Of course, in those days there were no mod cons," says Ruby Timberley, "and mothers would spend all day on Mondays at the wash tub having lit the copper fire, which was in a brick shed, to heat the water. The washing was all done by hand with hard Sunlight soap and soda. The ironing was done with a flat iron, which was heated on the fire in the kitchen range. In those hard-up days there wasn't so much ironing because nobody had many changes of clothes. But there was a certain contentment. No-one had anything to steal, so doors could be left unlocked all day, stealing was unheard of in our area."

(Above) Vigilant Cottages were at the south end of Whapload Road near Canary Cottages. In the 1930s, John Buck's family in this row comprised his uncle Frank Bunn in the house on the left, John Buck and his parents in the centre, and John's grandparents, John and Harriet Rose, next door.

(Right) Jubilee Terrace was a row of three houses situated close to Christ Church. The Boardleys lived in the first, Matthew Boardley being one of four children. "This house had two numbers. We lived at 1 Jubilee Terrace or 69 Whapload Road!" Jubilee Terrace was demolished in the early 1990s when the site became part of the Lowestoft Cold Store.

Mr E J Day concurs, "Doors were seldom shut or locked. We weren't afraid then of being done over like today."

Jessie Hitter remembers, "Saturday night you used to have to wash the clothes ready for Monday morning, because we never had extra clothes. You'd have a Sunday frock, you used to put that away with your Sunday shoes. Put them away till the next week, you weren't allowed to wear them during the week. We used to have a big old copper outside in the wash house, used to burn the old boots and shoes. Then there was the old mangle you'd have to turn for your mother and the scrubbing boards which were used to scrub the fisherman's clothes when they came in from the sea. It was hard work. I'd take linen down to the Denes if it was a fine day and put a linen line between the net posts. You weren't afraid anyone would steal your sheets and they were down there all day, no-one ever went and stole your things."

Edward Capps-Jenner could also recall net-posts being used for linen, although there were unwritten rules. He wrote, 'The use of anybody's net-drying posts was assumed for linen lines and carpet beating if not occupied by nets, provided no line was left out after dark, most important. If one was left out, it would be found cut in the morning; one lady found her line cut in six pieces. Probably a bad offender but I bet that "larned" her. It was probably the result of someone, when running down to the lifeboat, being caught by the line and flung onto his back on a pitch black night.'

(Left) There were many Roses in the Beach Village. John Buck's grandparents were Harriet Ann Jemima and John Rose, here at the rear of the Almshouses. John was a Beachman and lifeboatman and was also Jack Rose's grandfather's brother.

"After the Scots girls had finished each year, we used the pickling plots as our drying ground," says Bert Prettyman. "If it was a nice day and for some reason your mother hadn't collected her linen when it was dry, it would be taken in and folded and brought to your house so that the next person could put hers up. Sometimes it would be ironed too, that's the sort of people we were."

Mondays were wash days at John Day's home. "It took all day to do the washing, drying, ironing and hanging up. We had a scullery with a coal fire under a massive metal cauldron which my mother filled with buckets from a tap in the back yard and I played being lost in the fog when the steam began spreading up from the bubbling waters. We had one of those heavy cast iron mangles and heaven only knows how my fragile mother used to wring out sheets and blankets on her own."

"Then there were bath nights," recalls Michael Duncan. "The long galvanised bath hung on the outside wall in the backyard, and had to be brought into the dining room, put in front of a blazing coal fire and filled with hot water. When my younger brother came along, it was quite a long job getting bath night out of the way. The coal-fired boiler in the kitchen used to work overtime supplying hot water for baths and washing clothes. I remember helping my mother on wash days by turning the handle on the mangle. If I remember rightly, she did most of the fisher girls' laundry and their bed linen."

Jessie Hitter remembers having a tin bath in front of the fire. "I used to bath all my kids on Saturday. You used to have to fill your kettle and saucepans up with water, and after I bathed them I used to fill it up with some warm water and kneel down and wash all the kids' school clothes ready for Monday morning. Nine o'clock I used to finish after that lot. I used to get the kids to bed after I bathed the four of them."

Norma Wilson was one of three sisters in their Wilde's Street home, "When one of us washed our hair, the others would run out and get the water. We used to clean our teeth outside because the drain was right in the middle of the backyard. Our Dad used to walk down to the lifeboat shed or one of the pubs while we had our wash, that was his excuse!"

Houses on The Grit began to have electricity for the first time in the 1930s, but previously there were paraffin table lamps or wall lamps and before that candles. Mrs Fisher (née Thurston) was born on 22nd July 1904 and she recalls, "I lived in a house on Whapload Road, at the bottom of Crown Score. It was a one up, one down, and had a little staircase with a candle at the top."

Miss George lived in Snowling's Buildings. "This was the row of houses near Christ Church which they pulled down when they built the Central School. They were little houses, one room downstairs, one room up. There were benches inside to sit on, and a water tap outside."

Joy Pearce grew up in the 1930s. She recalls, "We had the gaslight, and the mantles were ever so fragile. You had two chains, either side of the lamp, to regulate the light." John Day meanwhile seemed unabashed by this new technology. "I loved lighting the gas mantles which would pop up at times," John says, "and when our outside toilet got a flushing system, I played pulling the chain for hours."

Even when electricity was connected it was usually only partially, and the older residents were unsure and uncomfortable with it. Colin Dixon's grandmother lived at 4 Wilde's Street before she moved to Hopelyn Cottage, next to the Almshouses in 1941. "My grandmother's name was Katie Hull, her sister was Jessie Hitter and her brother was Tom Harper. Grandfather decided to have electricity put on the Wilde's Street house which cost him seven pounds and ten shillings. But that was only one main room with an ancillary room, the whole house wasn't electrified. There wasn't anything in the scullery, which was the kitchen, and we still went to bed with candles although we had electricity. One of the funniest things about Grandma was when she went to bed, she would pull the cord to turn out the light in the main room, what we'd call the lounge now, and she'd pull the cord but still blow at the same time as if to extinguish the last bit of gas that was coming out."

"Most families used oil lamps and candles," recalls Ruby Timberley, "but some had gas lamps although they couldn't afford to use them as they had to buy gas mantles. The streets were lit by gas in the 1920s. We had a gas light very close to us on the corner of Strand Street and Anguish Street. The lamplighter used a long pole and went to each street light in turn for the lighting-up time, returning in the morning to put the lights out. He seemed a solitary figure, seldom speaking to anyone."

In the 1930s, gas cookers could be hired from the gas board for a shilling a week and were a lot cheaper to run than electricity. Coal fires were used in all houses as anything could be got rid of by putting it on the fire. "I can remember the men with coal sacks," says Jean Mitchell, "on their head and shoulders, unloading the coal. We used to take a barrow and pick up all the bits they dropped. And every Friday we used to go and get a barrow of coke for about a shilling from the gasworks, which smelt terrible."

Money was still tight after the war, and in the early 1950s when Doris James was running the Kumfy Kafe, she had her own method of getting coal, "One of the drivers at the gasworks used to come in the café and sometimes he'd say 'I'm on duty this morning, just watch out,' and he used to swing round the corner and lumps of coal flew off and I used to run and pick them up!"

Poverty and hardship had always been part of the Beach Village life. In the 1930s there was no family allowance, social security or old people's homes. "My father was a fisherman," recalls Jessie Hitter. "He died young and left my mother with ten children. There was no relief then, and old man Jarrold came round and saw my mother and he say 'If you can't manage, put some of your boys in the home'. My mother say to him, 'While I've got a pair of hands to work, I'll work for my children', and she did. If they were hard up they used to pawn the old man's suit to pay the rent, used to go down Lark's, the pawn shop. They'd all run to the pawn shop to pay the rent with, if not they'd be turned out. But we weren't unhappy because everyone was poor the same. We weren't envious, no-one was jealous of one another then because none of us had anything."

Most of the people on the Beach used the pawn shop at some time, as Ronny Wilson remembers. "They'd pawn the old man's suit. Then we used to get paid a ha'penny to run

down to the market, have a look out to sea and see what boats were coming in. If you recognised one of the boats, you'd run and tell the woman and she would nip and get the old man's suit out of the pawn shop before he got in. There were no rows in the house that way."

"No-one had much money," Ruby Timberley agrees. "No state aid then. Mrs Burwood would sell one pennyworth of rice or pickles or other bits and pieces. Some women took in washing from better-off families to earn a few shillings. There was a Mr Buck, a cobbler, he was kept busy repairing the boots and shoes of neighbours. Our Dad mended all our boots, he had a last. For a shilling, we could buy a piece of good leather from a shop in the High Street, perhaps enough for two pairs of boots. Dad also cut our hair and Mum's. We all had a basin put on our head to get the shape and boys and girls ended up with a fringe."

Being the main produce of the area, fish was the staple food in all the homes on The Grit. "My grandfather would say, 'Go down the market and ask for my fish'," says Leonard Boyce, who was brought up at the *East of England* public house. "Prime fish it was, anything, whatever he wanted. Of course, Ayers, being part-owner, said he could have it – they used to throw it at you nearly."

Jack Moore also recalls hard times. "Sometimes Mother ran out of money when Dad was away and what we used to do was get some fish for our dinner. We had several different methods of getting her some fish. First one – we used to go down and annoy the Scots girls by running along the barrels and kicking the bungs out. And as we ran along they used to throw herring at us. And we'd pick them up and take them home for tea. Another method was down the market where they unloaded the fish, anything that fell out of the baskets as they unloaded was fair game, you were allowed to pick it up, no-one stopped you. Any fish that dropped out of the fish baskets was there to be taken. Just take what you want and get away with it. Another method – now you might think this was illegal... Jones' fish-house was opposite us. Next to the fish-house was the Bethel. In between the Bethel and the fish-house was an opening. And you know the smoke houses had no top of them, so the smoke could

(Left) Nos 4 and 6 Wilde's Street. Colin Dixon's grandmother, Katie Hull, lived at No 4 until she moved to Hopelyn Cottage, and Miss Adams lived at No 6.

(Right) Looking up Anguish Street circa 1900. The row of houses on the near right of the photograph was where the Dalleys lived at No 4, next door to the *Suffolk Fishery Tavern* on the corner. Buck's shoe repair shop occupied the small building where the crowd of people are standing. The premises which would become Moss's sweet shop is on the next corner.

(Left) Ruby Timberley (née Dalley) with her family at a Christ Church outing to Corton in 1931. Standing at the back (left to right) Ruby, Lionel and May. At the front, Jack and Claude on the lap of his mother, Lydia Constance.

(Right) T Jones & Son fish curers were near to East Street. By the 1960s they were in business for the third generation.

go right out of the top there. Well, when my Mum used to run out of money, my brother Stanley (my middle brother), he used to go up that wall till he come to the open top. He'd sit on the wall, fill a bag and come down. Now, no-one bothered with that, even the fish-house people. They'd often send a boat back out and dump all the fish. Or put them in a truck and dump them on the land for fertiliser. They took it for granted that no-one complained about that, so no-one bothered when people helped themselves to the fish. That weren't classed as illegal, they just done it. And it always got us a feed."

Charles Ellis recalls, "In those days they used to bring home as much fish as they could carry and even if you hadn't got a lot in the house, it wouldn't be long before someone was round with a cracked plate, with three or four cod or skate, saying, 'Mum says we've got too much fish, would you like any of this?' and you'd got a couple of dinners there for everybody in the house, beautiful fresh fish. That sort of thing happened. I remember my father worked at Maconochie's who used to make sweets, and he used to bring jars of broken sweets home. All the kids used to come down to my house before they went to school and they'd all get a handful of sweets."

Michael Duncan grew up in Wilde's Street, next door but one to the *Gas House Tavern*, until the 1953 flood. I remember luxuries were very few and far between, but one thing we did have for tea was chocolate spread. It was my responsibility with my sister to set the table and clear away and wash up afterwards. Once when I went to the pantry to get the chocolate spread out, whoever had put it away after use had left the top off. A mouse had gotten onto the shelf and into the tub and all I could see were its hind legs and tail. The mouse was stuck and dead."

"A friend of mine was ill," recalls Hazel Boardley, "so my mother said, 'Take her this egg custard,' and when I ran in with it, her mother said, 'Quick, I've just sent my little boy to get an egg and I shan't need it now,' and I had to run after this boy to stop him spending the money. It could only have been a penny-ha'penny but she couldn't afford to spend it."

(Above) A Beach reunion at Jack Rose's retirement party in 1991. (Left to right) Billy Keith, Jack Reynolds, Jack Rose and Gus Jensen.

(Left) Beyond the *Gas House Tavern* were Nos 19 to 33 Wilde's Street. No 19, where Jean Mitchell's mother lived, can be seen on the far left at the end of the row, while Vernil Tuck and his family lived at No 27 which is the house with the white door in the centre.

"After the war my mother used to work in a fish-house to help feed and clothe us," Jean Mitchell remembers. "We often used to buy two penn'th of seconds (kippers) for our tea, and at Slater's boneyard we used to buy six penn'th of chitlings." Jean was born and bred on The Grit, meeting her husband, Brian, at the Coastal Boys' Club which had been started in the Little Bethel by Charlie Curtiss in 1948. "We married in 1951," explains Jean, "when my husband went into the RAF to do his two years' National Service. We carried on living with my mother and brother at 19 Wilde's Street... Almost a year after our daughter was born, we were able to buy our first house at 8 Wilde's Street. My husband was out of the RAF by then and as he had qualified as a bricklayer and plasterer before going into the RAF, he was working in the building trade with Leighton's in Belvedere Road. We bought the house for £175 from Tom Battrick who had a shoe shop in the High Street. He let us pay him at £1 a week. He didn't charge us interest but used to get Brian to do little repairs for him. It was a two-bedroomed house, with a front room, middle room and a tiny kitchen with a sink and cold tap. The toilet was outside in a yard shared with two ladies, the Adams sisters. We moved from the Beach to Europa Road in about 1965 when a compulsory purchase was put on our cottage for which we received £350, so we made 100% profit on it. By now most of the people had been moved for the development of Birds Eye."

Since the end of the Beach Village in the 1960s, an almost mythical status has been given to the area and many, who have no knowledge of The Grit and its people, seem to imagine it as a cosy fishing village with picturesque cottages. It was the people who made the place unique, and the indomitable spirit of the Beach community is still very much alive and in evidence in the surviving Gritsters. In 1993 the first of many Beach Reunions was held, arranged by Bert Prettyman. It was a well-attended gathering of old friends, many of whom had not seen one another since the outbreak of the Second World War, but who still shared this bond, a friendship unbroken by the intervening years. What brings these people together? Why was the Beach Village so special? "There was more spirit than today," says Charles Ellis. "The Beach community had the spirit and when you think of the Depression in the 1930s, that was a depression, and they needed that spirit all right."

"They say about the good old times, well, they were good times, but they weren't good in some ways," admits Lenny Norman. "Money was so scarce. I can remember people going to sea for weeks on end, and coming back with nothing. The Beach Village was a community of good people, everyone helped each other."

"Beach people loved one another," explains Harry Harper. "If someone was ill they cared, they'd help you, take your washing in and iron it for you. They were like that."

"You look back now," says Billy Keith, "and think, 'How did they survive with all the work they did?' but it was entirely different to what it is now. Everybody knew each other and it was a community, the friendship was greater than it is today. You try to compare it, but it was just so different."

Aerial view of the Beach Village circa 1967. The Birds Eye complex of factories is spreading northwards towards the net drying posts. St Peter's Court (top left), Lowestoft's 15-storey high-rise, is under construction.

The plan was to rehouse Beach residents in the tower block but it wasn't completed until 1968 and most families had moved by then. The new Fishermen's Almhouses on Church Green was the only housing scheme offered.

14. GRIT RISING

It's 2019 and I'm adding a new chapter to the book.
Times have changed. People are living on The Grit again.
They're building houses, converting old net stores into flats.
New industries too – the biggest wind turbine in the country...
from *PEARLS FROM THE GRIT* (2018)

Brian Springer was born in 1941 and is one of the last generation of 'Gritsters'. Brian says, "I come from two big families. My Dad was a fisherman, he didn't come from Lowestoft, he came from Milford Haven. He met mother during the War when he was posted to Lowestoft in the minesweepers. My mother was the youngest of 16. But they didn't all survive. Her maiden name was Prettyman. All big families. Well, they didn't have television did they!"

Interviewed in 2019, Brian is surprised when other Beach Village residents question it being known as 'The Grit'. "An old boy say to me, he must be 90 now, he say, 'Why do they call that The Grit now?' I say, that's always been that. He say, 'That weren't called that when I was down there.' That was! People who live up the town, they'd say 'He's off The Grit'. Sometimes I was called a sand-chomper too!"

Another former 1930s East Street resident, Jack Moore, verifies: "That was called The Grit. That had several different names. That was known as the Beach, the Beach Village, the Town Under the Cliff. But The Grit was one of the names."

Talking on a BBC Radio Norfolk interview at the time of the publication of the first edition of *The Grit* in November 1997, Jack Rose explained the reason for the name. "Why was it called The Grit? Well sand is grit int'it? And there were a lot of unmade roads. And you needed a lot of grit to live there! All the old people used to say The Grit, those that lived when the fishing was gorn' strong before the First World War."

It is now 20 years since Jack died and half a century since the clearance of The Grit in the late 1960s. Jack remained angry about the loss of the Beach Village all his life. In the same radio interview, he said, "With all this here lot coming down in the sixties, they demolished what would have been the biggest tourist attraction, all the old fishing houses, all the old cottages. They done themselves more harm by pulling them down, than by keeping them up, because they could have been done up, in their original form."

Jack had said so back in the 1960s and wasn't alone in his dismay at the time. Outspoken architectural journalist and TV broadcaster Ian Nairn gave a lecture in the town at the *Royal Hotel*. Nairn praised the old cottages in the Beach Village and described Whapload Road as having a 'honky tonk vitality'. He went on to say that The Grit was the only part of Lowestoft which was really worth saving.

(Top) Anguish Street leading to Rant Score East. Hugh Lees heard there were plans to retain this road and wrote, 'So now we have come to the corner of Rant Score East, this alone of all the streets leading off Whapload Road will remain when the development takes place.' It is now the site of the Birds Eye factory.

(Bottom) In the Lowestoft Archaeological & Local History Society report in 1967–68, Hugh Lees wrote, 'Next came the Fishermen's Hospital Houses (Almshouses). These were built in 1838 with two additional ones added in 1907. Several stone plaques were removed in 1964 and placed on the new Almshouses erected near St. Margaret's Church, which replace those on the Beach pulled down 14th February 1968.'

It seems that some of those in power had agreed with Nairn, and it was stated in the East Suffolk Planning Act that some of the cottages in the fishing village should be preserved as an example of their distinctive architecture. But by 1970 it was too late and it became clear there were no plans in place to save any of The Grit on the east side of Whapload Road.

During the clearance of the area in 1966/7 there were still some hopeful rumours that a few properties might be saved or even rebuilt. 'Only the *Rising Sun* remains at least for the time being,' wrote Hugh Lees in 1967, 'for this too is to be pulled down and rebuilt, being set back several feet upon a new building line. Whatever goes up in its place, it will never have the atmosphere of the old *Rising Sun*.'

New industries would need big lorries and Whapload Road would need widening – another reason why many of the houses facing onto the east side of the road were demolished. Any hopes of the last of the 13 pubs being rebuilt quickly faded, although lifeboatman Jack Stoddart did manage to keep a small part of the *Rising Sun* alive. Before demolition work started, Jack removed the exact section of the bar where he used to stand and had it fitted into his house in St Margaret's Road!

In the early 1960s Edward Capps-Jenner, born in 1889 and son of the lifeboat coxswain, had written an account of his life on the Beach Village. Ten years later he added one last paragraph before his death in 1974. 'Every formerly occupied house east side of Whapload Road has now, May 1972, been demolished. Nelson Road is now completely obliterated. And so the Beach of my recollection is no more and will shortly be obliterated altogether by very desirable commercial development and not even the streets and roads will be discernible. The houses were very largely bad and unfit for human habitation by any modern standard. I do not weep for it as much of it had served its turn.'

By 1970 both The Grit and the herring industry had gone. Families who had lived and worked there for generations had gradually been leaving since the Second World War, although many remained until the end of the 1960s. And they left to be scattered around the town. In the mid-1970s Anne Barratt was studying the Beach Village community for her PhD and spoke to the area's Housing Manager to ask him about the rehousing policy of Beach residents which been carried out by the council. Anne wrote, 'He said there had been no plans to rehouse the Beach people together, they had in fact been put into houses as

(Bottom left) October 1967 and children had rich pickings on bonfire night as the *Gas House Tavern* and Cumberland Square are the latest Beach Village properties to fall. In the background, the North Beach Bethel is still standing – but not for long.

(Middle) With rubble cleared and new roads laid, a new decade and whole new era began. Ron Rushmere was one of the first to secure a plot of land for his DIY supplies business.

they had been built... The only rehousing scheme, he said, which had been carried out with the people in view had been the building of the new Fishermen's Almshouses on Church Green. Rehousing was a big problem at the time and the Housing Manager and the County Welfare Officers did not consult each other.'

There had been an idea that St. Peter's Court, the new modern block of flats in north Lowestoft, could rehouse many Beach Village families. But it wasn't ready in time and the scheme fell through, although some Beach people still ended up there when the flats were finally completed in 1968.

The last house Brian Springer and his family lived in on The Grit was in Wilde's Street. Brian says, "That house was never condemned, it was compulsory purchased. I left in 1963 and I was still 21. When we moved out of 5 Wilde's Street, someone else moved in, after us. By the time we'd left, they had started to pull down a lot of the houses."

"Several of the old Beach families moved up to the Gunton estate. But they weren't all in one heap together, they were in several different roads. Some went the other end of the town. All over they went. Family was alright, cos you'd go visit them. But neighbours, you'd only speak to them if you saw them in the town. There was never any get together. Not for years."

But never doubt the enduring community spirit of The Grit. In the new century the Beach Village has found a new home – a virtual one, online, on Facebook. Created in June 2017 by Lucy Martin and Terry Down, just two years later the group has more than 1,300 members all over the world. It's an opportunity to share photographs and memories and update stories since the 1960s. In 2019 it's been possible to ask the last generation of Gritsters …

WHERE DID YOU LIVE? WHERE DID YOU GO & WHY?

SUE ARMES

"We lived at 7 Wilde's Street and moved to Rosevine Villa, Whapload Road after the floods. My great Aunt, Ann Burwood, had previously lived at that address. Then in 1966 we moved to Montgomery Avenue. My Grandparents and Uncle lived in Darby Villa, Anguish Street, next to the *Gas House Tavern*. They were Herbert James, Susan James and their son, who was also called Herbert James. Both the men were called 'Darby' by everyone. Uncle Darby lived there till about 1965 and moved to a flat off Normanston Drive. I now live in Tasmania, Australia."

TREVOR BOWDITCH

"My wife and I plus baby were moved from 53 East Street to a maisonette in Telesia Court. Council rehousing, 1964. My memory was the tide mark that bled through the wall paper, picture rail height, on the damp on cold days. Reminds me of those floods in 1953."

GAEL BOYNTON

"Mrs Ethel Ridgeway of 44 Whapload Road, forced out due to compulsory purchase order, moved to Montgomery Avenue. I remember the yard, it was tiny,and the smell of carbolic soap. My Aunt told me the night of the flood they had to climb out of the bedroom window and get on the roof. It was a dear little house, we spent many a happy hour there. I remember walking around the Beach Village and seeing all the empty houses. At the time I didn't realise the significance of this village. It's only as I got older that the full impact of what happened there hit me."

AMANDA CALLAIS

"We lived at No. 3 Newcombe Road. My maiden name was Harris. I moved away to Germany but my parents and brothers and sisters stayed. I now live in Florida. It was Bethel House, had 3 floors, 2 attic rooms then second floor with its own bathroom and kitchen so could be used as a flat. My Nan and Grandad came to live with us there from London, we lived on the first floor. Had an outside bathroom when we moved in but my Dad converted it to a inside one later. No frontyard to speak of but a big back yard, there was some kind of workshop above some our backyard, had to enter through big double doors. We used the underneath of it for storage and a play yard. I remember it was creepy coming home at night (no light under there)."

JOHN DAY

"We lived at 2 Canary Cottages, Whapload Road. After the flood the water never left. We got bumps coming through the plaster. The Health & Housing came down, put their little rods in the bubbles which broke and all the water was still in the walls. And I can remember the people coming in, knocking the plaster off and spraying something on it to try and stop the damp. Then we started getting rats, I can remember chasing them out into our little backyard, where they used to run along the fence and up to the roof of the toilet. We still lived there though, I didn't leave until 1958 when I joined the RAF and my mother didn't leave until the 1960s, when she moved to Council property in Lorne Park Road."

TERRY DOWN

"My parents bought No 4, Dunedin House, in 1934 and had to leave in 1968 due to Council muppets putting a demolition order on those fine-built homes. I still have the cast iron name plate on my house, here in New Zealand where I emigrated to in 1962."

PAM FINCH

"My husband David Finch lived at Cumberland Place until the 1953 floods with his Grandad, Uncle and his Mum and then was moved to 393 Whapload Road where his Mum lived until she passed away in 1982. We moved to Kent in 1965 after our marriage in October 1964. Nobody lived in the house in Cumberland Place after the floods because it was too badly damaged. 393 Whapload Road is still standing. It's on the road, at the bottom of Lighthouse Score."

TINA HOLMES

"Paternal grandparents, Arthur Knights ('Pop'), born 1 Seaview Cottages, East Street, Beach and Emma Maud Waller, born 2 Nobbs Buildings, Whapload Road. My Dad, Frederick William Knights (Freddy or Bill), was born in Spurgeon Street, my Mum, Molly Ora Eveline Curtis was born in 24 Old Nelson Street. As far as I know they all came off the Beach after the 1953 flood. Paternal family went to St Peters Street. Nanny lived on Long Road for years."

BARRIE HORTON

"We lived at 65 East Street. The house/cottage had three tiny bedrooms with a front room, middle room and a kitchen. I remember the house being narrow but long and we had a mangle over a fire burner at the back of the house. We moved out in 1967/8 as the whole area was being demolished. We were one of the last families to leave. We then moved to Clapham Road (demolished in the 1970s), approximately where the DHSS is now."

The junction of Whapload Road and Wilde's Street in the 1960s. The two houses on the right are Sadie Villa and Darby Villa. Brian Springer said, "Sadie Villa had three rooms downstairs but the kitchen was really small. More like a scullery. And two up with an attic. But you couldn't use the attic very much cos the floors weren't that good."

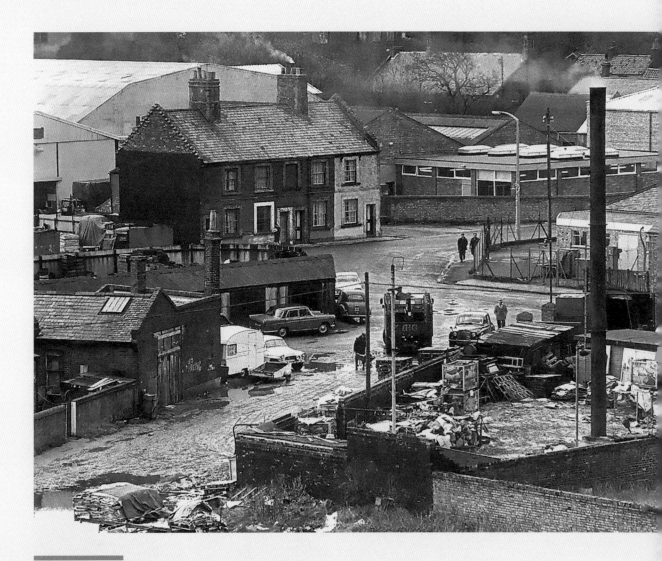

Whapload Road and Crown Score in 1966. In the distance, the white house on the corner of Crown Score was home to Mr and Mrs Boon. Daughter Gillian remembers, "We had a backyard with a coal-house and outside toilet. Tin bath and mangle too. A weekly bath was taken in front of the fire or in the kitchen."

LEE HUGMAN

"My parents lived in No 3 Vigilant Cottages, Whapload Road. They moved to Breydon Way in 1962, to a new-build house, climbing up the property ladder."

GILLIAN READ

"Mr & Mrs Boon and family lived at 177 Whapload Road and had to move because a compulsory purchase order was served and moved to 33 Marham Road. Our house was on the corner of Crown Score and the row was demolished in the 1960s when Birds Eye took over and built on the land. The front room had been partitioned off to make a hallway, with stairs leading up to three bedrooms."

JOY M RUSSELL

"My Nan, Grandad, Mum, Aunts and Uncles, were the 'Dells' and all lived at 52 Whapload Road Next to the *Rising Sun*. They moved to Northgate in 1963-ish due to industrialisation. My Mum remembers years after the flood having an explosion in the house due to the salt water eating away at the wires. She remembers my Nan pointing out that dogs would yelp walking past the lamp-post outside when it rained and it would always dry up faster near it than anywhere else."

SANDRA SMITH

We lived at No 1 Newcombe Road, the first house in the row. My maiden name was Sandra Ball. Our family lived in the top flat. George Anthony in the bottom. When George moved my Uncle Billy (Parker) took the bottom one. We lived there around 1945. I was born there in 1947, so was my sister in 1955. We moved out when they got pulled down. My daughter was born there in 1967, so it was a couple of years later when we had to leave and moved to Europa Road and then to Texas."

STEVE WARD

"We lived at 4 Wilde's Street from 1961 to 1964. My Dad, Jack Woodard, worked at Churchman's Fat & Bone company. Mr Churchman lent my Dad the money (£850) to buy his first house which was 155 The Avenue. We moved to The Avenue in 1964. My dad stayed at Churchman's for a little while longer until he moved on to be a long-distance lorry driver with Bowell & Harper of Fnstone Road."

HEATHER WELHAM

"My mother was born at Norfolk House, Newcombe Road in 1910 so my grandparents must have lived there prior to that. They moved to Seago Street during the Second World War. Their names were Frederick and Caroline Hobart. My Grandmother's maiden name was Breach. I can remember my mum talking about Ned Ellis who lived in the same row. The Breaches in Hastings House were relations. Mum worked there and referred to 'Uncle Jack'. She also worked at The Shoals."

NORMA WILSON

"We lived at 27 Wilde's Street. I left in 1963 when I got married and my parents Vernil and Florence Tuck moved, when the houses were demolished, to Lighthouse Score. Being a lifeboat man this was the closest they could get him so he could still bike down to the lifeboat."

ALAN YOUNGMAN

"I lived in Nelson Road, right opposite the Church. Ethel Cottage that was called. We moved there just after the 1953 flood. My father worked for Jones fish merchant and Jones owned Ethel Cottage so the house came with the job. We were there from 1954 to about 1967, right to the end. They pulled them down after that. We moved to Telesia Court. It was like a palace for my Mum. All our neighbours up Gunton Estate were from the Beach."

It's easy to think that the Beach Village has all gone because of the clearance of the east side of Whapload Road and all of the surrounding streets. However, the Scores, the net stores, the net posts and some houses do still remain and their preservation is essential. There can be no excuse to lose these vital visible links with the town's heritage.

Being on the west side of Whapload Road meant that Hastings House remained standing into the 1970s, but with the spread of new industrial buildings, its demise was imminent. Billy Whybrow remembers, "The house never recovered from the '53 flood. Up to about three or four feet of the plaster on the whole bottom floor had to be taken off. But the damp got into the bricks. They replastered it, but you couldn't keep paper on the wall, you couldn't keep paint on the wall. It was a continual effort to decorate it. All that brickwork got salt in it and decayed. And I think that was the main reason they pulled it down." His brother Bob agrees, "I remember my Dad putting tar on the walls and then put on anaglypta paper and then gloss paper but it still came off, didn't it."

Jack Moore has a longer memory of the Beach Village in the 1930s, but he doesn't blame the floods for The Grit's demise. He takes a different view. "It wasn't the flood that ruined the Beach because they'd had floods all their life. They were used to them. The Council wanted the place for Birds Eye. That was the reason the Beach Village got destroyed and everything was pulled down to make way for people like Birds Eye. Big money spoke louder than keeping the little places."

The 1970s saw the regeneration of the Beach Village into the Beach Industrial Estate and for the remainder of the 20th century, Birds Eye were one of the biggest employers in Lowestoft. 70 years since the company's arrival in Lowestoft, the Birds Eye factory now

(Left) The Whybrow family, outside Hastings House in the early 1950s. (Left to right) Mr Chilvers, Mrs Chilvers, unknown, Emy Chilvers, Arthur Howell, Laura Whybrow, unknown, and on the right, Bill Howell, Harry Chilvers and Whiskey the dog. Standing at the front is Bill Whybrow next to Gertrude Howell (holding Robert Whybrow).

(Right) The last generation of Beach boys – David Perrett, Peter Davis and Norman Bucknole on Christ Church Green in 1964 with Mr Grieve's shop in the background.

By the 1960s the Belfast Ropeworks would be neighbours to Birds Eye for not much longer. Where once Whapload Road had been the home for fishermen in caps or fisher girls in shawls and headscarves, in the 1960s Whapload Road was full of men in white coats and trilby hats walking between Birds Eye's many premises.

covers a 26-acre site and produces 450 tonnes of frozen produce everyday, including frozen peas, battered fish and chicken dippers.

In the 21st century, the most easterly point has become a centre for renewable energy, as symbolised by the arrival of a new iconic landmark. Where once you could identify The Grit by the gasworks, the lighthouse or the spire of Christ Church, an impressive wind turbine dominates the skyline. A competition in the *Lowestoft Journal* resulted in the name of 'Gulliver' and it took just four days to erect before the turbine was up and running at 6pm on Friday 10th December 2004. Standing 126 metres (413 feet) tall it was officially the tallest wind turbine in UK and commercially the first of its kind in Suffolk, producing 2.75MW of electricity, enough to supply over 1,500 homes.

Gulliver was soon followed by the arrival of the £9.4 million Orbis Energy Centre, which opened in November 2008. The five-storey building was built at an angle to maximise daylight, using recycled or recyclable materials where possible. The 'most easterly office building in the UK' was constructed with a raised first storey – on stilts – to cope with possible floods caused by sea level rises in the future. Just over 10 years later the building houses 62 businesses including major wind farm developers SSE and Scottish Power Renewables and other support companies. The energy industry has certainly put down roots in the town.

What other comings and goings has the area of The Grit seen since this book was first published in 1997? New housing has been built on Whapload Road and the Homeport development was the first of these early in the 21st century, with some of the properties incorporating an old flint and brick wall. A social housing project, Homeport, was aiming to build a small community living in a modern day 'square'.

It seems incredible that Gibbs', the last original Beach Village shop, was still open for business well into the early 2000s, over 70 years after it opened in 1931. Iris Gibbs died in 2008 and No 283 Whapload Road was demolished and three more social housing properties were built in its place, again with a raised first storey to accommodate flooding.

And more recently, in 2018, work began to convert and refurbish Lancaster Place into 18 apartments. Formerly a net store, the property has undergone many extensions and alterations over the years, with some of the oldest parts of the building dating back to the mid-17th century. Now luxury apartments, Lancaster Place is described as 'a stone's throw from the beach' having 'balconies with sea views'. Living on The Grit has become desirable!

Leisure and tourism have always sat alongside industry on The Grit. Sparrows Nest Gardens and a swimming pool were once built next door to the net posts and pickling plots. And in 2019, right next to Birds Eye, there's to be a new park called The Ness. This wide strip of green land will lead to Ness Point, and the ambition is to make this most easterly location in the UK as popular with tourists as Land's End and John O'Groats. As well as maintaining the area's existing wildlife and unique flora and fauna, The Ness will have a play and picnic area and, it is hoped, will become a vibrant space for arts, education and heritage events. By celebrating the history of the Denes, The Ness will also help to secure the future of the net drying racks.

(Left) GritFest filled Sparrows Nest Gardens in May 2018 as over 2,000 people of all ages came together to celebrate the Beach Village.

(Middle) An exhibition featuring photos from The Grit drew crowds to the main marquee.

(Right) 'I won't forget Lowestoft's Beach Village' was across the True Grit on-stage banner. The Strumming Seagulls were one of the local groups who performed on the bandstand.

These days tourism and heritage are ever more closely linked, as vividly demonstrated by the popularity of the first GritFest in May 2018 which was part of the year-long Grit project funded by the National Lottery Heritage Fund and run by Poetry People. GritFest drew over 2,000 people to Sparrows Nest Gardens and was opened by Lowestoft-born BBC broadcaster Zeb Soanes with some specially-written Grit News Headlines. A free programme of events included live music, group activities (GritKnit, GritQuilt), heritage talks, archive films from the Lowestoft Movie Makers, and a special Grit exhibition in the main marquee. The lighthouse was opened to the public by Trinity House for the first time in many years and there were demonstrations from the International Boat Building Training College and the Excelsior Trust. GritFest involved 20 local businesses including traditional smoked and wet fish food stalls. Zeb Soanes tweeted, "What a wonderful community event @LowestoftGrit is! A celebration of Lowestoft's lost fishing village and our town's rich character and heritage. So lovely to be a part of it."

Rich evidence of the fishing industry can be found in the Lowestoft & East Suffolk Maritime Museum in Sparrows Nest Gardens which also houses the Royal Naval Patrol Service and Lowestoft War Memorial Museums. The Heritage Centre in Wilde's Score has an interactive 1930s model of the Beach Village, built by Nigel Purdy in 2003/4 and added to in 2016. "It shows just how much was down there and brings it all to life," says Nigel. "People who lived on the Beach Village are proud to say that's where they come from."

(Left) The Beach Village 1930s model, in the Heritage Centre, showing Whapload Road and the Almshouses.

(Below) The Beach Village model was built by Nigel Purdy and measures 3.6m x 2.7m, has interactive features including rocking steam drifters, moving trams and lights from the houses and gas lamps.

(Above) Happy Welham (David Redgrave) takes to the stage during *Pearls from The Grit* to re-enact the night he won a barrel of ale at a singing contest at The Hippodrome on 9th November 1905.

(Right) Blundeston Primary Year 5 visited the Lowestoft Maritime Museum as part of The Grit project in November 2017. As one 10 year old boy said, 'It makes me feel that Lowestoft is a very special place.'

Over the last 50 years, many new names have been attached to the place. It's still called the Beach Industrial Estate although that seems to have been superceded by the aspirational 'PowerPark' which unites The Grit with Hamilton and Waveney Dock. It's also known as 'the most easterly point', Ness Point and now there's a new park christened, The Ness. In the old days it was the Beach, the Beach Village, The Grit or the Town Under the Cliff. Like a fisherman with many nicknames, it will answer to any of them!

In 2019 one of the oldest living Gritsters, Jack Moore, says: "When people say they come from the Beach, I always ask them if they were born there. I mean lots of people came after the war, but I didn't class them as Beach people. I thought, and I still do, that you have to be born in a place to claim the name of it. And like I say, I am a Beach Boy and I was born there." One of the last who can lay claim to this is David Finnigan, born 2nd January 1964 at 52 Whapload Road next door to the *Rising Sun*. His family moved out soon after and he has no memory of living there but is proud to say he is a true Beach Boy. The Beach people who can remember the village and the fishing industry are now in their late sixties and older and becoming few and far between.

Brian Springer's father Sadie had a Beach Village house named in his honour. "I was born in East Street, then we moved from there to No 2 Cumberland Square and then to 5 Wilde's Street and that was what they called Sadie Villa. That belonged to Gus Jenson. When Gus done them up, he asked us and the James family, if we minded calling these two houses Sadie Villa and Darby Villa (after Darby James). And that's what he called them, they had a plaque over the house."

Interviewed in 2019, Brian said, "I still walk down there. Not every week. On the sea wall on a Sunday maybe, and walk through where the gasworks is. Look at my old plot where I used to live. Pass the old *Flowing Bowl*. I can picture it all. When my stepson come to visit he say, 'Can we go and have a look at that new windmill?' I say, 'If you want.' We were driving along where East Street was, so I say, 'Hang on Gary, stop the car.' He say, 'Why do you want to stop here for?' I say, 'So we can go and have a pint.' That's where the *Gas House Tavern* used to be!"

Lowestoft heritage and industry side by side – Gulliver, Birds Eye and the net drying posts on 24th March 2019, the day the Excelsior Trust took the sails of their famous ship to be dressed on the historic site now called The Ness.

THE GRIT RISING

You may think we're history
long-lost village by the sea
like dust beneath your boots
but between you and me

board up all the windows, but like the sun we'll rise.

Dunwich is more romantic
church bells chimin' neath the sea
we had three churches n'thirteen pubs
an' we're talking recent history

board up all the windows, empty all the houses
but like the sun we'll rise.

Bombs dropped around the gasworks
a flood tried to push us orf
but the council went and finished the job
all those memories lorst

board up all the windows, empty all the houses
dig up all the roads, but like the sun we'll rise

It's not our fault the fishing's gorn
We worked right hard night and day
They built new houses round the town
old families moved away

board up all the window, empty all the houses
dig up all the roads, scatter all the people
but like the sun we'll rise.

I'll tell yer where this village was
you won't find much left there
a turbine marks the spot
and there's something in the air

board up all the windows, empty all the houses
dig up all the roads, scatter all the people
turn the place to rubble, but like the sun we'll rise.

DEAN PARKIN, from *PEARLS FROM THE GRIT* (2018)

CHRONOLOGY

1400–1800 EARLY HISTORY

1400
During the reign of King Henry IV (1399-1413) fairs and markets at Lowestoft were held below the cliff.

1500-1600S
A row of fish-houses was located at the bottom of the cliff, connected by paths or 'scores' to the fish merchants at the top.

1624
The town's first low light, lit by candles, stood at the bottom of Swan Score (now Mariners Score). Another structure – a 40 feet high and 20 feet round, brick and stone lighthouse – would be built in 1676.

1644
10th March, 'a great and terrible fire which consumed dwelling houses, fish-houses, and goods' as stated by Edmund Gillingwater in his *An Historical Account of the Ancient Town of Lowestoft in the County of Suffolk* (1790).

1650
Large iron coppers stood out on the Denes, in which cod livers were boiled to extract the oil.

1717
Another sudden fire broke out, destroying fish-houses belonging to Captain Josiah Mighel.

1735
The first movable timber low light was erected on the Beach. It was replaced in 1779.

1737
King George II landed on the north beach in January, having been forced ashore by a storm at sea.

1750
Beach Companies in Lowestoft were mentioned in documentary sources around this time and by the 1780s three Beach Companies emerged – Denny's, Lincoln's and Reed's.

1800–1850 THE BEGINNINGS

1791-1806
Lowestoft's fishing industry began to grow and more houses were needed for the fishermen. Gillingwater records that 76 tenements were constructed below the cliff during this time. These were the beginnings of the Beach Village.

1801
27th February, the first Lowestoft lifeboat arrived. However, the Beachmen preferred their own yawls and the following year the vessel was moved to Gorleston.

1810
More houses were built, though the area had no street plan and the buildings were scattered over the site.

1824
An RNLI station was established in the town. The Bath House was built in Hamilton Road.

1831
27th May, a year after the first bridge was built, the town's harbour opened. A new school room was built at Wilde's School (the date marked out on a wall with the bottoms of bottles).

1837
The town's first gasworks was built near Ness Point.

1838
The Fishermen's Hospital – later known as the Almshouses – was built on Whapload Road.

1844
The fishing industry continued to grow, helped by Samuel Morton Peto, a Victorian businessman who rebuilt the harbour and built the railway station.

1851–1900 GROWTH

1851
The Grit was inhabitated by 1,117 people (583 male, 534 female), living in 218 houses (Lowestoft population 10,150).

1860
The Scottish fishing fleets started to arrive each autumn for the herring fishing season, along with the Scots fisher girls who travelled to the town by train.

1863
Beach Village streets on the east side of Whapload Road were given official names, for example Anguish Street, Cumberland Square and Nelson Road.

1865
The Trawl Dock opened and in 1867 the low light was moved to Ness Point. The old wooden structure was replaced by one of tubular steel, capable of being moved around the beach.

1869
Christ Church opened in Whapload Road, built for fishermen and their families.

1881
The recorded population of the parish of Christ Church was 2,755 living in 441 houses, according to White's Suffolk (1885).

1882
28th October, tragic loss of life suffered on Black Saturday when the lifeboat crew refused to launch during the storm. As a result, the private lifeboat Caroline Hamilton was bought to prevent a similar tragedy happening again, although the vessel proved difficult to handle.

1883
Waveney Dock was opened to cope with the growing number of fishing boats.

1886
In a Lowestoft guide book written by Arthur Stebbings, the population of The Grit was estimated at 2,400 (Lowestoft's population was around 21,000).

1891
The Denes were purchased by the Town Council

1892
Christ Church School was built.

1897
Sparrows Nest, formerly a private house and garden, was opened as a park. 28th November, the whole of the Beach Village was flooded and the lifeboatmen returned to find their homes several feet deep in water.

1899
July, the model yacht pond on the Denes was officially opened.

1901–1914 HEYDAY

1901
An estimated 2,500 people lived on The Grit (Lowestoft population 23,385). Each October, the population of the fishing village doubled with the arrival of Scottish fishermen, fisher girls and industry workers for the herring season. Two of the old Beach Companies joined forces – the North Roads with the Young Company.

1902
After years of flooding on The Grit, work began on Lowestoft's first sea wall. To celebrate the coronation of King Edward VII on 9th August, the town's 'biggest ever bonfire' was built near to the Bath House. 14th September, The North Beach Bethel in East Street held its opening service.

1903
Hamilton Dock opened.

1907
Lowestoft's Regatta hosted its last yawl race, staged between the Beach Companies.

1911
The 1911 census disclosed that the population of Lowestoft Christ Church Ecclesiastical Parish was 1,997 (Lowestoft population 33,777). Cottages in Christ Church Square were demolished to make way for a new high school.

1913
A record catch of 535 million herring were landed at Lowestoft. The combined Scottish and East Anglian drifter fleet consisted of 1,650 boats.

1914–18 FIRST WORLD WAR

1914
A high school was built in Whapload Road, later renamed Central School. A site next to Hamilton Road was picked for the War Signal Station.

1916
25th April, the town was bombarded from the sea by the German fleet – shells landed in Lighthouse Score but didn't explode. Abnormally high tides caused widespread flooding and wrecked sea defences.

1919
A welcome home feast for 3,500 soldiers and sailors was held on the Denes.

1919–1939 HARDSHIP

1919
After the First World War all exports of herring to Germany and Russia stopped – a massive loss to Lowestoft's fishing industry.

1921
7th July, the Denes swimming pool was opened, with the Denes Oval being laid out four years later.

1923
A new sea wall was built. Before it was completed, a record 24-foot high tide flooded The Grit again to a depth of about two feet.

1925
25th November, another high tide of 24 feet caused the whole Beach Village to be flooded to a depth of about two feet.

1927
The sea wall was completed and used for motorcycle and car races.

1933
The council described houses on The Grit as 'old, worn-out and dilapidated beyond repair'and designates it 'a clearance area'.

1937
As part of a scheme to build a new housing estate on the Beach Village, houses were built in Lighthouse Score to replace the old cottages. The rest of the plan was never completed.

1938
February, the pickling plots and Hamilton Road were severely flooded.

1939
The end of an era as both of the old Beach Companies recorded the last launches of their yawls – the Old Company (1939) and the Young Company (1940).

1939–1945 SECOND WORLD WAR

1940

3rd July, Lowestoft's first daylight raid – 3 Beach Village residents were killed, the first fatal casualties of the Second World War. The Beach Village was on England's frontline and was subject to 105 bombing raids. The north beach was sealed off and the area laid with mines against possible invasion. Sparrows Nest became the Central Depot of the Royal Naval Patrol Service, renamed HMS Europa. The army used the deserted streets and houses on The Grit to train Allied soldiers in house-to-house fighting.

1941

3rd May, a parachute mine fell on the sea wall causing damage to 450 houses.

1941

13th June, Central School, used for military accommodation, was bombed. 14 soldiers and one civilian were killed.

1943

12th May, Wilde's School was destroyed during an air raid.

1946–1970 DECLINE

1946

After the war, compensation for the loss of Beach Company property was used to establish the Lifeboat Social Club in East Street.

1949

Birds Eye opened its first factory in the town on The Grit, with further investment and growth to follow.

1951

The census showed a population of 699 living on the Beach Village.

1953

31st January, water swept through 400 homes on The Grit in the worst flooding in the history of the east coast. The flood proved a huge blow to the area, causing many people to leave forever.

1955

'First Stage of Slum Clearance Programme' of the fishing village was announced in the *Lowestoft Journal* and demolition work began.

1958

After the demolition of the Eagle Brewery, Birds Eye redeveloped more land.

1958

Only one curer, I & J Dunbar, arrived in Lowestoft for the herring season and did not then handle a single herring during their stay.

1960

1st December, Prince Philip visited the Birds Eye frozen food factory. At peak periods, the company employed 1400 people on their site in Whapload Road.

1961

The census showed a population of 611 still living on the Beach Village.

1964

The old 100-foot chimney at the gasworks was demolished. The following year a new gas holder was built with a capacity of one million cubic feet.

1964

The *East Anglian Daily Times* describes The Grit as 'a relic of less prosperous days'. More Gritsters moved to new housing estates in the town. It was reported that there was only 150 people living on the Beach Village, 50 occupied buildings, two shops, 70 unoccupied dwellings.

1965

The Lifeboat Social Club was opened in Hamilton Road to replace former premises in East Street.

1966

Many former Beach Village residents were rehoused in new housing estates in the town.

1967

October, demolition work continues with the *Gas House Tavern* and five cottages in Cumberland Square among many buildings to be demolished.

1968

The *Rising Sun*, The Grit's last pub, closes 4th November prior to demolition.

1968

The Lowestoft Maritime Museum moves into the cottage in Sparrows Nest Gardens, leased from the Council.

1969

March, clearance of the area continued – the former premises of Belfast Ropework Co were demolished with Birds Eye building on the site.

1971–2019
INDUSTRIAL ESTATE & HERITAGE SITE

1971
February, the houses on the corner of Whapload Road and Old Nelson Street were demolished. Few dwellings remained on the east side of Whapload Road, with the streets re-laid and new industrial buildings built on the site.

1972
Houses to the south of Herring Fishery Score (near Christ Church) were demolished, including the building that was formerly the *Mayfly Inn,* to make way for the police station.

1975
The old gas holders were pulled down.

1977
The roundabout at the junction of Whapload Road and Old Nelson Street was laid out.

1978
Prince Philip visits the Lowestoft & East Suffolk Maritime Museum to open the 'Bill Solomon' room.

1979
22nd June, new police station opened in Old Nelson Street.

1984
An extension to the Birds Eye factory was built.

1987
The last surviving member of the Old Company, Vernil Tuck, died.

1988
Birds Eye transferred their entire vegetable repacking operation to the Whapload Road factory. A third potato line would be added the following year.

1991
After much controversy and debate, Birds Eye were given permission to build a new factory on the Denes, which opened in 1993.

1993
The first Beach Reunion arranged by Bert Prettyman, was held in Christ Church Halls.

1997
Birds Eye had 1,500 employees working in five main production buildings covering over 31 acres.

1997
October, *The Grit: The Story of Lowestoft's Beach Village* by Dean Parkin & Jack Rose was published and became a local bestseller selling 3,500 copies.

2000
A new social housing project, Homeport, was built in Whapload Road.

2001
24th February, Jack Rose died. Author of 11 books about Lowestoft, he was born into a 'Beach' family and worked as a longshoreman, trawlerman, drifterman, lifeboatman, fish worker and school caretaker.

2004
7th December, construction began on 'Gulliver', the county's first commercial wind turbine built on Ness Point. It took three days to build and started generating energy for the National Grid in January 2005.

2008
November, the Orbis Energy Centre opened as 'the most easterly office building in the UK'.

2010
The newly-refurbished Lowestoft & East Suffolk Maritime Museum was opened by Princess Anne.

2018
Renovation work began on Lancaster Place, a former net store, to turn the building into 18 apartments.

27th May, GritFest in Sparrows Nest Gardens attracted over 2,000 people for a day of performances, demonstrations, activities, archive films, exhibitions and talks to celebrate the community spirit and heritage of The Grit.

October, first performances of new theatre show *Pearls from The Grit* by Dean Parkin. This touring production, featuring a professional cast and the voice of Jack Rose, sold 1,200 tickets for nine shows in seven Suffolk venues.

2019
The 70th anniversary of Birds Eye's arrival in Lowestoft is marked by a BBC television documentary, *Inside the Factory,* presented by Gregg Wallace.

Work began on The Ness, a new park on land near to Sparrows Nest Gardens and leading to Ness Point.

THE SCORES

In the days of The Grit there used to be 12 'official' Scores, but since the demise of the fishing village Lowestoft has lost one full Score and half of two others. In 1979 the new police station was built over Frost's Alley Score, which was the oldest in the town. The lower half of Wilde's Score was taken by Birds Eye, and Maltsters Score was diverted into Spurgeon Score. There was also a thirteenth 'unofficial' Score.

In 2001/02 the Scores were part of a major regeneration scheme which involved the creation of the Lowestoft Scores Trail and the introduction of some sculptures, including Paul Amey's *Giant Mackerel* (in Spurgeon Score) and *Invasion of The Crabs*, actual size metal crabs which could be found either side of the path in Crown Score. The Mackerel has long-since disappeared, but some of the crabs can still be found.

There is also now a popular annual Scores Race which has become something of a local tradition, the route of which takes the runners up and down the Scores. Originally held in the 1930s, the gruelling event briefly restarted in the 1970s, before it was revived again in 1996 by Waveney Valley Athletics Club who still organise a senior and a junior race each August.

FROM NORTH TO SOUTH...

CART SCORE

The most northern Score was formerly known as Gallows or Gibbet Score. It's now a one-way road leading from Whapload Road up to Yarmouth Road.

THE RAVINE

Listed as Gunton Score on a 300-year-old map and later known as Park Hill. It has also been referred to as Sandhill Score, Grene Score, Lopham Score, Girdle Score and Jesuin or Hailwater Score. The Ravine is now one-way, leading down to Whapload Road.

THE SCORE

This 'unofficial' Lowestoft Score is no longer in evidence. It led from the rear of Arnold's House down to Whapload Road and was only ever used in emergencies, such as during flooding.

LIGHTHOUSE SCORE

Once known as Lighthouse Hill and taking its name from the lighthouse to which it leads. Two of the Score's most well-known residents were Arthur 'Happy' Welham who lived at No.16, and lifeboatman Vernil Tuck, the last surviving member of the Old Company.

MARINERS SCORE

Believed to have been named after Samuel Mariner who owned property there. Earlier it had been called Swan's Score due to the *Swan Inn* which stood there. This was the inn where Oliver Cromwell is said to have stayed when he visited the town in 1644 to put down the 'malignants'.

CROWN SCORE

Named after the pubs or inns that the Score led to – previously Lion Score because of the *Lion Inn*, it later became known as Crown Score because of the *Crown Hotel*, also located in the High Street.

MARTIN'S SCORE

Named after a worthy of the town Thomas Martin, but was formerly Gowing's Score, presumably named after Gowing's Ropeworks. At the top of the Score can be found a small post, marked 'TM'. This post is known locally as the Armada Post or the Revolution Post, thought to be either a boundary marker or connected to the Spanish Armada in 1588 (the date of which is also on the post).

RANT SCORE

Has also been called the Blue Anchor Score and Youngman's Score, due to Youngman's brewery which was located here in the late 1800s. The current name connects to a Christopher Rant who owned property at the top or bottom of the Score in the early 17th century.

WILDE'S SCORE

Also known as Denny's Score and School Score. This Score is named after John Wilde who died in 1738 leaving all his money to start a school which was run until the start of the Second World War. The bottom half is now covered by Birds Eye; the top of the Score is where the Heritage Centre can be found, in one of the former school buildings.

MALTSTERS SCORE

Named after the *Jolly Maltster* public house. Once known as Salter's Score, after a local merchant, this led down into Salter Street in the Beach Village, where presumably the merchant and his premises were located. Although partially built on, near the top of the Score still stands a crinkle crankle wall. A traditional Suffolk design, the zig-zag wall is particularly good at withstanding strong winds. It was also cheap to build and is only one brick thick.

SPURGEON SCORE

Named after a worthy of the town, but was also previously known as both Titlowe's Score and Acton Score. The Score was another that once featured a crinkle crankle wall, but this disappeared after the Second World War. In the 1920s three cottages in Spurgeon Score were said to have been home to three families with 70 children between them.

HERRING FISHERY SCORE

Now the most southern Score, it took this name after the pub at the top end, although today is also frequently called Christ Church Score because of the church at the bottom end. In the past it's also been called Porter's Score, Spendlove's Score and Nelson Score, having once led on to Nelson Road on the Beach Village.

FROST'S ALLEY SCORE

Was also known as Bowlers Score and Brown Score until just after the mid-1800s. This was Lowestoft's oldest Score and said to have formed the seaward end of a prehistoric pathway. It was cleared in the mid-1970s for a new police station to be built on the site.

THE DENES

by David Butcher

The term *denes* is an earlier version of *dunes*. It derives from OE *dūn*, meaning "a hill", and became applied to coastal sandhills during the late medieval period – being first identified in a printed source dating from the year 1523. In Lowestoft's case, any undulating effect may never have been very great as a result of tidal action and the effect of the wind, and the progressive development of scrub-growth of one kind and another would have moderated this even further. With Gunton Score (much later, to become known as The Ravine) acting as the northern boundary of the parish in the coastal sector, anything further to the north lay in the parish of Gunton itself – a new creation of the century following the Domesday Survey (1086), formed from land previously belonging to Lowestoft and Corton and not found in recorded, official documentation until the year 1198.

It is probably safe to assume that the Denes became of primary importance in the history and development of Lowestoft after the community moved from its original site somewhere in the north-eastern sector of what is now the municipal cemetery (bounded by Normanston Drive and Rotterdam Road) during the first half of the 14th century. The area constituted the largest of

the town's seven areas of manorial *waste* (or common) – land that was of little use for agriculture, but served as a valuable resource for other purposes: the rough-grazing of livestock, the taking of small timber and brushwood for a variety of purposes, the extraction (where permitted) of sand and clay, and the cutting of bracken for animal bedding, Controlled access was available to residents, but was supervised by the manor's steward (or bailiff) and fees were charged for the use of facilities and materials. One thing strictly forbidden to users, however, was the capture of rabbits – and even as late as the year 1712 a local farmer, Charles Boyce, was fined the sum of 5s in the annual manorial *leet court* for poaching the animals out on the Denes. Another infringement of the rules was the digging of sand and gravel, with a 3d fine imposed for anyone caught doing so.

This particular area was always the most strictly controlled of the town's commons – providing rough grazing only, out of the traditional uses of such land. However, its main importance quickly became use as an open-air wharf to service fishing activity and maritime trade, as both these enterprises assumed growing importance and significance during the 14th and 15th centuries.

Until the first harbour works were built (1827-30), Lowestoft had no man-made port facilities. Ships had to anchor offshore between the beach and outlying sandbanks, and cargo of all kinds had either to be sent out to them or brought inshore by ferry-boats. Even after the first harbour-works had been completed, their limited facilities meant that such use continued. It was only after Samuel Morton Peto had greatly expanded dock-capacity and brought the railway to Lowestoft, during the 1840s and 50s, that the Denes were no longer needed for their traditional maritime function. Even the shipbuilding, which had traditionally been carried out on the shoreline (from Crown Score southwards), was able to move into the inner harbour west of the bridge.

Records of the Late Medieval and Early Modern periods show widespread trading contact with other north European nations – much of it unlawful in strict legal terms. Great Yarmouth was the local head-port and Lowestoft was supposed to conduct its trade through that town. Obviously, this was both inconvenient and expensive in terms of both time and carriage, so Lowestoft "did its own thing" and traded directly offshore from where it was situated. This led the Great Yarmouth officials to describe its rival as "a place of great smuggling" and it wasn't until 1679 that more than three centuries of argument and strife were finally resolved. In the January of that year (with further privileges confirmed in May), Lowestoft was granted port-status in its own right – thus freeing it from Yarmouth's supremacy and interference.

Apart from the maritime trade in goods of a widely varying nature (coal, timber, pitch, hemp and cordage, canvas, pig-iron, grain, malt, bricks, pantiles, butter, and linen and woollen cloth), there was also much activity centred on fishing. This consisted of two main methods of capture: drift-netting for herrings in the autumn and early spring and for mackerel during the late spring/early summer, and hand-lining for cod and other demersal species during the winter and early spring. The ferry-boats mentioned two paragraphs above doubled up as longshore fishing-craft, propelled by either oars or sails, while the larger vessels combined fishing further from shore with overseas trading-voyages according to seasonal activity and the dictates of economic opportunity. For over three hundred years (from the early 15th century to the middle of the 18th), Lowestoft ships, in varying numbers (never large), sailed northwards every spring to Faeroe and Iceland to fish for cod and ling – a venture that must have been

hazardous, but which also yielded good profits in the event of the voyage being successfully completed.

All the catches made, of whatever type, were landed directly onto the beach and processed in buildings situated at the bottom of the cliff or on the first terrace above (all gear and other materials were also stored there). Limiting this account strictly to the two main species caught (herrings and cod), the former were either dry-salted on the ground or brined in vats before a lengthy period of smoking turned them into red herrings, while the latter were further salted (having undergone that treatment on board ship to preserve them) and dried prior to being cooked in a manner of different ways. An important by-product of the cod fishery was the livers. These were put aside, after gutting and salting, and stored in small, sealed wooden casks. Once the boats had returned, the casks were opened and the livers boiled in large iron coppers located on the northern sector of the Denes. The oil thus produced was known as *train-oil* (from a Dutch word traen, meaning "oil") and was used to fuel household lamps and provide a dressing for newly-made leather.

The trench housing the fire-pits where the process was carried out is mentioned by Edmund Gillingwater in

his *An Historical Account of the Ancient Town of Lowestoft* (1790) and is still detectable today. It is situated near the surviving net-drying racks and is about 80-90 paces long (on a north-south alignment) by 3-4 paces wide. It was filled in at some point with material different from the gravelly deposits underlying the Denes and makes its presence known by a slight depression in the ground and differing vegetation from that surrounding it. It is vital, regarding any kind of development which may take place hereabouts, that this feature undergoes thorough archaeological investigation. Lowestoft does not have a good record when it comes to loss of heritage caused either by inattention or calculated disregard.

The net-drying racks themselves (usually referred to in earlier times as *spars*) are of more recent historical origin, dating from the late nineteenth-early 20th century. They remained in limited use right into the 1970s, latterly supporting trawl-nets rather than the herring gear they had been originally designed for. Close scrutiny of the structures reveals that many of the uprights are split railway-track sleepers, with the horizontal cross-pieces made of re-used telegraph poles. Trawling, of course, was a late arrival in Lowestoft, coming into the town from Thames-side Barking and from ports in Kent and Sussex during the middle of the 19th century – an arrival triggered by the availability of excellent, unexploited fishing-grounds in the East Anglian-Dutch sector of the North Sea and by the harbour improvements introduced by Peto, referred to above.

Regardless of type, however, all fishing-gear (in the days before plastic filament became the norm) required regular treatment against the damaging effect of constant immersion in salt-water. The earlier tanning agent used before *cutch* (resin from the *acacia catechu* tree) was introduced for cotton-fibre was a solution of either ash, or oak, bark steeped in water – much the same as was used to produce leather from raw cow-hide. The hemp-twine nets were soaked for a while, then spread out on the ground to dry. Manorial records of the 17th century show that townspeople were allowed the privilege of drying their nets without any charge being made, but fishermen from other parts of England paid one shilling and four pence as a seasonal fee and foreigners had to find two shillings and eight pence. A common misconception, still prevailing, is that "common land" belonged to local people. It didn't! It was part of the manor: open to public use, but with *fines* (fees) payable for the services granted.

Given the size and appearance of the Denes today, it may be appropriate to reproduce the words of Thomas Howard, the third Duke of Norfolk, written in a report concerning local coastal defences in May 1545 as

the country prepared for war with France. Modern spelling is used, but the original grammatical structure retained. 'At Laystofte [*sic*], for small ships of 10 or 12 foot draught are two very good roads called the North Roads and the South Roads, in either of which a number of mean ships may ride against all winds. Between the landing place and the town is at least 40 score tailor's yards, and the landing place is more than half a mile in length. The town have made bulwarks of earth at each end of the road and in the middle, with three or four small pieces in each. The town is as pretty a place as I know any few on the sea coasts, and as thrifty and honest people in the same, and right well builded; but surely if an army royal [large force] should have come thither, considering the bulwarks, which should beat the road, be but of earth, as banks made of turves, and so far distant from the town, I think it should be no great adventure for a good puissance to land there and burn the said town.'

A number of things strike the reader – not least of which are the compliments paid to the architectural quality of the town and the prosperity and good character of its inhabitants. But perhaps the most revealing comment concerns the size of the Denes, at the time. A *tailor's yard* was forty-five inches long and 'forty score' (800) of these measures out at 1000 yards – more than twice the width of the area today. Then there are the references to the three earth-and-timber gun emplacements, which guarded the sea-approaches. One was at Ness Point itself, with

the other two located at a distance on either side, and all of them contained medium-range cannon (the 'pieces' referred to) known as *slings*. The manufacture of these guns during the month of February 1540, in the Tower of London, is recorded in the *Letters and Papers Foreign and Domestic* series, as is the appointment of three gunners to man the emplacements – each of them to be paid 6 shillings per day for his services. It is also interesting to note that, in 2003, during archaeological excavations inside and outside the Old Schoolhouse located on Wilde's Score (now the Lowestoft Heritage Workshop Centre), a spherical piece of limestone about the size of a tennis-ball was found – almost certainly a piece of shot dating back to the 16th century.

Two centuries or more after the Tudor coastal artillery had been put in place, Lowestoft saw the Denes begin to assume another use – one devoted to leisure activity. During the 1750s and 60s, during an age of increasing social politeness, the town acquired an assembly-room, a soft-paste porcelain factory and sea-bathing facilities. It became a place of resort for local gentry and the increasingly affluent middle orders, and ink-and-wash studies by local artist, Richard Powles (dating from the 1780s), show both beach-area and Denes as places to enjoy for 'taking the waters' and for 'perambulation'. The latter activity took place alongside the grazing of livestock, but this particular use was no longer practised on such a scale as had once been the case. The manor still controlled the area, but the two parish churchwardens (elected annually) had taken on the responsibility of controlling the growth of scrub and of maintaining drainage (similar to their duties on Church Green), as well as seeing that the scores were kept in good order. One of the species of flora naturally occurring on the Denes was the sea pea (*Lathyrus japonicus*, var. *maritimus*), the pods of which were eaten by some of the local people – hence, the derogatory nickname *pea-bellies* once used by the inhabitants of Great Yarmouth for Lowestoft residents.

For centuries, the manor exercised strict control of the Denes, allowing no building to take place there, nor any extraction of sand and gravel. At the beginning of the 19th century, things began to change as the town grew in size and changed in nature, and new houses began to appear as the lord of the manor relaxed restrictions and released land for development. The number of dwellings remained relatively limited, however, and the major encroachment onto the southern sector of the area occurred during the mid-late 19th century, leading to the overall creation of the so-called 'Beach Village' – always referred to by the people who lived there as either *The Beach* or *The Grit*. It is no part of this essay's intention to cover what may be termed the industrial era's history of the Denes (including the arrival of the Birdseye Factory in 1949) and much has been left unsaid, including the rise and function of the town's three beach companies, which carried out salvage operations and

life-saving activity from the late 18th century onwards. The purpose here has been to produce a summative statement concerning the earlier history of the Denes and show the area's importance in Lowestoft's economic and social development.

There had been a handful of dwellings at the foot of the cliff since at least the second half of the 16th century (and possibly even earlier), but these had been randomly located between what is now Cart Score and No. 27 High Street. The best idea to be had as to what the layout of the The Grit's development looked like during its earliest phase may be found in a map of 1831 by William Cubitt, designer and engineer of the Lowestoft harbour works (1827-30). This shows the local coastline from Corton to Covehithe, with Lowestoft as the main focus, and the concentration of houses to the east of Whapload Road (between the bottom of what is now Old Nelson Street and what was later to become Rant Score East) shows the early stages of that most singular of communities which was to develop below the cliff. There is no structured street-plan in evidence – just a scattered collection of dwellings, placed at random on the ground. But a pronounced increase in the town's population from mid-century onwards, resulting from the boost in fishing and maritime activity, created by Samuel Morton Peto's railway links (Norwich in 1847 and Ipswich in 1859) and his harbour expansion and improvements at the same time, saw the whole area reorganised and set out on a geometrical grid-pattern. And it was

this regularised, re-structured area of housing which became so much a feature of Lowestoft's overall townscape and which forms the subject of Dean Parkin and Jack Rose's book.

As for the Denes, the surviving, unbuilt portion has great potential as a heritage-area – but any development there has to be set firmly within a sound historical framework. Far too much local history relies for its effect and its capacity to interest people on an accretion of myth and inaccurate information. The truth is just as good as (and, in many cases, better) than what is popularly believed!

David Butcher is a retired Lowestoft schoolteacher and former lecturer in the Continuing Studies Department at the University of East Anglia. He has published many books including a series of oral histories capturing the heyday of the British fishing industry and, more recently, *Medieval Lowestoft* (Boydell Press, 2016) and *Norfolk and Suffolk Churches: The Domesday Record* (Poppyland, 2019).

MAPS

The following maps have been researched and drawn by Ivan Bunn and are reproduced with permission from their original 1997 artwork. They show the Beach Village at pivotal moments – at its beginnings (1835), during its growth (1890), at its biggest (1930, 1935) and during the decline (1960).

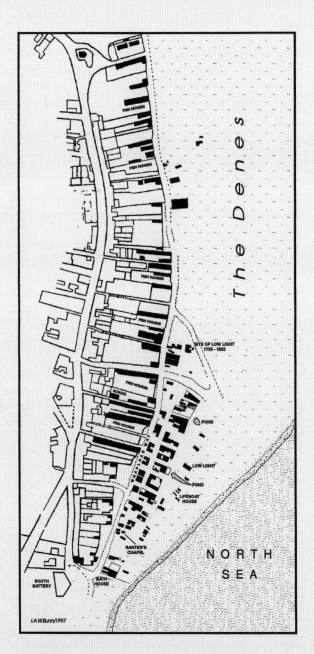

c. 1835

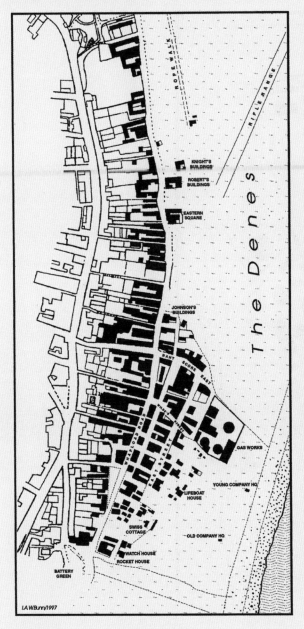

c. 1890

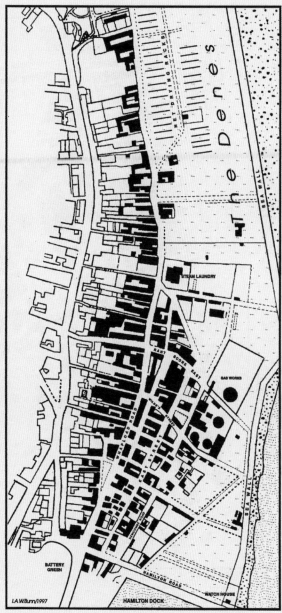

c. 1930

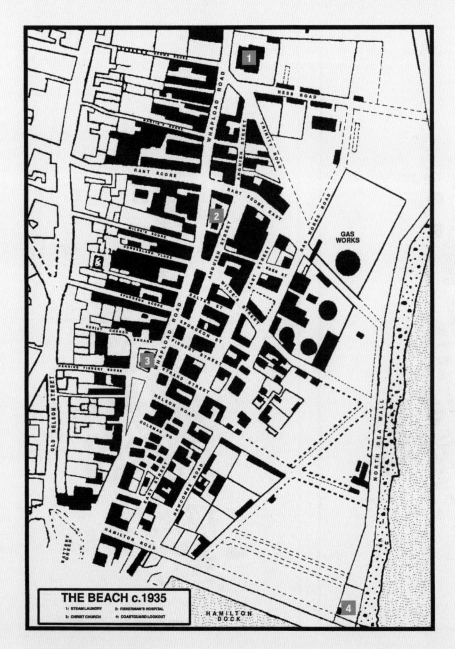

THE BEACH c.1935

1: STEAM LAUNDRY   2: FISHERMAN'S HOSPITAL
3: CHRIST CHURCH   4: COASTGUARD LOOKOUT

THE BEACH c. 1935

1. Steam Laundry
2. Fisherman's Hospital
3. Christ Church
4. Coastguard's Lookout

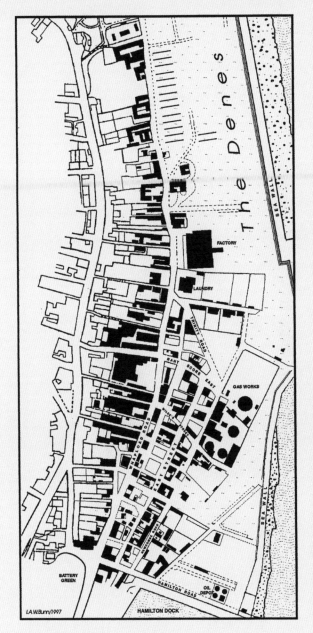

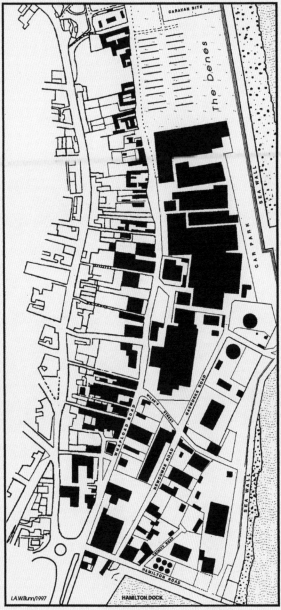

c. 1960

c. 1996

INDEX

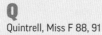

BIOGRAPHIES

DEAN PARKIN

Dean Parkin was born in Lowestoft in 1969 and left school to work at Panda Books in the town's High Street. In the 1990s he co-wrote, edited and published nearly 40 local history books, many of them under his own Rushmere Publishing imprint.

In 1999 he started his long association with the international Aldeburgh Poetry Festival and its organisation, The Poetry Trust, where he held various roles for 15 years, latterly as Creative Director.

Since 2015 he has worked as a freelance poet, writer and workshop leader. He has run sessions in schools, prisons, colleges, universities and residential homes, with every age from primary children to the over nineties.

In 2010 he wrote and performed his one man show *Dean's Dad's Ducks* at the Edinburgh Fringe Festival, followed by his *Poem for Suffolk* show across the county in 2014. He has published two poetry collections, *The Swan Machine* (2015) and *The Bubble Wrap* (2017) for children.

In 2016 he co-founded Poetry People which devised and delivered The Grit, a project to celebrate Lowestoft's almost forgotten fishing village. Supported by the National Lottery Heritage Fund, the project ran from 2017-18 and consisted of workshops in primary schools and residential homes, GritFest celebration day, and the creation of a new theatre show, *Pearls from The Grit*. Featuring three actors, a musician and Dean himself as the writer/narrator, performances drew sell-out audiences across Suffolk in October 2018. With Arts Council support, the show will tour Suffolk and Norfolk in November 2019.

Dean is currently working on two books which will be published in 2020 by Corner Street. A newly revised and illustrated edition of Jack Rose's autobiography, *Lowestoft Life* will be followed by *Suffolk Heart*, a collection of Dean's own stories, poems and illustrations of life in the most easterly county.

JACK ROSE

Jack Rose (1926–2000) was born in Lowestoft into a 'Beach' family. He worked as a longshoreman, trawlerman, drifterman, lifeboatman, fish worker and school caretaker.

His interest in the town began after he returned from service in the Second World War to discover how much Lowestoft had changed. In 1970 he began giving slideshows and talks in local venues, schools, clubs and old people's homes for the next three decades, regularly filling the Marina Theatre and raising money for local charities.

Jack never saw himself as an historian and preferred to be thought of as the 'last of the old characters' (Trevor Westgate, *Lowestoft Journal*). The first of his 11 books was published in 1973 and his favourite was always *The Grit* (1997) which, along with five of his other titles, he co-wrote with Dean Parkin.

In 2019 Jack's family appointed Dean as curator of the extensive archive of notes, photographs and slides. The Jack Rose Collection will now become the source for a number of forthcoming ventures including books, talks and heritage events.

To mark the 20th anniversary of Jack's death, a revised and redesigned edition of his long out-of-print autobiography – *Jack Rose's Lowestoft Life* (1991) – will be re-published in 2020 using materials from the archive.

SILK PEARCE

Peter Silk and Jack Pearce met whilst studying graphic design at The Royal College of Art and after several years of working in various design companies came together in 1984 to form Silk Pearce. The design group quickly gained a reputation for well-crafted ideas-based design underpinned by a feel for the subject matter. Their simple mantra of 'designing things that people like' has stood the test of time, and has drawn many to their doors including many arts organisations, not to mention the publishers of this book.

Silk Pearce's Creative Director, Rob Steer has taken the leading role in the design of *The Grit* book and has been at pains to project the character of the project, and indeed the community that it represents, becoming immersed in the subject as a whole and familiar with its stories and images. The strong use of black and gold used frequently on the sign-written nameplates of the fishing boats has been borrowed and is used throughout this book with no other colour. The illustrations are deliberately taken direct from the sketchbook in which they were drawn with no adornment, and in a departure from the modern inclination to retouch scratches or creases from photographs we have approached things differently, treating old photographs as precious artefacts, preserving their 'wrinkles', dog-eared corners and even some of Jack Rose's handwriting.

The result, we believe, is an authentic record of The Grit as a living place and a thriving community, the echoes of which are preserved well beyond these pages.

PAULA WHITE

Paula White is an artist, illustrator and printmaker who grew up and still lives in Lowestoft. Her family history is steeped in sea-faring, with one great grandfather a Lowestoft fishing skipper and another an adventurous Southwold sailor who rounded Cape Horn many times in the late 1800s.

After graduating in 2000 with a First Class Honours Degree in Design Crafts, Paula set up her own business as an artist and textile designer. In 2002 she began working in Further and Higher Education as a part-time lecturer, teaching drawing and printmaking for 14 years. More recently she secured a place on the Children's Book Illustration MA at the Cambridge School of Art, graduating with distinction in 2018.

In 2019 her children's book *Bread, Buns and Biscuits* was a finalist for The Templar Illustration Prize. These illustrations were chosen for the Snape Maltings Gallery winter exhibition, and litho prints inspired by Lowestoft's fishing heritage were selected for the Norwich Print Fair.

Her evocative drawings of Lowestoft's fishing heritage and its historic Beach Village led to the commission to produce a new cover and chapter illustrations for the revised edition of *The Grit*. Paula said, "It was Dean and Jack's book that captured my interest many years ago. So I visited the site at dawn and dusk many times, sketching and absorbing the atmosphere. I talked with old residents, sketched the brilliant scale model at the Heritage Centre, worked from my drawings and old photographs. I wanted to keep the artwork honest and true, showing intimate detail but also creating atmosphere with loose brushwork, pattern and texture where needed. The limited colour palette adds to the nostalgia and evokes a real sense of place, bringing the sights, sounds and smells of the Beach Village – and the past of many of our families – back to life."

BIBLIOGRAPHY

BARRATT, ANNE
The Beach –
A Community Study

BLYTH, JAMES
Edward Fitzgerald & 'Posh'
(John Long, 1908)

BLYTHE, RONALD
The Time by the Sea
(Faber & Faber, 2013)

BUTCHER, DAVID
The Cliffhanger: Landscape
and Fishing as Elements in
the History of Lowestoft
(EARD, 1983)

BUTCHER, DAVID
Following the Fishing
(Tops'l Books, 1987)

BUTCHER, DAVID
Living from the Sea
(Tops'l Books, 1982)

COOPER, ERNEST READ
Storm Warriors of the
Suffolk Coast (Heath
Cranton Ltd, 1937)

DUTT, WILLIAM
Norfolk & Suffolk Coast
(Methuen, 1909)

DYSON, JOHN
Business in Great Waters
(Angus & Robertson, 1977)

FLAXMAN, ROYAL
Wall of Water (Rushmere
Publishing, 1993)

GANZ, CHARLES
A Fitzgerald Medley
(Methuen, 1933)

GILLINGWATER, EDMUND
An Historical Account
of the Ancient Town of
Lowestoft in the County
of Suffolk (G. G. J. and J.
Robinson, 1790)

GRIFFIN, STANLEY
A Forgotten Revival
(Day One Publications,
1992)

HIGGINS, DAVID
The Beachmen
(Terence Dalton, 1987)

HUSSEY, FRANK
Old Fitz
(Boydell Press, 1974)

JENKINS, FORD
Port War: Lowestoft 1939-
1945 (W S Cowell, 1947)

KIRBY, JOHN
Topographical & Historical
Description of the County
of Suffolk (J Munro, 1829)

LEES, HUGH
The Chronicles of a Suffolk
Church (Published by
author, 1949)

MALSTER, ROBERT
Lowestoft East Coast Port
(Terence Dalton, 1982)

MALSTER, ROBERT
Saved from the Sea
(Terence Dalton, 1974)

MARTIN, R.M.
With Friends Possessed: A
Life of Edward Fitzgerald
(Faber and Faber, 1985)

ROSE, JACK
Changing Lowestoft
(Rushmere Publishing, 1994)

ROSE, JACK
Jack Rose's Lowestoft
(Panda Books, 1981)

ROSE, JACK
Lowestoft Album
(Panda Books, 1983)

ROSE, JACK
Lowestoft Life
(Panda Books, 1991)

ROSE, JACK
Lowestoft Scrapbook
(Tyndale + Panda
Publishing, 1988)

ROSE, JACK
Tales & Tall Stories
(Rushmere Publishing,
1992)

STEBBINGS, ARTHUR
Visitor's Guidebook to
Lowestoft & Vicinity
(1886)

TEMPLE, C.R.
Shipwreck: Wrecks &
Rescues off the East
Anglian Coast (Tyndale +
Panda Publishing, 1986)

TOMKINS, HERBERT W.
Companion into Suffolk
(Methuen, 1949)

WADE, STEPHEN
Lost to the Sea: Britain's
Vanished Coastal
Communities (Pen &
Sword, 2017)

WRIGHT, W A (ED)
Letters of Edward
Fitzgerald to Fanny Kemble
(Richard Bentley, 1895)